Germans and Jews

The Collected Works of
George L. Mosse

Germans and Jews

The Right, the Left, and the
Search for a "Third Force" in
Pre-Nazi Germany

George L. Mosse

With a critical introduction by
Sarah Wobick-Segev

THE UNIVERSITY OF WISCONSIN PRESS

Publication of this book has been made possible, in part,
through support from the George L. Mosse Program in History at the
University of Wisconsin–Madison and the Hebrew University of Jerusalem.

The University of Wisconsin Press
728 State Street, Suite 443
Madison, Wisconsin 53706
uwpress.wisc.edu

Gray's Inn House, 127 Clerkenwell Road
London EC1R 5DB, United Kingdom
eurospanbookstore.com

Originally published by H. Fertig under the title *Germans and Jews:
The Right, the Left, and the Search for a "Third Force" in Pre-Nazi Germany*,
copyright © 1970 by George L. Mosse
Critical introduction copyright © 2023 by the Board of Regents of the
University of Wisconsin System

Printed in the United States of America
This book may be available in a digital edition.

Library of Congress Cataloging-in-Publication Data

Names: Mosse, George L. (George Lachmann), 1918-1999, author. |
Wobick-Segev, Sarah, writer of introduction. | Mosse, George L. (George Lachmann),
1918-1999. Works. Selections. 2020.
Title: Germans and Jews : the right, the left, and the search for a "Third Force"
in pre-Nazi Germany / George L. Mosse ; with a critical introduction by
Sarah Wobick-Segev.
Description: Madison, Wisconsin : The University of Wisconsin Press, [2023] | Series:
The collected works of George L. Mosse | Includes bibliographical references and index.
Identifiers: LCCN 2022039084 | ISBN 9780299342845 (paperback)
Subjects: LCSH: Antisemitism—Germany. | Jews—Germany—Intellectual life. |
Germany—Politics and government—20th century.
Classification: LCC DS146.G4 M66 2023 | DDC 943/.004924—dc23/eng/20220923
LC record available at https://lccn.loc.gov/2022039084

The nervous nineteenth century has reached its end. There will not be another revolution in Germany in the next 1,000 years.

—Adolf Hitler, at the "Nazi Party Day of Unity," 1934

Contents

Acknowledgments   ix

A Critical Introduction by Sarah Wobick-Segev   xi

Introduction: The "Third Force"   3

1 Culture, Civilization, and German Antisemitism   24

2 The Image of the Jew in German Popular Literature:
   Felix Dahn and Gustav Freytag   43

3 The Influence of the Völkisch Idea on German Jewry   54

4 The Corporate State and the Conservative Revolution in
   Weimar Germany   80

5 Fascism and the Intellectuals   99

6 Left-Wing Intellectuals in the Weimar Republic   117

Notes   155

Index   177

Acknowledgments

Though this book was conceived as a unified work, the first five chapters first appeared as articles over the last decades. They have been extensively revised. Chapter 6 in a much-changed form was given at the annual meeting of the American Historical Association in 1964 and has not been published previously.

For facilitating the work on the additions and changes made in the various chapters, I want to thank the Wiener Library, London, and the library of the University of Wisconsin–Madison. I was especially fortunate in being able to use the archives of the Alliance Israélite Universelle in Paris, the Jewish National Archives and the Martin Buber Archives in Jerusalem. Howard Fertig and Ann Adelman did much to improve the quality of the manuscript. To my graduate students at the University of Wisconsin–Madison, and especially to Paul Breines, I owe a special debt for a constant critical dialogue from which I have learned much.

G.L.M.
Madison, Wisconsin
June 1969

~

For permission to reprint significantly revised copyright material, the author is indebted to the following:

"Culture, Civilization and German Anti-Semitism," reprinted from *Judaism* 7, no. 3 (Summer 1958): 256–267.

"The Image of the Jew in German Popular Culture: Felix Dahn and Gustav Freytag," reprinted from *Leo Baeck Institute Year Book* 2, no. 1 (1957): 218–227.

"The Influence of the Völkisch Idea on German Jewry," reprinted from *Studies of the Leo Baeck Institute*, ed. Max Kreutzberger (New York: Frederik Ungar, 1967), 81–115.

Acknowledgments

"The Corporate State and the Conservative Revolution in Weimar Germany," reprinted from *Gouvernés et gouvernants*, vol. 5, *Période contemporaine* (Brussels: Éditions de la Librairie Encyclopédique, 1965), 213–242.

"Fascism and the Intellectuals," reprinted from *The Nature of Fascism*, ed. Stuart Woolf (London: Weidenfeld and Nicolson, 1968), 205–225, The Graduate School of Contemporary European Studies, University of Reading.

A Critical Introduction

Sarah Wobick-Segev

The following collection can in many ways be read as a companion piece to George L. Mosse's seminal work *The Crisis of German Ideology: Intellectual Origins of the Third Reich* (1964, 2021).[1] Written largely between 1957 and 1968, the essays that make up *Germans and Jews: The Right, the Left, and the Search for a "Third Force" in Pre-Nazi Germany* reflect the gestation of a profoundly important and radically new direction in Mosse's thinking that would find full expression in *The Crisis of German Ideology*, namely Mosse's turn to ideology to account for the rise of National Socialism, a move that reflected his embrace of cultural history. The chapters chart the course of specific intellectual and cultural developments that crystalized in Europe generally in the 1920s, spotlighting important precursors and events in Germany, more specifically, during the Imperial era and the Weimar Republic. As Mosse makes clear in the introduction, the common thread that links the essays in this collection is the conceit that a perceived crisis of modernity was shared among two distinct and internally heterogenous groups of individuals—one with distinctly right-wing tendencies, the other drawn to the left of the political spectrum—who felt significant angst and distrust of the political status quo during the interwar years. These individuals attempted "to solve the problems of the modern age by creating a force that could eliminate the unpalatably capitalist and materialist present" (3).

Although they would seek out vastly different solutions, these same thinkers shared certain basic characteristics: first, they all held a profoundly negative view of modern society, which they saw as the very cause of their alienation and a direct and dire threat to the individual's personality and identity. Second, they took a common approach to the problem by embracing a strict idealism and rejecting materialism. They also, in keeping with their idealism, yearned to create utopias and scorned political pragmatism of any kind, causing them to break with or express deep discontent with existing political parties (5). Third, and in a sense as an outgrowth of their idealism, they shared a "revolutionary impetus" (12) and hoped to overthrow the bourgeois, capitalist present that was marred by pragmatism. To this end, they longed for strong leadership to bring them and society forward. Finally, they also all shared a similar disappointment with the political movements that would emerge ostensibly to solve the crisis they so yearned to overcome. Overwhelmingly, these individuals failed to find a political movement that they could claim as truly representing their own concerns and offering what they deemed to be acceptable (read, unpragmatic) solutions. These men—indeed, all of Mosse's examples are male thinkers—were thus in Mosse's reading representatives of a Third Force.

The chapters that follow the introduction approach the topic from a variety of angles: first exploring those on the right who popularized anti-semitic tropes and myths, then moving on to examples of German Jews who found inspiration in the völkisch movement and, like many non-Jewish Germans, believed that the modern age had stripped society and individuals of their authenticity. Later chapters explore the political dimensions and consequences of these attitudes by examining different intellectual groups that constituted Mosse's Third Force, including a chapter that examines the attraction of fascism among certain intellectuals and a final chapter on left-wing intellectuals.

Chapters 1 and 2 offer an alternative German literary canon. Instead of the land of Goethe and Schiller, Mosse presents a Germany represented by a gamut of authors, chief among them Felix Dahn (1834–1912) and Gustav Freytag (1816–1895), who enjoyed considerable popularity and proliferated an image of the Jew as Asiatic, "rootless," dishonest, unethical, and part of a perpetual conspiracy. At the heart of Mosse's analysis is the basic idea that "German antisemitism is a part of German intellectual history. It does not stand outside it. Above all, it became involved with the peculiar turn which German thought took after the first decade of the nineteenth century" (40–41). Mosse concludes, "All in all, the stereotype Jew that emerged from this segment of popular culture provided one of the most important roots of German antisemitism. It was an ominous image, the more so as it was in all instances associated not only with contempt but with actual cruelty" (53). Such cruelty was an essential feature of German antisemitism, and Mosse notes in this chapter that in each story, in each case, the figurative Jew comes to a bad end. For Mosse, the popularity of such antisemitic images and conclusions already in the Kaiserreich did not bode well for real-life Jews in Germany.

In his discussions on the continuity between antisemitism in Imperial Germany and under the National Socialists, there is a certain similarity though ultimate difference to Shulamit Volkov's famous essay on antisemitism as a cultural code. Both historians point to the longer history of German antisemitism, though Volkov highlights the changes to this ideology both in terms of its political rationale and its outcome. For her, antisemitism in the Kaiserreich was a political code that served as a form of shorthand for a variety of political opinions (e.g., militant nationalism, imperial expansion, and racism).[2] Only under the Nazis, she argues, would the once rhetorical political antisemitism become violent and genocidal. Mosse, by contrast, reads antisemitism in the Kaiserreich as "an escape valve from serious social and political problems" (53). Unlike Volkov, Mosse thus stresses the *non*-political nature of antisemitism and sees both its appeal and its danger precisely in this fact. He continues, "The image of the Jew was outside the range of serious political and social analysis, and that was its strength. In this way it provided the emotional basis for a totalitarian solution of these problems" (53). Moreover, antisemitism, for Mosse, was already violently predisposed during the Kaiserreich and did not have to wait until the National Socialists to reveal its violent side.

In the third chapter, Mosse examines in depth how an important segment of German Jewry found answers to the crisis of modernity in völkisch ideas (54). In a sense refuting Gershom Scholem's (1897–1982) famous rejection of the very possibility of a German-Jewish symbiosis, Mosse explores the extents to which Jews participated in this movement, taking examples from youth movements and the writings of such leading intellectuals as Martin Buber (1878–1965). By analyzing the Jewish engagement with völkisch ideas, Mosse reminds the reader that there was a time when Jews used, to use Robert Weltsch's (1897–1982) phrasing, the "same terms as those used by their fellow Germans" to describe their own situation (54). Here Mosse makes an important and still relevant point: German-Jewish history was an intrinsic part of German history, an idea that Steven Aschheim has taken further in his own writings on the co-constitution of German culture.[3] To be sure, Mosse also notes where the German and German-Jewish uses of völkisch ideology part ways: while both Weltsch and Buber employed "the vocabulary of the völkisch renaissance," they "looked upon the *Volk* as a stepping stone to a general European culture. Only by first becoming a member of the *Volk* could the individual Jew truly become part of humanity" (62).

In perhaps his most challenging and politically relevant essay, Mosse explores the meaning of popular participation and political representation in his fourth chapter. Focusing on what he calls "the conservative revolution," Mosse reminds the reader that many on the right did not seek to abandon democracy but to rethink it; they engaged in "a search for the new forms that popular representation might take, a quest for a different kind of democratic expression" (80). As Mosse argues, "Few wanted to do away with popular participation in government: the majority believed that parliamentary institutions were, in fact, inhibiting such participation" (80). If Adorno and Horkheimer had seen the roots of the demise of European civilization in the Enlightenment itself, here Mosse points to the negative and darker sides of democratic yearning.[4] Rejecting Weimar's representative parliament, these right-wing thinkers hoped for "a corporately structured *Volk*" that would serve "as the antithesis to the present 'anonymous' state" (84). Ominously, these same corporatist political ideas were wedded to economic and racist ideas: "The true community on which the state must be built was said to be Aryan in nature, and because this was essential for the proper working of politics and economics, it had to be defended against all enemies. Traditionally the Jew had been cast in the role of enemy. Thus the action necessary to implement true socialism was not a revolution as such but, rather, the elimination of the Jews, who came to represent the slavery of interest and the domination of unearned capital" (90). For all the apparent similarities to National Socialist ideology, as Mosse notes, and not without some irony, Nazism would reject this corporatism and focus instead on relationships to the leader (94). Advocates of this corporatist political model "soon found themselves not only excluded from participation in power but imprisoned or exiled. Adolf Hitler did not want their kind of German revolution" (97–98).

In the last two chapters, Mosse explores the relationships of the Third Force, first to fascism and then to left-wing political ideologies and movements. In both cases, Mosse writes how members of this Third Force felt betrayed by the political movements in which they had either placed their hope (as the case of right-wing thinkers) or with whom they might have found political allies to counter the rising threats from the right (as in the case of left-wing intellectuals). The last chapter, in particular, points to the political dangers of the idealism and consequent inaction of certain left-wing intellectuals: "Self-consciously intellectual, they believed that their task lay outside the normal realm of politics, beyond society and yet relevant to it" (136). Distancing themselves from everyday political action and the pragmatism that such political activities involved, they were nonetheless forced into exile and witnessed the burning of their books: "Here is the ultimate consequence of these attitudes, of the contempt for political reality without the attainment of a firm relationship to any actual part of it" (145). Though Mosse expresses clear sympathy with the ideas of those on the left, he cannot abide by their aloofness from political action: "The absolute of a categorical imperative distracted some of the best minds of a later generation from the task at hand. In condemning compromise, existing politics, and the exploitation of realistic possibilities, the left-wing intellectuals put forward a vision of society that seemed incapable of realization" (148). As we will see below, Mosse was not merely motivated by his desire to set the historical record straight but offered words of warning for contemporary society.

Why This Book Matters: The Reception and Legacy of *Germans and Jews*

When Mosse began writing the early essays that would make their way into *Germans and Jews*, much of the historiographical consensus on National Socialism and fascism insisted on seeing them in very different terms, especially in Mosse's country of birth. Methodologically, early postwar German historians tended to favor political historical approaches and the scholars themselves frequently held conservative political opinions. Some, like Hans Rothfels (1891–1976), focused their studies on conservative resistance to Nazism, whereas Gerhard Ritter (1888–1967) tried to explain Nazism as a pan-European phenomenon that was linked to excessive democracy, which had been only too easily taken advantage of by demagogues who sought to manipulate the masses.[5] Despite these differences, in both cases National Socialism was presented as an aberration, corralled off from the otherwise normal trajectory of German historical development. In a not dissimilar fashion, the esteemed German historian Friedrich Meinecke (1862–1954) suggested in his book *Die deutsche Katastrophe* (*The German Catastrophe*, 1946) that the rise of Hitler and the National Socialists was made possible largely thanks to chance ("böser Zufall") and by the actions of two specific men, Alfred Hugenberg (1864–1951) and Paul von Hindenburg (1847–1934), even if Meinecke was willing to admit that there might have been links between Hitlerism and Prussian militarism. As Steven Aschheim has rightly suggested, for the leading German historians of the immediate postwar era, "indigenous German traditions and developments played only a minor role in explaining the etiology and disposition of National Socialism; the real causes (and blame) were deflected outward onto post-1789 Europe, where the origins of a formless mass society and totalitarian democracy were to be found."[6] Although these early postwar German historians might have had their own very special political, intellectual, and perhaps even psychological motivations for their arguments, we must admit that these same interpretations have not stood the test of time, and today, in fact, carry little historiographical weight.[7]

To be sure, the historiographical and academic landscape in Germany did begin to change during the 1960s, roughly at the same time that Mosse would take his own cultural turn. Yet the shift among German scholars went in the direction of social history and more particularly structuralism. By focusing on structures and the primacy of unique and unrepeatable socioeconomic conditions, this new generation of German historians, while placing emphasis on events inside Germany, explored the rise of Nazism by means of non-agentic causes and sidestepped questions of personal guilt and responsibility.[8] Taken together, the postwar historiography in Germany well into the 1960s—in both its political- and social-historical guises—did not take ideas, especially National Socialist ideology, into account. Perhaps unsurprising then, this book, like *The Crisis of German Ideology*, was not particularly well received in postwar Germany. West German scholars rejected Mosse's ideas, preferring to hold to a strict functionalism that asserted that unique socioeconomic forces, and not ideas and the people who shared them, were the reasons for the rise of National Socialism. It has also been suggested, though not without some controversy, that the rejection of Mosse's thesis (and the ideas of other exile historians) also reenacted a debate about who belonged and who did not, and who was thus capable of truly understanding and interpreting German history.[9]

Mosse's reception was quite different on the other side of the Atlantic. There, not only would Mosse become a pioneer in a very different methodological approach, blending cultural and intellectual history to explore the origins of National Socialist ideology, but this approach would find a more receptive audience among American academic circles.[10] The topic of the (ideological) roots of Nazism was from the very beginning considered of merit; Fritz Stern (1926–2016) viewed it as "an imperative of historical investigation and moral understanding."[11] What made Mosse's work so radical and pathbreaking, however, was not only this methodological

distinction but his insistence on taking ideas, especially bad and dangerous ones, seriously. As he writes in *Germans and Jews*, "for if fascism were
merely a pragmatic, activist response to the immediate historical situation, the intellectual would have no real place either among the duped
masses or in the cynical political leadership" (99). In other words, the
presence and participation of intellectuals in the longer history of antisemitism, ultranationalism, and even National Socialism necessitate that
we analyze fascist and National Socialist ideology with the same academic
seriousness applied to other ideologies.

To be sure, the message that stood behind this radical shift was perhaps
central to the long delay between the publication of Mosse's key works
on the subject and their eventual recognition in Germany. After all, in
focusing on ideas, Mosse directly confronted Germans and Germany with
their own guilt. *Germans and Jews*, just like *The Crisis of German Ideology*, makes clear that the roots for National Socialism, and in particular
for the Holocaust, were already long present in German culture. Antisemitism, völkisch ideologies, and ultimately Nazism were not aberrations
but were integral, albeit repugnant, parts of German history. As he writes,
"The significance of racist thought is misunderstood if its absurdity and
bad taste are stressed and the continuation within it of an older, 'respectable' trend ignored" (39). In short, it was historically problematic, if not
simply wrong, to dismiss the longer history of these ideas, especially when
in so doing, one ignored the popularity and acceptance they had enjoyed.

In keeping with this position, Mosse vociferously argued against the
notion that National Socialism was a purely pragmatic political phenomenon and that the National Socialists had simply and cynically used these
ideas to manipulate the helpless and hapless masses. Instead, Mosse high-
lighted the deeper roots of ideas that were held by wider swaths of the
population—again, including intellectuals—who in turn disseminated and
popularized them.[12] The following essays thus represent Mosse's careful
analysis of the writings and thoughts of a broad group of intellectuals
who represented not only the elites but, as Philipp Stelzel has called them,
"figures of high and popular culture alike."[13] In so doing, Mosse gives
weight to popular culture and does not focus merely on "great minds."
Simultaneously, he demonstrates how widespread these ideas were in pre-
1933 Germany.[14] Here we can locate one of Mosse's most important,
though relatively unspoken, arguments as it emerges in the introductory
chapter: namely, the idea that intellectuals, too, not just the "masses,"
could be caught up in the allure of fascism—that they could hold the
"wrong" and even dangerous opinions. Here Mosse returns the individual,

even the thinking individual, to center stage and gives them agency, thereby making them complicit in some of the greatest crimes of human history. While this message is far less surprising to audiences today, at the time of publication it was revolutionary. Indeed, to today's readers the arguments presented in the early chapters of the book might appear somewhat pedestrian. To be sure, this by no means reflects the simplicity or lack of novelty of Mosse's ideas; instead, it serves as a testament to the extent to which Mosse's ideas have become accepted wisdom in the historiography.

In addition to the book's clear ground-breaking importance for the field of cultural history in general and the study of fascist ideologies more specifically, *Germans and Jews* includes a message of warning for the present. The book brings together a series of reflections on political roads not taken and lessons learned only too late. Mosse's historical enterprise always tended to monumental history—that is, that which sought to inspire the present.[15] *Germans and Jews* is the story of a time of crisis and of the many people from different sides of the political spectrum who were troubled by it and sought a radical solution to address it. Yet, just as Mosse offers cautionary warnings against right-wing ideologies and their pervasiveness in the culture of early twentieth-century Germany, he also points to the failings of many on the left to do anything about it.

In this regard, *Germans and Jews* emerges as a series of cautionary tales for the present, which he makes explicit from the beginning of the book: "We can sympathize with the dilemma of these left-wing intellectuals and respect their ideals, which exalt that which is noble in humanity, but we must also realize the dangers inherent in idealism that stresses the purity of absolute values and is apt to retreat into its own circumscribed world in the face of a reality that will not bend to the intellectuals' desire" (22). Mosse does not speak generally or hypothetically but gives concrete examples in his book, citing recent cases of states or movements that had tended toward or articulated elements of fascism, like Peronism in Argentina and Nasser's Egypt. In one brief section in the middle of the book and then in a lengthier passage in the last chapter, Mosse takes a step forward, linking the subject of his study with his contemporary political landscape (i.e., the US of the 1960s). Here he again reveals his own basic sympathy with the general concerns of left-wing intellectuals who sought meaning and asserted that "Man is good" (136), while at the same time castigating them for refusing to engage in pragmatism. Mosse thus seeks to criticize but also to point to a common trajectory shared by left-wing intellectuals in the United States of the 1960s and intellectuals from interwar Italy and Germany. Fascinatingly, the comparative aspect (even as he highlights the critical differences between the different times and places) again sets the history of Germany squarely into what he would call "Western civilization" (153) and further complicates Mosse's own position on the Sonderweg debates.

Finally, *Germans and Jews* offers a glimpse of themes that Mosse would develop more fully in his later publications. In the third chapter, on the influence of völkisch ideas on German Jews, we can see the beginnings of Mosse's interest not only in nationalism but in its intersection with masculinities, a topic that Mosse would return to in ground-breaking works like *Nationalism and Sexuality* (1985, 2020). The following essays also reveal an early awareness of the role of emotions in political processes, making Mosse an often-overlooked pioneer in the field of the history of emotions. As John Hutchinson has noted, unlike "materialist scholars, who at the time viewed fascism as an irrationalist melange of ideas employed as part of an opportunist drive for power," Mosse came "to understand fascism (and its predecessor nationalism) as not so much a rational ideology like liberalism and Marxism, but as a *Weltanschauung* that appealed to the emotions."[16] Here we can thus also see the beginnings of Mosse's more anthropological approach—an attentiveness to the role of popular culture in historical processes.[17]

How to Read This Book

Readers seeking fast and easy definitions of the phenomena under study will be quickly disappointed. Indeed, it has become almost de rigueur for scholars reviewing Mosse's work to point out that he rarely, if ever, offered straightforward definitions for key concepts or took pains to offer detailed explanations about his methodological approaches.[18] In the case of the present work, Mosse, for example, only gives a clear definition of "intellectual" along with their key ideas and ways of thinking in the last chapter, albeit spread over the span of several dense pages (118–122). Employing phrases such as "völkisch mystique," "crisis of modernity," "intellectuals," and even "fascism," Mosse appears almost evasive, preferring to delve into deeper analyses of individual figures and exemplaries of the very same phenomena he describes rather than to define such broad categories. Indeed, the term "Third Force" itself remains elusive. And it seems fair to ask if we can really place such widely different thinkers side by side. Yet such acts of defining appear to have been incongruous with the man and scholar Mosse was. This is a book, like all his works, that was written by an intellectual-cultural historian who was deeply learned in the major philosophical writings and movements of the modern era and had, as well, profound familiarity with the many "obscure," even mediocre thinkers of the nineteenth and early twentieth centuries.[19] The force of his argument comes thus not through an overarching "meta"-level analysis or a limited discussion of the ideas of a small elite but through the sheer weight of numerous examples of thinkers and writers who criticized the society around them.

The subtle brilliance of Mosse's argument comes in his ability to point to the widespread, simmering discontent with modern society that was shared by members of very distinct political movements, revealing a broad base of people who felt alienated by contemporary society. Moreover, these same figures, as writers and intellectuals, gave voice to this sense of alienation and wrote about specific solutions, popularizing both their discontent and their (dis)utopian visions. As Mosse suggests, those on the political right who fell into his category of the Third Force did not find common cause with National Socialism. Nonetheless, their belief in völkisch nationalism—with its yearning for authentic community—reflected what appeared to be a solution to modern society's challenges and was all too adeptly harnessed by the National Socialists for their own ends. The völkisch nationalists thus played vital roles in spreading ideas that helped the National Socialists take power. In this way, Mosse presents a broader spectrum of individuals who were susceptible to Nazism's ideological claims, and in so doing, points to how the movement gained greater ground by the end of the 1920s and early 1930s.

Writing history for Mosse was, as Karel Plessini has noted, a "civic mission," a necessary precondition for making "well-informed life choices on a political as well as on a personal level."[20] If we return to the presentism that undergirds *Germans and Jews*, we must acknowledge Mosse's continued timeliness and the importance of his warnings. For all the differences between today's political landscape, the era in which Mosse wrote these essays, and the period that he studied, we cannot help but note recurrent themes and social-political challenges. Whether we agree with all of Mosse's characterizations and terminology, as Mosse's longtime friend Stanley Payne once remarked, "the historian can only study recent past phenomena and trends, with the apprehension that violent authoritarian movements, whatever their exact form, may have a flourishing future."[21]

Germans and Jews

Introduction

The "Third Force"

A century ago historians used to publish collections of their essays without giving much thought to the cohesion of their subject matter. Random articles on a wide variety of subjects were put between hard covers. During recent decades random collections have become infrequent and, where they exist, the authors have made an effort to focus on a historical problem or to center their interest on a specific historical period. I have attempted to give the essays in this volume a unity in terms both of the historical problem with which they are concerned and of the time span which they cover. This has meant some revisions in essays that had been published previously, as well as the inclusion of material that has not been published before. In addition, this introductory chapter is designed to define the specific problem in humanity's existence which must concern us and to give some historical background to what follows in this book.

We shall be dealing with the attempt to solve the problems of the modern age by creating a force that could eliminate the unpalatably capitalist and materialist present. The time span encompassed by this book extends from the last decades of the nineteenth century to, roughly, the beginning of the Second World War. The urge toward a society that was neither capitalist nor materialist was strongest in those years which witnessed the climax of the industrialization of Europe and which have at times been designated the age of bourgeois predominance. The form which modern German nationalism took is closely related to this effort, and so is the attempt of the Jews to affirm their own identity. Furthermore, many European intellectuals shared similar desires, whether they were left-wing intellectuals in Germany or those who made a commitment to fascism. We are concerned with proposed solutions to a dilemma that all individuals of this century were forced to confront.

3

Introduction: The "Third Force"

The existential dilemma of modern humanity has often been described in very general terms: the quest for identity in a world in which the "vulgar rationalization of life" threatens to swamp the individual personality, and the advances of technology as well as the progress of urbanization and industrialization produce a feeling of alienation. However, I am concerned with a more specific reaction to this state of affairs, a more precise view of humanity's existential dilemma and its solution. Though this book discusses such varied subjects as German nationalism, left-wing intellectuals, and fascism, all these attitudes toward the modern world have basic factors in common which must be stressed from the very beginning of this study.

The dissatisfaction with one's place in the world was part of a wholesale rejection of modernity and led to a flight from society and from the traditional pursuit of politics. The individual personality was suffocating, and the existing political parties provided no satisfactory alternatives. The individuals whose attitudes fill the pages of this book sought to free themselves from the bourgeois age, which they blamed for their alienation—an age in which, in the words of Nietzsche, "ordered society puts the passions to sleep."[1] To be sure, Marxism with its anti-bourgeois impetus and its own condemnation of the bourgeois age lay readily at hand, and many turned in its direction. But not the people with whom we are concerned. They saw a Marxism embodied in the Social Democratic and Communist parties, which had become a part of the "ordered society" that produced the alienation of modern individuals.

We are here talking about the left-wing intellectuals and also those who retreated into a national mystique. Both considered themselves a "Third Force," despite the differences which existed between them. Certainly the left-wing intellectuals wanted to abolish capitalism, while the others fulminated against all capitalism but meant to destroy merely finance capitalism: the banks, stock exchange, and large-scale enterprises. However, both were at one in rejecting bourgeois society and materialism on behalf of an idealistic commitment that stood above and beyond present reality.

In many cases, opposition to existing reality was closely tied to the background of most contemporary intellectuals. Rejecting traditional modes of thought and society, they found, in art and literature, a way out of the hostile present. The artistic movements which sprang up in the late nineteenth and early twentieth centuries gave them such a refuge. Whether Expressionists or Dadaists, these artists at first had little ambition to change society itself. Their protest was strictly individual, without any

4

definite aim other than to rediscover the individual's personal creativity or soul.[2] This protest was not principally aimed at discovering new artistic forms. Rather, its purpose was to find a new manner of experiencing one's inner drives.[3] Obviously, society and its political institutions had no place here. But the protest could not maintain itself in a political and social void. An Expressionist could write that even within a group, each must remain a unique, independent individual—but, in fact, aesthetic appreciation could not remain forever apart from its milieu.[4] All long for a *point d'appui*, a point of support for their inner drives, and an escape from chaos. These men and women found this in a "Third Force" that would transform society—whether via a socialism that rested upon the Kantian ethical imperative or with the aid of a nationalist mystique. They came to believe in a utopia neither capitalist nor properly speaking Marxist, rejecting any and all materialism.

The social and economic basis of the Marxist analysis of society seemed close to that materialism which these men, left or right, despised as part of the bourgeois present. Moreover, the Marxist contention that change must come from the "maturation" of present society seemed to imply an acceptance of the reality of that society and to involve an exercise in patience until such a society was ready for revolution. These individuals wanted to solve the existential dilemma of humanity here and now. Revolutionary tactics and the compromises of political parties within a parliamentary setting seemed cut out of the same cloth. Both made people a means and not an end in themselves. The road to Marxism was blocked to them, as was any meaningful participation in political parties. Small wonder that they constituted a group that consciously stood outside present reality, ready at any moment to overthrow it.

No history of this "Third Force" exists and yet, especially in the years between 1918 and 1939, many Europeans shared its longings. The essays in this book are intended to contribute to an understanding of this phenomenon. The propagators of the "Third Force" were for the most part thinkers obsessed with the importance of absolute values and opposed to the "hypocrisy" of political tactics and compromise. The nature of these absolute values runs from the mystique of the *Volk* to the ideal of Kant's categorical imperative. In spite of such differences, however, all those with whom we are concerned rejected the present, and the immediate past as well, for an invigorated idealism: the German nationalists rejected the traditional saber-rattling worship of the state; the Jews the ghetto from which they had recently escaped; and the left-wing intellectuals the orthodox

Marxism of their immediate predecessors. The ideal they had all fashioned for themselves must be put into practice uncontaminated by a history gone wrong.

The intellectuals were the heirs of the *idéologues* of the French Revolution: people who were themselves concerned with ideas and with placing "ideal" aims before the "material interests" on which society had rested.[5] The primacy of mind over matter which Kant and Hegel had firmly established in the German philosophical tradition provided a deeply held belief for the adherents of the "Third Force." The term "ideology," which will often appear in this book, means a worldview that holds that ideas and ideals are primary, for the mind rules sovereign over the world of matter, including systems of government and economics. The "Third Force" provided a retreat into ideology, representing an escape from a world that seemed dominated by capitalism on the one side and by a materialistic Marxism on the other.

What about this ideal, the absolute to which these men paid allegiance? There were left-wing intellectuals who attempted to infuse socialism with uncompromising humanist values, rejecting any and all nationalism. We will deal with them toward the end of this book. But there were others, in the majority, who in upholding their system of absolute values in an evil world retreated into a nationalist mystique. Most of the chapters that follow concern German nationalism, which provided this ideal for so many men and women within the German-speaking lands. The term "völkisch" has come to be associated with this national impetus, and because it is so significant to our analysis, we must be certain of the meaning and complexity of this ideal.

The word "völkisch" derives from "*Volk*," which, in its simplest translation, means the people. But this translation is not quite accurate in this case, for here the *Volk* became a metaphysical entity, an eternal and unchanging ideal which encompassed all the German people. The use of the word "*Volk*" to describe a system of absolute values dates back to the rising national consciousness of eighteenth-century Germany. Within a disunited Germany, many longed for an unchanging ideal of peoplehood to which they could relate themselves, and they found it in the concept of the *Volk*. Johann Gottfried Herder (1744–1803) stood at the beginning of the evolution of völkisch ideas, and he can serve to illustrate the meaning of the concept.

Herder saw in the German *Volk* an entity whose spirit was eternal, coursing underneath all the changes that history had wrought. Just as individuals had a soul, so there existed a *"Volk* soul," which, like a person's soul, gave the *Volk* its unique and unchanging character. The German *Volk* had its own soul, which must find expression once again. Herder contrasted this soul with the present and artificial reality: the true nature of the *Volk* is wild and dynamic, based on the emotions rather than on a tortured intellectualizing. The progress of history had obscured the genuine völkisch impetus.[6] Herder agreed with his contemporary, the publicist Justus Möser (1720–1794), who in his *Deutsche Geschichte (German History,* 1773) demanded that the German national character be liberated from the layers with which the advances of history had covered it.[7]

Such men looked back nostalgically to a historical period in which the soul of the *Volk* still had free play. In völkisch thought, this was the Middle Ages. Möser calls the early part of that age the "golden time," when the peasants owned their own farms and were their own masters and when "nothing else mattered but the honor of the nation." Subsequent history had obscured this foundation upon which the *Volk* was based, until in modern times the cities provided "anomalous bodies" typifying the lack of a genuine soul.[8] Herder included Möser's interpretation of history in one of his own books: both men agreed that the agrarian, rural spirit was the only true setting for the *Volk.*

The concept of the *Volk* was thus defined in opposition to the present. These two shared a longing for the "genuine" as against a human-made, "artificial" environment. We can trace this theme in much of eighteenth-century thought. The longing for the genuine did not lead to praise of the "noble savage" but rather of the ancient Germans, who, removed from modern civilization, had practiced a true völkisch life. Such a life was not merely that of the peasant tilling the soil, however, but also encompassed a true human creativity. The early proponents of a völkisch revival stressed the importance of art and literature as an expression of the *Volk* soul. To be sure, they were intellectuals, but there is an added reason for this interest: in a disunited Germany the common language and the common folk arts were the only concrete elements that bound the nation together. Herder stressed the importance of language, and his lifetime saw the publication of ballads and fairy tales that had come down through the centuries. This was "genuine literature," as opposed to the works of Frenchmen like Pierre Corneille (1606–1684) and Jean Racine (1639–1699), whom Herder accused of fabricating dramatic fiction.[9]

National unity was conceived in cultural terms and the binding force of a common language continued to play a major role in völkisch thought.

Introduction: The "Third Force"

The Frankfurt assembly of 1848 proclaimed: "*Was Deutsch spricht soll Deutsch werden*" ("Whoever speaks German shall become a German"). Territorial boundaries were meaningless here, and the criterion of a common language was vague enough to leave the door open to a multiplicity of conflicting claims. The emphasis on a nationalist mystique conceived in cultural terms remained strong even after Germany had found territorial unity in 1871. Not only were there many people, supposedly German, who had been left stranded outside German territory, but the very advance of urbanism and industrialization seemed to negate the potential inherent in the new nation. Therefore, even after 1871, the national mystique continued based on the völkisch idea and even increased its momentum. Organic growth was contrasted with human invention; only through organic development could the *Volk* truly unfold its potential. The *Volk* must grow like a tree from its roots in the historical soil, striving toward a genuine creativity within the collective whole. Such a concept of the *Volk* brought about a weakening of those national values which so many in the eighteenth century had prized. However, the emotional base of völkisch thought led to a head-on confrontation with the constricting process of reality, for not only was national unity denied to Germans, but traditional personal bonds were being eroded by the steady advance of modernity. Just as medieval social relationships had been replaced by the institutions of the family, preserving humankind from an unbearable moral solitude, so the family was now menaced by the increasing social mobility and urbanism of eighteenth- and early nineteenth-century Europe.[10] Father Johann Friedrich Ludwig Christoph Jahn (1778–1852), whose *Deutsches Volkstum* (*German Volk*, 1810) was a seminal work in the development of völkisch thought, made the family the chief biological foundation of the *Volk*. The maintenance of meaningful, genuine personal relationships was basic to a restoration of the collectivity of the *Volk*. But the family was not the only kind of personal bond which had to be restored. Morality must be reinforced within the dissolving framework of traditional society.

Johann Gottfried Herder, Father Jahn—indeed, all the proponents of völkisch thought—believed that the virtues of honesty, probity, and the inviolability of women must once again become common currency throughout the nation. They saw embedded in the roots of the *Volk* this traditional morality, which presumably had been practiced by the peasant society of bygone days. This view of morality accompanied völkisch thought throughout the nineteenth and twentieth centuries, together with the concept of the *Volk* as the genuine and unchanging collectivity whose roots were in a past that knew neither cities nor industrialization and in which personal relationships were filled with meaning. The shadow of materialism had not darkened the creativity of the original *Volk* and must never be allowed to do so.

This view of the *Volk* attained a new importance toward the end of the nineteenth century. At this point many völkisch intellectuals no longer attempted to assert that the family must be the biological foundation of the *Volk*. Since the times of Father Jahn, the family had been ever more hard-pressed as an institution, and while some advocates of völkisch thought still clung to its revival, others no longer believed it so vital. For the family had become an integral part of the bourgeois, capitalist society which they despised, and was consequently robbed of personal appeal. The restoration of true relationships among people must be attempted instead from a different direction. The collectivity of the *Volk* itself would take the place of the family; relationships would be restored within this mystique. As we shall see in the last chapter, even left-wing intellectuals held passionately that their faith would lead to the formation of groups that would in turn restore meaningful personal relationships. The institution of the family was abandoned to the bourgeois by many völkisch thinkers, and a mystical community was substituted. This movement detached the *Volk* still further from the historical reality of the time. Here was a concept which could have no relevance to existing political parties, for they divided a collectivity that must be united.

Admittedly, those who held these views saw the necessity for the existence of the state. Father Jahn called a *Volk* without a state an organism without a body, a mere Utopia. But for all these figures the state was an organ of the *Volk* and could have no separate existence outside that collectivity. *Volk* symbols were held to be primary, and Father Jahn proposed a series of festivals, such as the day of the victory of the Germans over the Roman Legions (*Hermannsschlacht*) or a celebration in memory of the peasants who had risen against the princes and bishops in the early Middle Ages (Battle of Merseburg, 933).[11] These occasions would inspire the *Volk*, which had once triumphed against great odds. Indeed, the peasants *were* the *Volk* which had risen against tyrants who had suppressed the *Volk* soul. The state was never foremost for the advocates of these theories; their orientation was toward the absolute ideal which the *Volk* represented, and they thought of this ideal in terms of morality, creativity, and an ideal community rather than in relation to the kind of pragmatic politics the state would have to pursue.

Father Jahn's proposed festivals continued a Greek and Roman tradition which had been renewed in the eighteenth century by Jean-Jacques Rousseau (1712–1778). In his *Lettre à M. d'Alembert sur les spectacles* (*Letter to M. D'Alembert on Spectacles*, 1758) Rousseau advocated republican festivals which would uplift the public and private morals of the citizens. During the French Revolution such festivals were instituted as a means of social control: the Goddess of Reason or the "Tree of Liberty" symbolized the new regime toward which the people's loyalty must be directed—a consecration to the goals of the revolution which would replace the Christian symbols of the ancien régime. For Father Jahn, public festivals also symbolized the ideal community, but a community whose roots and goals were diametrically opposed to the civic festivals of the Jacobin dictatorship in France.

Nevertheless, here was an adaptation of an already familiar device to German conditions. Both revolutionary and counterrevolutionary forces were to use public festivals as a means to control and manipulate mass movements. The abstract collectivity needed symbols to make its existence concrete and tangible to the mass of humanity. Thomas Nipperdey (1927–1992) has recently demonstrated how the national monument also served this function. For example, the monument erected in 1913 to commemorate the Battle of Nations against Napoleon presented the völkisch ideology in stone and mortar. A massive pyramid-like construction, it was meant to show that the nation was anchored in the irrational beyond the comprehension of reason, and simultaneously in the cosmos. The heroic figures within the monument represent the Germanic virtues of bravery, readiness for sacrifice, a strong faith, and the Germanic power of will (connected, in this case, with the joy of bearing the nation's children). Significantly, this and other national monuments stressed the inner directedness of the *Volk* spirit, its ethos and idealism.[12] Popular festivals, symbols in stone and mortar, were added to literature and philosophy in order to strengthen and encourage the *Mythos* of the nation. This idealism could and did provide a framework for many of those who desired a society that was neither capitalist nor materialist; a collectivity that would find new forms to express its true and eternal mystique.

Up to this point we have discussed the common basis of völkisch thought, but on this base there existed a variety of viewpoints, all related to the mystique of the *Volk*. Not all völkisch thought was aggressive. Herder, for one, held that every people had its own *Volk* soul and that it must be respected by all. This lack of aggressiveness does not end with Herder. At the end of the nineteenth century, for example, middle-class

German youth organized its own Youth Movement, which envisaged a world wherein all separate peoples would exist peacefully side by side—each with its own unique concept of the *Volk*. Small wonder that Zionist youth was attracted to this kind of nationalism.

Yet aggressiveness against the outside world frequently found an important place within this ideology. The very idea of national uniqueness meant separation from the foreigner, and emphasis on the soil and land-scape as the unchanging sources of völkisch inspiration led to a provincialism that once again excluded those who were outside the collectivity. The concrete dilemmas faced by many Germans from the eighteenth century onward added to the inherent exclusiveness of völkisch thought. Greater social mobility seemed disturbing, especially as it affected the commercial interests within German society. A concern on the part of the intellectuals for the uprootedness of the growing middle classes runs throughout the chapters that follow. Such troublesome mobility reinforced the ideal of rootedness and led to a condemnation of those who were not rooted in the native soil.

This condemnation was directed toward those who pioneered the new commercial and urban development, and not necessarily toward any foreign enemy. Oswald Spengler (1880–1936) in his *Der Untergang des Abendlandes* (*Decline of the West*, 1918–1922), written during the First World War, specifically condemns imperialism as part of "civilization" and not "culture," by which he meant that it was part of the externalization of life, irrelevant to the development of a *Volk* soul.[13] However, cruelty and aggression could also be generated by this spiritual impetus. Thus a leader of the German Youth Movement wrote (1920–1921) that "people who preach humanism, the right of everybody to happiness, and the progress of mankind . . . cannot be taken seriously." Such people were shallow captives of reality. It was necessary to look beyond the present to a cultural impetus.[14] The *Volk* soul was embattled against those who sought to destroy it, but they were more often internal than foreign adversaries.

Within this nationalism there were differences over the tactics of battle against the enemy, though the common ideal of the *Volk* was kept intact. The conservative wing of völkisch thought believed in organic evolution and was opposed to revolutionary action. But another element within the movement believed in revolution: radical action was needed to overthrow the present order in the name of the *Volk*. After the First World War and Germany's defeat, these two viewpoints confronted each other. The völkisch conservatives, who abhorred revolution and sought to maintain social and political respectability, were by that time causing some dissent within the German National Party (Deutschnationale Volkspartei), while the revolutionary-minded völkisch men and women pitted themselves against the Weimar Republic to seek an immediate restoration of the *Volk*. We have devoted a chapter to these revolutionaries who, curiously enough, also called themselves "conservatives": because through their revolution they wanted to recapture a völkisch past uncontaminated by modernity.

They are important, for it is often forgotten that this national mystique could lead to a revolution of the right and that the left was not the only revolutionary impetus in the twentieth century. Indeed, the longing for immediate action and violence attracted many intellectuals to the fascist movement. Völkisch thought could at times support a conservatism which, though revolutionary, nevertheless stressed the importance of social hierarchy, the family, and personal property. It believed in a pluralistic society, but expressed this belief not by advocating parliamentary government but by emphasizing the corporate nature of society and politics. This corporatism stressed the harmony necessary for the unity of *Volk* and society. It sought to reorganize politics by grouping people by profession: the owner and the laborer within one industry or profession would be united in one organization. There would be no class struggle; instead, a consensus would emerge. Such a reorganization of politics would produce a true group rather than an artificial one, without destroying social and economic hierarchies. As we have seen, the *Volk* was at times also based on the family structure, and many who worshipped the *Volk* also saw in corporatism a feasible way to reorganize society and approximate the guilds of the Middle Ages. But the revolutionary wing of the völkisch movement wanted to right the wrong turn history had taken—not when the time was ripe but here and now.

However, the concept of a social hierarchy, dear to many in the movement, conflicted with the equality which all believed should prevail within the collectivity of the *Volk*. The revolutionary wing of the movement sought a more genuine social equality among all Germans. They tended to discard social hierarchy, replacing it with a leader who would incorporate within himself the mystique of the people. He would be the archetype of the *Volk*. After the Revolution of 1848 there are many descriptions of the "New Men" who would save and redeem the *Volk*. Hopes for creating a united Germany on a liberal foundation were now buried, as capitalism made ever greater inroads among the German people. From a host of such "heroes" we can take Adalbert Stifter's (1805–1868) *Witiko* (1865) as one example: he is rooted in his native landscape but leaves the native soil to taste the outside world. He refuses its temptations, however, and

12

makes his way back to his native region. There he recaptures his own soul and becomes the savior and example to the community. German literature at this time is filled with Witikos who lead the *Volk* back to its own true self, triumphing over the evils of modernity and the temptations of the outside world.

With the growth of mass politics after 1870 a new element was added. The masses of the *Volk* must be involved in the völkisch movement through myths and symbols that would appeal to their deepest instincts; the magic of leadership could then direct these instincts toward action. Völkisch thought had always been preoccupied with myths and symbols, for the ancient legends, sagas, and tales which rested deep in the *Volk* soul had been closely tied to a set of emotion-laden symbols. The irrationality that was basic to the völkisch experience led to a belief in magic, represented by the old Germanic gods of the *Volk*. The leadership ideal became part of this complex of völkisch thought. While the more conservative völkisch elements believed that slow organic evolution would bring about the völkisch ideal without running the risk of upsetting social hierarchy or property relationships, the revolutionary wing of the movement dreamed of a leader who would bring about a völkisch revolution.

This ideal was always foremost in the thought of these völkisch men and women. The hero is the embodiment of the soul of the *Volk* and of its morality: strong, brave, honest, and free of modern hypocrisy. He symbolizes an archetype of which Carl Jung (1875–1961) has given us a good definition—whose psychological correctness may perhaps be doubted but which summarizes very well the approach to life we are discussing: archetypes are like the riverbeds which the water has left but to which it returns after a long time. The archetype, then, was like an ancient riverbed in which the waters of life have coursed for centuries, and the longer they have lived within it, the greater the likelihood that they will find their way back.[15] The hero, the leader, as an archetypal phenomenon is thus tied to the deepest levels of the feeling of the *Volk*.

Völkisch thought moved in stereotypes—of its own image and the image it fashioned for itself of those who supposedly opposed its liberation. The Jews come into völkisch thought in this manner. The "image of the Jew," to which we have devoted two chapters, was defined in antithesis to völkisch ideology. The Jewish stereotype provided the focal point for the feeling of aggression inherent in the ideology. But, as chapter 1, "Culture, Civilization, and German Antisemitism," shows, this image was not necessarily motivated by racial feelings. Rather, it provided a foil for the völkisch ideal of rootedness and morality and became the symbol of völkisch anger with history. By the end of the century racial thought would take over this Jewish stereotype, yet it continued to exist hand in hand with the nonracial stereotype.

Stated in more concrete terms, this meant that even those who held to the stereotype were willing to exempt certain Jews from it. In mid-century, Gustav Freytag described the "ugly Jew" (as we shall see in the chapter devoted to Freytag) and at the same time drew up plans for the complete assimilation of Jews in Germany. Similarly, when at the end of the nineteenth century German youth organized its Youth Movement, it accepted Jewish members in spite of the völkisch orientation of the movement. There were those within the völkisch movement who believed some Jews capable of rising above their Jewishness, though this Jewishness was a fact and was, according to them, hostile to all the *Volk* stood for. These groups held that Jewishness was bad and inherently un-German, yet they did not regard the condition of the individual Jew as hopeless. To be sure, assimilation was possible for only a small number of Jews; the majority would remain a foreign, hostile element within the nation. Though by the end of the century racism increasingly closed the door even to this minority, it was never completely shut within the völkisch movement.

The völkisch ideal predated the development of racism. Blood and soil were wedded in the thought of many völkisch adherents only toward the end of the century, particularly after Germany's defeat in the First World War. But even during the Weimar Republic some völkisch groups (especially among the Youth Movement, but also in the German National Party) stood apart from this marriage and exempted certain individuals from the general condemnation of Jews. And among nationalists a variety of attitudes held sway. Some believed that a few Jews could be assimilated; others saw in the Jews a separate *Volk* and carried through Herder's idea that each *Volk* deserves respect. These groups denied the possibility of Jewish assimilation and advocated a "clean separation" between Jews and Germans. All variations in the tenor of völkisch thought must be borne in mind, for they will make their appearance in the chapters that follow. We must not read the National Socialist emphasis on "blood and soil" into the whole völkisch movement, for this nationalist emphasis developed over more than a century.

Nevertheless, the Jew became the foil for the evolution of this nationalism. The emphasis upon a person's inner drives, upon their soul, which we will discuss in the next chapter, was meant to establish a system of values that stood outside and opposed to present realities. These values, embodied in the *Volk*, were to be set up against the capitalism and materialism symbolized by the Jew. The attempt to preserve the purity of the *Volk* against all establishments that might oppose it became opposition against the merely "external" forces of objective reality. Personal and political renewal must come through the triumph of the *Volk* which, rising up from the Germanic soul, would lead to Utopia. The Jew stood for the shallow and insincere adaptation to external reality, opposed to all that was true, genuine, and beautiful. Antisemitism thus provides an excellent approach to this nationalism which, as a force opposed to the establishment (though it would attempt to capture one or the other political party), could supposedly open the gate to creative and meaningful politics.

This nationalism is the soil from which National Socialism took much of its nourishment and whose ideology Adolf Hitler used in his struggle for power.[16] The controversy over Hitler's belief in völkisch ideas will never be resolved, but there can be little doubt that he advocated this ideology. Some historians still believe that Hitler's triumph can be ascribed to his "naked will to power." Surely this represents a clinging to nineteenth-century concepts whereby thinkers like Leopold von Ranke (1795–1886) saw the idea of power as determining the struggle among European states. But power does not exist in isolation, separate from aims and ideals which infuse a concept with energy and meaning. Even in Ranke's Europe statesmen had to obtain support for their power politics by appealing to such ideals as nationalism or social harmony. We can no longer sunder power from context and hold it up as a self-contained principle; for even those who are often credited with advocating pure power did not use force and tactics in isolation from the purpose these were designed to serve. After all, Niccolò Machiavelli's (1469–1527) Prince used his power for the sake of a united Italy regenerated through Roman morality, and Ranke saw power in terms of God's immediate concern for all men and nations. Adolf Hitler desired power—desired it fanatically—but even there the attainment of power served a functional purpose; the völkisch ideology provided the ideal which gave the quest for power its aim and purpose.

People's actions are based on their attitudes toward life and what life holds for them. Attitudes of mind are crucial in that regard. The völkisch ideology—indeed, all the systems of thought with which we are concerned—may seem abstract and unrelated to reality. The development of this ideology took place against the backdrop of exceptional vicissitudes in German life; its attraction was precisely that it seemed to explain them in an unchanging and absolute manner. The penchant of thinking in absolutes was not confined to intellectuals. In the "age of the masses" the use of myths and symbols became of prime importance in forming political movements, and these had to rest on an unchanging appeal to man's equally unchanging wishes and desires. José Ortega y Gasset (1883–1955) has referred to the "vertical invaders" of society: hundreds of millions of men and women who were injected into the political scene as a result of the Industrial Revolution. These masses had no firm traditions themselves, but they longed for traditions to which they could relate, within which they could end their alienation from society and indeed participate in determining its fate.[17]

Such traditions had to be created for them through myths and symbols that would appeal to their longing for security and action, and to their prejudices. The nationalistic mystique of the völkisch movement was very well attuned to the "revolt of the masses," and so was the whole fascist movement. It was never a question of day-to-day reactions but of capturing the "soul" of the people through a national myth resting on an irrational base. We have already mentioned the importance of public festivals. Even Maximilien Robespierre (1758–1794) in the French Revolution found that to wed the masses to the ideal of reason, it was necessary to transform that very ideal into an irrational myth—and a Goddess of Reason was fashioned in the Tuileries for the people to worship. Many socialists after 1918 felt their movement was bogged down in an aggressively rationalistic orthodoxy that focused on an analysis of present society rather than on an unchanging and unadulterated ideal that could bring about Utopia. The socialist movements had a much more organized following after the First World War than the völkisch groups did. But the ideal of the *Volk* existed, to a great extent, outside any political entity, and in nations like Germany it undermined the socialist parties until they gave up the struggle. The left-wing intellectuals had, in any case, stood outside these parties because they no longer seemed to represent an unchanging ideal but rather an adjustment to society through strategy and tactics.

These factors make it difficult to assess just how deep the völkisch movement went in Germany. It has been pointed out repeatedly that even during the economic crisis that ended the Weimar Republic, no overtly völkisch party (and this includes the Nazis and the German National Party) ever received more than a bare majority of votes in any national election. But once we turn from such a narrowly political analysis, the picture changes. Certainly among the most articulate German youth the ideology had found a home. Not only the nearly half a million youths organized in Youth Movement groups, but the students at the universities, had accepted völkisch thought as a way out of Germany's dilemma. The official German students' organization (Bund Deutscher Studenten) elected a National Socialist president in 1931, well before the Nazis achieved success at the polls. Even before this date, the more conservative German National Party had won a majority of student elections. Perhaps there existed a völkisch underground, an attitude of mind which did not readily translate itself into national politics and which found its most vital supporters among German youth. For them it was indeed a "Third Force," outside the maneuverings of the left- or right-wing establishments.

The question also arises to what extent völkisch ideas had penetrated the democratic and even the socialist parties. Though no definite answer can be given, it is certain that the kind of mind that thought in German and Jewish stereotypes made inroads here as well. For example, Friedrich Stampfer (1874–1957), the editor of the official Social Democratic newspaper (*Vorwärts*), shared with other German Jews the shock of making contact with the mass of Polish Jewry during the First World War. He called this a "new world" of dirt, misery, and decay. For the first time he experienced the Jew "en masse" and realized that a Jewish problem existed. Stampfer, a socialist, concurred in an image of the Jew which, through the stereotype of the East European ghetto, played such a large part in antisemitic völkisch thought from the mid-nineteenth century on.[18] There were others, liberals and socialists, who shared this experience. This did not mean that they became völkisch in the full meaning of the word, but such attitudes could exist alongside the worship of the *Volk*. This point is worth making, though it is impossible to tell how many such individuals took the full plunge into the völkisch movement. Certainly the left-wing intellectuals avoided such a catharsis.

We are concerned here with an attitude of mind that produced a certain atmosphere in the nation: any examination of how deeply this penetrated can only lead to a hypothesis based on a variety of examples. Chapter 3, "The Influence of the Völkisch Idea on German Jewry," has some importance in this connection. Once again young people were involved, young people who accepted the non-racial aspect of völkisch thought: the "clean separation" leading to a unique peoplehood or the possibility of a more complete assimilation. Why should such young Jews take to völkisch ideals unless the pull of this ideology was strong, even before Germany's defeat in the First World War? Why should one of the leading theoreticians of Jewish nationhood, Martin Buber, be so close to völkisch ideas at this point in his life? Völkisch thought was not favorable to Judaism. Yet many young Jews who wanted to emphasize their unique *Volk* turned to this body of ideas for inspiration.

This völkisch atmosphere was not confined to the traditional German lands. Certainly Austria and German-speaking regions such as Bohemian Sudetenland made important contributions. But it cannot be said that völkisch ideas emerged principally through the racial conflicts that dominated the border regions of the Austrian Empire.[19] Neither Herder nor Father Jahn lived in Austria, and most völkisch writers mentioned in this book were Germans concerned with specific German problems. The fact that Hitler derived much of his völkisch thought from Austria must not lead to a single-minded concentration upon the Austrian Empire. German Austria was a border region, facing the Slavic world—but so was the eastern frontier of Germany. Hitler reacted to the immigration of East European Jews to Vienna, and Gustav Freytag reacted in a similar manner to this immigration in the Silesian town of Breslau.

To be sure, the völkisch movement in Austria and Bohemia was from the first more aggressive, repudiating the non-racial side of the German movement. Austrian university fraternities, for example, had excluded Jews from membership by 1890, long before the German fraternities decided to do so. The border regions of the German-speaking lands made important contributions to völkisch ideology, especially to its more radical elements. However, the dynamic of the movement and its principal strength derived their inspiration from the German heartland. Perhaps it is best to ignore political boundaries altogether in an analysis of the völkisch movement. The myths and symbols that were to renew the Volk knew no geographical limitations.

How uniquely German was this ideology? There is no doubt that the nationalism growing up in Eastern Europe during the nineteenth century shared many völkisch attitudes, transposing them to its own mythical and historical bases. Moreover, völkisch ideology must be grasped as part of the totalitarian impetus of the twentieth century. The totalitarian nature of that völkisch thought which sought a leader and which wanted to overthrow existing society is obvious. But the relationship of this thought to the fascist movement is still controversial, though many historians have viewed völkisch thought as it climaxed in National Socialism as an integral part of the fascist movement. Yet the differences in fascism in the various European countries must not be lost from sight.

All fascism shared an organic worldview and believed in a hierarchy defined in terms of service to the Volk or nation as exemplified by the leader. All fascism also held that the fascist revolution was a spiritual revolution, one of attitudes, and consequently subordinated social and economic considerations to the nationalist mystique. Moreover, all fascisms

18

put the emphasis on youth, virility, and a dynamic which, under the leader, would lead to the elimination of the degenerate present. The fascist revolution was supposed to be a "moral act," and the morality which such an act exemplified was the morality for which the *Volk* supposedly longed. Völkisch thought and fascism, in the twentieth century, were a part of the same nationalism, which was geared to solve the dilemma that people and nations faced within their society.

The differences between Germany and Western Europe must not be minimized, however, in attempting to reach a synthesis of the fascist movement. Everywhere fascism presented itself as the "Third Force": transcending evil capitalism and unpalatable Marxism. But though it did so on the basis of a renewal of the nation, the content of this unchanging ideal varied. Admittedly, it was always emotional and centered on human creativity as transmitted and released through association with "genuine" national spiritual values. But there were differences in the way in which the nation was defined. Every nation had its own tradition and lived within its particular historical situation, and this was bound to affect the "Third Force," however much it claimed to oppose present reality.[20]

Italian Fascism differed from the German national mystique in obvious ways: the *Volk* was not pitted against the state, for the symbol of the state, the king, remained in office. Moreover, the Italian nationalist tradition looked to Giuseppe Mazzini (1805–1872) with his ideal of humanity rather than to Herder for inspiration, aggressive though this turned out to be in the end. Because Mussolini's early fascism had a left-wing revolutionary character, and because *Il Duce* had to abandon most of this impetus on his way to power, Italian Fascism proved to be more eclectic than German völkisch thought. For the *Volk* the eternal and unchanging truth was "given," and upon it the nation must be rebuilt. But for Mussolini that truth was far less clearly expressed, and concepts such as the "heroic will" had much greater scope. The ideal of rootedness in the mystical collectivity of the nation was certainly there, but the rhetoric of a Nietzschean dynamic never left the movement.

There were many Europeans who saw in fascism a "permanent revolution," a viewpoint which was barred to those Germans who adhered to the ideal of the *Volk*. Italian Fascism during its early phase could have a revolutionary impetus which was denied even to völkisch revolutionaries. For such conservative revolutionaries ended up in the arms of a völkisch, racial mystique in spite of their revolutionary longings.

However, some fascists in France and Italy continued to believe that existing reality could be destroyed in one instant, while others wanted to go to the "limits of fascism, where all possibilities are open."[21] No doubt these fascists meant it: here was permanent revolution which was not bogged down in dogmas or party programs. But even here we can detect anti-urbanism and at times the mystique of the soil. In France, Robert Brasillach (1909–1945) spoke often and at length about the love of adventure and the dynamic of fascism, but in his novels he shows great admiration for the peasant stock and its ties to the soil. He loved Paris, but for him the city was an assemblage of separate small towns, each with its own characteristics and experience.[22] Fascism always had in it a strong romantic component, which led to an exaltation of activism or rural nostalgia or a mixture of both. It was always based on the ideal of a spiritual collectivity, a true camaraderie among men. But in German and Eastern European fascism, this base had a more definite content derived from the idealization of the *Volk*. Here also the marriage of this ideology with racism was, in the end, more firmly rooted than in Western fascism, some of which for a time bypassed racism and even overt antisemitism.

These variations within fascism are important, for they help explain the many different kinds of people who were attracted to the movement. In this book we are primarily concerned with the attraction which fascism as a "Third Force" held for the intellectuals. When we have dealt in a general way with the ideals to which some of them committed themselves, we must return to the individuals themselves as a group. They will emerge in this book as writers and artists as well as political theorists—always seeking to infuse a system of absolute values into the pragmatic present and dedicated to keeping these values intact. Chapter 5, "Fascism and the Intellectuals," gives some of the reasons why such thinkers adhered to the movement, what they saw in it, how it met their needs, and how they became captives of their commitment even when it no longer lived up to their ideals.

Fascism and National Socialism were myths in which such people put their faith and which they themselves helped to transmit to the masses. The fascist mystique obviously answered their individual needs, but beyond this, the kind of ideology for which the movement stood was closely linked with the general search on the part of intellectuals for identity in the postwar world. It is necessary to dwell on this fact, for it provides a link between the majority of the themes in this book and the final chapter "Left-Wing Intellectuals in the Weimar Republic."

Intellectuals pioneered the search for a future that would be neither capitalist nor materialist. Left-wing intellectuals shared the "anti-capitalist longing" of which some fascists spoke so eloquently, but they related this longing to ideals of equality and universal justice. The individual must always be an end in themself, never merely a means. In their eyes this was the ideal that must infuse all mass movements and political tactics. Here also the ideal aims were put before any purely material interests; and this concern for absolute values dominated any specific socialist programs which the intellectuals might advocate. Moreover, creativity and the primacy of individual consciousness informed this idealism. Even when they joined communist parties, the task these intellectuals set themselves was to watch over the ideals represented by the communist revolution—a revolution which they were apt to see in spiritual terms. This held true for the Surrealists in France and for those in Germany who are discussed here.[23] Many refused to join communism or the Social Democrats because they could not fulfill their tasks within these ranks, and many who did join left in disillusionment by the 1930s.

The concept of a "spiritual revolution," writ large in these pages, was not merely a German nationalist phenomenon; from time to time we have referred to examples from other nations. No doubt this concept made the fascist revolution acceptable and attractive to many in the West, especially to the middle classes. A change was possible in the present which would not vitally disturb property relationships and which would guarantee order amid the danger of chaos. By concentrating on a change of attitude, fascism seemed to avoid the dangers which social and economic revolution might bring—dangers that were exemplified by Soviet Russia. This facet of the movement which was congenial to middle-class longings also had a more positive appeal. The "spiritual revolution" seemed to avoid the materialism of both right and left and to concentrate on absolute values—ideals which must take precedence over immediate and pragmatic concerns.

The ideals of the left-wing intellectuals were, of course, different from those of the völkisch or the fascist movements, but both looked to ideology to solve the specific concerns of present society. Both movements personified "poets of revolution," as Léon Degrelle (1906–1994) characterized the fascist leadership, even though their verses ran differently.[24] Left-wing intellectuals abhorred the nationalism and the idea of struggle inherent in all fascism; they had little overt sympathy with the rejection of rationalism. Yet, when one reads the last chapter in this book in conjunction with what has gone before, one can see a certain convergence of opinion among these bitter enemies. Not only was there in both an utter rejection and an absolute criticism of existing society; there was also a tendency toward irrationalism even on the part of the left, one of

21

whose members spoke of the "mysticism of the ratio."[25] Idealism bound together the two movements, and the vagueness that runs through even the concrete programs of the völkisch movement and of the left-wing intellectuals also forged a chain that bound them together. Contemporaries realized this, but it has never been clearly stated.

Because this whole argument is controversial, it seems best for the reader to draw their own conclusions. The material presented in this book will enable them to do so. We can sympathize with the dilemma of these left-wing intellectuals and respect their ideals, which exalt that which is noble in humanity, but we must also realize the dangers inherent in idealism that stresses the purity of absolute values and is apt to retreat into its own circumscribed world in the face of a reality that will not bend to the intellectuals' desire. Such intellectuals are in constant danger of becoming a sect, whereas fascism became a mass movement precisely because it was willing to compromise with reality and to take in popular prejudices and desires. The very integrity of the left-wing intellectuals kept them apart from the masses they so desperately wanted to lead.

The final chapter, on left-wing intellectuals, is an integral part of the discussion of human attitudes which fills this book. They all worked upon the canvas of modern technical society and all of them wanted to eliminate the present in favor of an ideal that was to infuse all human life. These intellectuals were not content to build bridges from the present to the future, but rather sought to bypass such dreary work and leap across the stormy river. Yet their ideals are still with us, and the search for a "Third Force" has not been concluded. Fascism can still provide an ideology and the momentum for societies in danger of chaos and dissolution. There seems little doubt that Peronism (Juan Perón, 1895–1974) in Argentina and the Nasser (1918–1970) regime in Egypt (at least in its early stages) contained elements of fascism. In other areas of the so-called underdeveloped world ruling elites have had recourse to fascist ideas.[26] Völkisch thought had its base in Central Europe where it still has many adherents, even though they are scattered and agitate beneath the political surface.

The dilemma of the left-wing intellectuals has continued in the West. Because it is especially acute in the United States, the chapter on left-wing intellectuals concludes with a discussion of their present state as related to the past. Here I have gone beyond the chronological boundaries of the book; it seemed important to do so. These essays all deal with problems that are relevant to our time, but for those of us who live in the United States the continuing impetus of the left-wing intellectuals is especially striking. So much has been written about the "New Left" that it is sometimes forgotten that the New Left belongs to a historical tradition, one that has never been properly investigated. I am aware that the ideology of the present-day New Left is not static and that many different traditions went into its making. Their attitudes are constantly subject to change: new ideas of leadership, as well as a tendency to return to greater Marxist orthodoxy, can be discerned on the horizon. The problem of influences exists throughout history. Here we may have no firmly established direct line of influence but instead a parallelism which is immediate and startling. The background provided for the New Left by the left-wing intellectuals discussed in this book is significant, and once this is realized, our discussions can take on a new dimension; those who are on the New Left can then perhaps become aware of some opportunities and dangers inherent in their position as a "Third Force."

It seemed proper to conclude this book on a contemporary note—not only to demonstrate once more the close connection between past and present but also to lend perspective to the existential dilemma faced by some of our most sensitive and committed intellectuals. In this way, we can give an added dimension to the ideologies which have concerned us and which—whether left or right—present a shared approach to the materialism of our society.

1

Culture, Civilization, and German Antisemitism

In this chapter, German antisemitism is examined within the framework of a more general trend of German intellectual history. Whereas the social and political roots of German antisemitism have been thoroughly investigated, its intellectual foundations have received scant attention. Above all, the image of the Jew as it evolved in an important segment of German thought has not yet received sufficient analysis. The image of the Jew which had formed in many German minds goes far to explain the surrender to National Socialism's antisemitism by even the more respectable elements of the population. This theme is part of an intellectual history that has not yet been written. The very absurdity of the image of the Jew, drawn in racial terms, has stood in the way of close analysis.

Solomon F. Bloom (1903–1962) perceptively points out that Western scholars have rarely been at home with *outré* subjects, and no subject is more *outré* than the National Socialist view of Jew and Aryan.[1] Yet these views did not seem at all absurd to many respectable members of the community who embraced them. Such racial attitudes, ridiculous to most Western intellectuals, had in fact been prepared by popular novelists for more than a century before National Socialism came to power.

It can be demonstrated that the image of the Jew in nineteenth-century German thought is not basically different from the image of the Jew in National Socialist belles-lettres. It is significant, moreover, that the nineteenth-century image is not necessarily associated with the idea of race; it is not even the prerogative of reactionary forces.[2] Popular writers such as Gustav Freytag and Wilhelm Raabe (1831–1910) were liberals. We are, then, dealing with a specific trend of thought which put forward a consistent image of the Jew. At first this image did not depend exclusively

24

or even principally on racial ideas. One could hold this image of the Jew and not be a racist. This fact is frequently overlooked, just as it is often forgotten that this manner of thought made it possible for people to surrender to National Socialism who did not believe in the Aryan myth or in Alfred Rosenberg's (1893–1946) *Der Mythus des 20. Jahrhunderts* (*The Myth of the Twentieth Century*, 1930).[3]

If race is not the key to this image of the Jew, what does characterize the concept of the Jew in this intellectual development? It is the idea that the Jew was devoid of spirituality and feeling, even if this was not necessarily explained as an unchanging racial characteristic. But why should this particular view of the Jew have such importance? The answer is that in German intellectual development the emphasis came increasingly to be on "feeling" and on the "inner man and his condition." This emphasis is part of the völkisch thought which has been discussed in the introduction. The *Volk* was a spiritual ideal based on a nationalist mystique. The soil, the native landscape provided constant inspiration, and the inner-directedness of an individual soul was thought to be analogous to the soul of the *Volk*. Through such ideas many Germans rejected materialism in any form and envisaged humanity and society as filled with irrational and spiritual drives.

Oswald Spengler is symptomatic of this development. His *The Decline of the West*, contrasting culture and civilization, soul and intellect, sums up a way of thinking which was of cardinal importance in forming Gentile attitudes toward the Jew. A culture possesses a soul, civilization is the dead-end state of a culture, the "most external and artificial state of which . . . humanity . . . is capable." Spengler held that cultures are living organisms, whereas civilization is the corpse of a culture. Civilization destroys the living organic form of human life on earth, taking over when such life has become stifled and fossilized.[4] Above all, civilizations lack the essential aspect of a vital culture: religion. Every culture must ultimately be religious if it is to be truly creative. Civilization is irreligious, strictly materialistic, "unspiritual, unphilosophical, devoid of art [and] clannish to the point of brutality, aiming relentlessly at tangible success."[5] It is within this framework of thought that the image of the Jew must be placed.

The emphasis in German thought on true feeling and on culture as equated not with externals but with inward spiritual growth has many different roots. It is a flight from reality which can be traced back to the beginning of the nineteenth century. This escape took the form of a search for a new security. Some writers sought in it the glorification of national roots, as, for example, in idealized peasant novels. Others found their roots in the glorification of provincial life, in a retreat from the turmoil of the city to the life of the stable, provincial middle class. Thus, Gustav Freytag rejected the uncertainty of the industrial and political world for a glorification of the bourgeoisie engaged in steady, honest work. It is characteristic that this mid-century writer who glorified *petit bourgeois* life was hailed by his contemporaries as the "most representative writer of our time."[6]

This retreat into feeling and the life of the soil was furthered by a fear of the masses which became more general among the educated classes after the Revolution of 1848. Georg Gottfried Gervinus (1805–1871) in his *Einleitung in die Geschichte des neunzehnten Jahrhunderts* (*Introduction to the History of the Nineteenth Century*, 1852) states typically that the "movement of the times is carried by the instincts of the masses"; the influence of great individuals in the affairs of men has been eclipsed. Since Napoleon, there have been no "truly outstanding geniuses in politics."[7] Gervinus feared this development in the 1850s, just as Jacob Burckhardt (1818–1897) was to fear it in the 1870s.

How does this bear on the image of the Jew? Presumably, since he lacked the necessary spiritual impulse, the Jew came to stand for all that these figures feared: materialism, progress, the big city, and the sober rationalistic mind that could have no sense of the beautiful. This is clearly illustrated by two of the most popular novels of the century, both written by liberals, men who were not racists. Gustav Freytag's *Soll und Haben*, (*Debit and Credit*, 1855) is similar in character and plot to Wilhelm Raabe's *Hungerpastor* (*Poor Pastor*, 1862). In both novels two young men go out into the world, one a Christian, the other a Jew. Both are unsuccessful in achieving the high aims which they had set for themselves. But here the similarity between them ends. The Christian makes his way honestly, and if he does not gain his earthly goal, he arrives at the end of the novel contented, settled, and, above all, spiritually enriched. In Freytag's novel, Anton Wohlfahrt finds this enrichment in the steady life of a provincial merchant house; Raabe's Hans Unwirsch finds the same spiritual satisfaction in life in the "hunger parish"—in a lonely outpost by the sea. In both cases true culture is found through a retreat from the world, living a life dedicated to eternal values without participating in the revolutionary upheavals which form the background of both books.

The Jew makes his way dishonestly. He does not retreat in the face of the world but takes advantage of its dishonesty and weaknesses of character. Moses Freudenstein, in *Poor Pastor*, dabbles in politics and plays both sides in order to satisfy his worldly ambitions and lust for power. Veitel Itzig's commercial dealings in *Debit and Credit* also take advantage of worldly realities in order to satisfy his lust for riches. Obviously, both Jews are incapable of spiritual enrichment, indeed of any spiritual feelings. Both end in oblivion. Itzig drowns in a dirty river, and Moses Freudenstein, his ambitions thwarted, dies in bourgeois imprisonment.[8]

The crux of it all is that Jews have no feeling. This accusation is repeated in its sharpest formulation in one of the most violent National Socialist novels, Tüdel Weller's (1902–1970) *Rabauken! Peter Mönkemann haut sich durch* (*Peter Mönkemann Fights His Way*, 1938). After Weller has depicted Jews committing every conceivable crime and engaged in every kind of underhanded dealing, he remarks: "How can one speak of ideals when one speaks of the Jews?"[9] Given the intellectual context already described, this one accusation could explain all else; in the debate on the Jewish Question in the Prussian Diet of 1880 one deputy warned that the absence of feeling (*Nüchternheit*) among Jews allowed them to employ immoral means to enrich themselves.[10]

Where did this accusation of a lack of spirituality originate? It was bound up with the attitude toward the Jewish religion, and this well before racial thought came on the scene. Judaism was considered a fossil, an image familiarized by Arnold J. Toynbee (1889–1975) in our own day. When Judaism was viewed from this perspective, it became evident that its people, who were once the "people of the Book," could no longer have any ethical foundations. It will not do to say that such an attitude reflects a general hostility toward every Jew, for this concept of Judaism antedates the emergence of racism. Voltaire (François-Marie Arouet, 1694–1778) hated Judaism but not individual Jews. For the Enlightenment, Judaism, like all religions, was a dead issue. Yet it was the Enlightenment, it must be recalled, which emancipated the Jews. This separation of Judaism and the Jew was at the root of future difficulties. A look at the work of the great champion of Jewish emancipation, Christian Wilhelm von Dohm (1751–1820), *Über die bürgerliche Verbesserung der Juden* (*About the Improvement of Jewish Citizenship*, 1781), is illuminating here. The gist of his argument was that through emancipation the Jews would become educated and useful members of the community. This meant that Jews must shed their superstitions. Because Jews had only superstitions, not true ethical and spiritual roots, they must be given new roots from which to develop into good citizens—they must become peasants and craftsmen. "Let them cease to be Jews" was Dohm's solution to the problem.[11] Dohm had all the stereotyped prejudices about the Jews but he believed that as they shed their "Jewish habits" and superstitions they could and would become good citizens.

The Jewish problem could be solved through the reeducation of the Jews. The *philosophes* of the Enlightenment believed passionately in the capability of the human mind to triumph over the forces of superstition and to arrive at a rational understanding of the universe. The process of education was directed toward developing a critical mind in each person, and this meant battling the forces which impeded it. The *philosophes* saw in Christianity the greatest adversary of the critical mind, the power which had to be crushed. Judaism had provided the foundations for Christianity, and as such it was part of that "infamous" religion's conspiracy of deception: the false myth which opposed independent inquiry. The Jew who was faithful to Judaism was wholly corrupt, an evil force in society, who must be reeducated to shed his religion and enter the age of progress and enlightenment.

Dohm shared this attitude, and it outlasted his own times. As the new century opened, Joachim Heinrich Campe's (1746–1818) popular *Wörterbuch der deutschen Sprache* (*Dictionary of the German Language,* 1807) showed no trace of the new nationalism which is so often assigned the sole blame for the development of modern antisemitism. But his judgment on the Jewish religion was severe. The synagogue was called the "Jew School" (*Judenschule*) because, like unruly schoolboys, the worshippers mumbled to themselves in an "unlovely" way. Jewish services were dubbed noisy and chaotic. Campe was repeating a word (*Judenschule*) that had long been in popular use, and defining it conventionally. But he did so as a man of the Enlightenment who in general rejected "superstitious traditions."[12]

How, then, were the Jews to be reeducated? The enlightened Emperor Joseph II (1741–1790, r. 1765–1790) of Austria (who freed the serfs in his domains) set the tone. Traditionally, Jews had had to obtain the Emperor's permission to marry. Joseph II eased this cruel requirement but substituted a new regulation for the old: permission was to be given automatically to Jews who had attended a primary school where German, not Yiddish, culture was taught. The proposals put forward in Prussia for new Jewish legislation contained similar provisos for German schooling. The "advanced" culture of the age was to replace ancient superstitions as a prerequisite for Jewish emancipation.

The attempts to "civilize" Jews went one step further. As long as Jews clung to their religion they represented a stereotype even to the enlightened: a stereotype of antisocial behavior and devotion to usury. Therefore, Dohm emphasized the necessity of directing Jews away from trade and toward activities that would aid them in becoming moral individuals. Jews must become peasants and craftsmen. This opinion represents a curious clinging to tradition on the part of men who in other respects rejected the medieval past where these occupations had predominated. Romantics were to glorify the peasant and craftsman in contrast to industrial society; men of the Enlightenment such as Dohm did so mainly when confronted with the Jewish problem.

The Jew must be radically transformed on their way to full emancipation: this was the crux of the matter. They could be urged forward along this road, but not persecuted. Dohm believed, in true Enlightenment fashion, that evil "political or religious enthusiasm and allegiance are perpetuated solely through persecution." Yet the sophisticated, anti-Christian *philosophe* Georg Christoph Lichtenberg (1742–1799) could write: "Next to my own wanton lusts, it is the Jews who have given me the greatest trouble."[13] There can be no doubt of the ambivalence of the Enlightenment toward Jews and Jewish emancipation. Judaism was immoral, superstitious, and produced an undesirable Jewish stereotype. The individual Jew could be made fit for participation in society only through reeducation. We can, from this point of departure, clearly envisage the accusation leveled against Jews in the nineteenth century: You have become a citizen but you have failed to reeducate yourself, and because you have chosen to re-main imprisoned within Judaism, the process of emancipation has failed.

The Enlightenment's ambivalence toward Jews was not merely a product of the imagination of the time; all ideologies have roots in reality. In the eighteenth century Jews lived apart from the rest of society, within their own culture, which, though influenced by outside forces, seemed to Gentiles strange and parochial. The ghetto walls had not yet fallen. However deeply they were influenced by their surroundings, Jews seemed a foreign element living on European soil. They differed in their way of life, habits of thought and dress from the rest of the European population. It is from this point of view that we must view the reaction to Jews, first in the eighteenth century when the ghettos still existed, and then throughout the nineteenth century when the ghetto walls had fallen but the masses of Eastern European Jewry still seemed to continue the life associated with an earlier epoch of history. This is the historical reality against which the *philosophes* formulated their solution to the Jewish problem. Their ambivalence, so significant for the future of the Jews, was intimately connected with the ghetto period of Jewish history—which itself continued to haunt the relationship between Jews and Christians in the nineteenth and twentieth centuries, even when, in the West, emancipation seemed to have triumphed.

Thus, at the very outset of Jewish emancipation the dualism between the "fossil" of Judaism and the hope of assimilation for the individual Jew appears. It is this theme which was carried into the nineteenth century. Gustav Freytag, for example, drew up elaborate plans for complete Jewish assimilation (1893). He has high praise for his friend Jacob Kaufmann (1814–1871), the "Bohemian Jew boy," who had taken the final step and "integrated himself completely with our nation."[14] Yet in his writings Freytag depicted Veitel Itzig as a Jew who had remained a Jew and had not assimilated. Freytag shows clearly how hope for Jewish assimilation was combined with a belief in the stereotype of the Jew. Judaism was a fossil; the only way for the Jew to become an ethical person was to acquire new roots, the roots of his adopted land, through honest work (to use Dohm's phrase).

The Jews who did not fulfill this hope were the ones who formed the core of the popular image, and as the optimism of the Enlightenment began to fade, all Jews were associated with them. Especially when after the Revolution of 1848 the great fear gripped writers, the dualism between Judaism and the Jew was no longer tenable. No Jew could now share the ethical roots of the Germans, which they, in their search for stability, proudly reserved for themselves. Dohm at the end of the eighteenth century had believed that the Jews could acquire new roots by becoming German craftsmen or peasants, but by the middle of the nineteenth century the atmosphere had changed. This is made clear in Heinrich von Treitschke's (1834–1896) remarks about the Jew Berthold Auerbach (1812–1882), father of the peasant novel. Auerbach's peasants were only Jews in disguise. When it came to depicting the feeling of a people, the voice of nature could not be adulterated by artificiality. And Auerbach's peasant must be artificial creations, for Auerbach, as a Jew, could have no genuine relationship to the tillers of the soil. The Jew had no feeling and thus no rapport with the real *Volk*.[15]

The dualism between Judaism and Jew was abandoned. Judaism determined the character of the Jew, and here it became plain that the Enlightenment had not fundamentally improved the popular image of the Jew; indeed, it had materially contributed to the creation of the stereotype. Voltaire could be cited on Judaism, and now that the dualism of the Enlightenment had become inoperative, the "fossil" description blanketed all individual distinctions. Court preacher Adolf Stoecker (1835–1909) summed it up at the end of the century when he described the Jewish problem as an ethical rather than a religious one; since Judaism was not a proper religion, Jews could have no ethics.[16] It is significant that in his attack against the Jews, Dietrich Eckart (1868–1923), the earliest National Socialist ideologue, posited as his first point that Judaism is not a religion at all, because it is without soul and centered on this world.[17]

Like many other writers, Freytag and Raabe delighted in equating the observance of the Jewish religion with unethical acts. The twentieth-century antisemitic literary critic Adolf Bartels (1862–1945) called Auguste Hauschner's (1850–1924) *Die Familie Lowositz* (1908) the best novel for an understanding of Jews. The essence of that work is the episode in which the family is celebrating Passover. How superficial is this observance! The members of the family hate each other, and in business the Lowositz clan makes its money with utter disregard of honesty. Hauschner summed it up in her conclusion: the Jewish religion was not a true worldview, and everything else springs from that.[18]

In mid-century, Judaism began to exert a certain fascination on writers, without, however, gaining in ethical stature. It was the mystical element in Jewish ritual that interested them, but not with the kind of seriousness that marked the interest of the Humanists of the sixteenth century for the Cabala. This mysticism was informed by a certain concept of the East European ghetto, combined with the fear of the unknown. East European Jewry entered German literature through Jewish authors. Leo Herzberg-Fränkel (1827–1915) saw in the ghettos of Poland both intellectual and spiritual poverty. He condemned Jewish orthodoxy, which, he said, furthered ignorance. In his *Polnische Juden* (*Polish Jews*, 1867) he blamed these conditions on the social and political milieu. Nevertheless, his ghettos wielded a fascination; not by reason of their spiritual life, but because of the appeal of caftaned figures moving about the narrow, dirty streets. In Karl Emil Franzos's (1848–1904) stories, his native Jewish regions of Bucovina and Galicia were depicted as "half Asia."[19] The world of the ghetto was opened to German readers by Jews who had little understanding of it and who wanted to purge themselves of the past. Authors like Herzberg-Fränkel and Franzos were undoubtedly sincere in their description of the East European ghetto civilization. Certainly their viewpoint was shared by many official Jewish organizations in Germany. When, for example, a committee was formed in Königsberg in 1869 to help the poverty-stricken Jews of Belarus, its report stated unequivocally that such Jews had a "low level of culture in general" and that all progress of modern times passed them by. This Jewish committee echoed a general German prejudice of the times by emphasizing that "only the possession of general cultural standards can guarantee economic prosperity." In the eyes of the committee these Jews did not possess such "general cultural standards," by which they meant the standards of liberalism and the Enlightenment. For the wealthy Jews on the committee were not infected by völkisch thought, but clung to a liberalism which derived from the Enlightenment. Here we see two cultures actually colliding within Europe: this fact, it seems to me, provides the most important insight into the role which the ghetto played throughout the nineteenth century in the formation of the Jewish stereotype.

A sensitive observer could feel the deep spirituality which coursed beneath the crowded conditions and poverty of the Jewish settlements. Many German Jews, such as the writer Alfred Döblin (1878–1957), were deeply attracted to the vitality of intellectual life within the ghettos. Toward the end of the century the young Zionists felt strongly drawn to the Jews of Eastern Europe, for they represented the core of the Jewish *Volk*. Their enthusiasm did not embrace the religiosity of the ghetto but was centered on a national impetus, much of which derived its inspiration from German sources. This is a point to which we shall return. For all that, Goethe's reaction to the ghetto as a child in the 1750s was more typical for most Gentiles and many Jews: what he saw was "lack of space, filth, milling crowds, the accents of an unpleasing language."[20] This was indeed a "foreign" people, living at the border of Germany and infiltrating the so-called higher culture of the Western nations.

The ghetto theme was taken up by German writers, for it fitted in with their view of Judaism. Raabe in his story *Holunderblüthe* (*The Elderberry Blossom*, 1863) imbued the old ghetto of Prague with an aura of romance. Yet he, too, stressed the dirt of the streets, and he described the people as "ugly as the night."[21] The Romanticism of these writers tended to be transmuted into a fear of this unknown world. Hermann Goedsche (1815–1878), who wrote under the pen name of Sir John Retcliffe, typified this development. Once more the ghetto of Prague was depicted, but in his novel *Biarritz* (1868) it was stripped of its romantic elements and became simply Emil Franzos's "half Asia" within Europe. The mystic fascination crystallized for Goedsche in the meeting of the Jews (the Sanhedrin) in an ancient cemetery, to plan a Jewish world conspiracy.

The fear of a Jewish world conspiracy had roots reaching far back into the centuries. It gained added popularity when seen in the light of the supposedly mysterious and evil nature of Judaism as exemplified by the ghetto. The aim of this conspiracy was to take power, to destroy all non-Jews. *Biarritz* has been called the sharpest antisemitic attack of the nineteenth century. Johann von Leers (Omar Amin, 1902–1965), a Nazi propagandist, reissued the ghetto section of the book after Hitler had assumed power in 1935. Goedsche's ideas were taken up in France as well, though much of French antisemitism (especially that represented by influential Catholic publications) as a rule paid little attention to antisemitism movements outside its own boundaries.[22] Judaism was here associated not only with unethical behavior but also with the crowded conditions and filth of the ghetto. The stereotype of Jewish physical ugliness which Freytag and Raabe had stressed was now related to the way of life of the masses of Eastern Jewry. An element of mystery took shape as the "world conspiracy" grew within the ghetto walls. Increasingly, this appeared to be a true revelation of both Judaism and the Jews.

Gustav Freytag's Jewish figures represented the Eastern Jews as he saw them penetrate the city of Breslau from nearby Poland.[23] In National Socialist times, Eberhard Wolfgang Möller (1906–1972), winner of the national book prize for 1934–35, represented Eastern Jews as "the Jews," without any further qualifications. Tüdel Weller, in his preface to *Rabauken!*, showed how Franzos's "half Asia" seemed best to describe the Jewish milieu in general. He quoted a spurious letter from Benjamin Franklin to Congress: "I warn you gentlemen . . . the Jews, gentlemen, they are Asiatics."[24] Alfred Rosenberg's periodical *Die Judenfrage* (*The Jewish Question*) put it succinctly: Eastern Jewry was the reservoir of modern Jewry and the root of its strength.[25] What a contrast these roots provided with the roots of the German and the spiritual enrichment that grew out of them. Jewish roots were set in a religion without ethics, in surroundings of dirt and filth, and in an atmosphere of world conspiracy.

This theme was exploited in National Socialist belles-lettres. In detective stories the brave sleuths fought the Jewish world conspiracy. For example, Pieter Coll (Hans-Walter Gaebert, b. 1905)—a prolific writer of detective stories—in *Die Menschenfracht der "Ano-Wati"* (*The Human Cargo of the Ano-Wati*, 1939) had his detective hero fighting such a Jewish conspiracy and the Jews were portrayed as people without sense of beauty or cleanliness and, of course, without scruples. Nor was the triumph of justice final; some Jews were caught, but the conspiracy went on.[26] Here, once more, the fear of the unknown has appeared. At times a deeper, more medieval note was struck. Thus, Hans Hauptmann (1865–1946) in *Die Memoiren des Satans* (*The Memoirs of Satan*, 1929) had the devil buy the Jews to do his work on earth. He called this book a satirical novel but his theme was built on the ancient relationship between the devil and the Jews.[27]

After the First World War, the Jewish world conspiracy came to be linked with the communist conspiracy. Surely, communism was the kind of ideal the Jews were incapable of experiencing. The theory was that Jews were communists for the sake of their conspiracy to take over the world, not out of concern for the oppressed. Fritz Halbach (1879–1942) in *Genosse Levi* (*Comrade Levi*, 1921) made this plain. The young communist agitator was really on good terms with his father, a wealthy banker. Both wanted the same thing, world power, and both were willing to use any means to obtain it.[28] Thus, Judaism was equated with communism.

A celebrated völkisch novel, Nathanael Jünger's *Volk in Gefahr* (*Volk in Danger*, 1921), sums up these trends.[29] Jünger was the pseudonym of the evangelical minister Dietrich-Johann Rump (1871–1941). For him, too, the roots humanity had acquired were all-important, and these were found in the *Volk*. He was in agreement with the novelists who after 1848 sought out these roots, for roots gave men culture. Jünger's other, less-known works dealt with such subjects as the struggle of the peasants to remain on the land, German colonization in the East, and the conflict between modern materialism and the fundamental belief in Christian revelation. He also wrote war novels, concerned chiefly with the German fleet, and works extolling the simple life of the rectory.[30] This is an important point, for Jünger's output is fairly typical of that of most völkisch novelists in the early twentieth century. The theme is always centered on the rootedness of the *Volk*, its ethical consequences, and the need to defend and protect these roots from the foreigner.

Volk in Danger exemplifies these themes. In this novel the Christian Mendelsloh family spends the evening in harmonious discussion around the dinner table, ending their day with a reading from Scripture. They have feeling and lack guile and deceit—so they are easily deceived by the Jewish Klosters family. Of the two Klosters brothers, one wants assimilation and the other is orthodox. Jacob is the religious Jew and appears at first as a pure and noble character who denounces the rest of his family for their unscrupulousness. But as the novel progresses, Jacob's true nature is gradually revealed. He denies that Jews can be assimilated and, because he is a Jew first and a German second, he is dismissed from the German army. He has a closer bond to his French fellow Jews than to the Germans he is supposed to defend. Jacob is convinced that the Jews will always be aliens in Germany.

This leads to the denouement, in which Jacob is revealed as a member of the Jewish world conspiracy. On the surface he may appear to be honest and upright, but the orthodox Jew simply does not have the ethics and roots of the German. Jacob is really cut from the same cloth as his unattractive brother, the assimilationist Bernhard. Bernhard, a later version of Veitel Itzig and Moses Freudenstein, wants power and does not care how he gets it. In the end, symbolically, the two brothers meet. It is not the kind of family gathering the Mendelslohs were fond of. Rather, the brothers meet to establish the Communist Party in Berlin, behind the front, during the First World War. Here the religious ideas represented by Jacob are shown once more to be without ethical foundations. The Jewish world conspiracy is in tune with Judaism, and Jews are Jews regardless of their professed religious attitude.

There is another side to this: the Jews are depicted as a city people who have no understanding of the settled life of the provinces. Here the provincialism that had been called a flight from reality reappears. Father Mendelsloh, happy in his small, provincial town, believes that the "big cities are the tomb of our people."[31] The only Mendelsloh son who survives the war goes out to become a peasant as the sole way to strengthen the life of the nation. From Dohm to Jünger this peasant ideal persisted, along with the ideal of the small, provincial town.

The theme of the glorification of the peasant and the *petit bourgeois* (as in Freytag) is now further expanded to take in the rootless, big-city Jew. In Fritz Claus's (Martin Jaeger, 1853–1923) *Der Wucherer* (*Usurer*, 1890) and in the famous *Der Büttnerbauer* (*The Peasant from Büttner*, 1895) by Wilhelm von Polenz (1861–1903), the Jew comes down from the city to trick the peasant.[32] The city stood for civilization as opposed to culture and was, therefore, the enemy of the people. Tüdel Weller in his *Rabauken!* made a point of saying that völkisch ideas could best be spread in the provinces. There the people had roots. Berlin was the domain of the Jews.[33]

The retreat from reality, so marked in the second half of the nineteenth century, meant a rejection of material progress, along with an opposition to materialism in general. The stereotyped image of the Jew is part of this emphasis on the soul as against the city. It is no coincidence that all writers who use the ghetto theme stress its urban nature, the narrow streets, the desert of stone. Once more the ghetto symbolizes Jewish emptiness, in contrast to the spirituality and solidity of the German peasant or the German *petit bourgeois*. This was the German glorification of the Philistine, and here Jew had no place. Yet the very fact that it was the Philistine who was being glorified was also an attraction. Most Germans saw themselves praised in the picture of the narrow, provincial life which these writers depicted for them. The denigration of the Jew not only bolstered their self-esteem but was an integral part of the glorification of their own humdrum lives. Franz Mehring (1846–1919) may be right in saying that no hero in the whole of German literature is as boring in his Philistinism as Anton Wohlfahrt. But he has to admit that Freytag's *Debit and Credit* was one of the most widely read novels of the century.[34]

The Philistinism underlying this literature emerges clearly in the way in which these writers treated the man they all abhorred: Heinrich Heine (1797–1856). Raabe in his *Hungerpastor* gratuitously introduces Heine in order to comment on his mockery of the German humiliation and disgrace that followed the Napoleonic Wars.[35] Heine, so runs the accusation, is in himself sadly ironic, but he makes fun of others: he is sacrilegious in his attacks on the Philistinism that other writers glorify. He has no sense of shame, loyalty, truthfulness, or reverence.[36] One critic, writing about Heine's travel sketches, pictured the Jew boy, hands in his pockets, standing unashamed before an image of the Madonna.[37]

Heine's skepticism frightened these writers. One of them called it the poet's "inherited drive toward negation."[38] They saw in Heine's wit an attack on the foundations of the culture that lent them security. According to them, Heine's "unfeeling" nature mirrored a restless spirit with no true culture; "one never knows where one stands with him."[39] All this was due to Heine's Jewishness. Heinrich von Treitschke (1834–1896) gave away the basic fear underlying this criticism of Heine. Heine, he said, had prepared the Revolution of 1848 by sowing discontent with the things Germans should hold most dear, with their deeply rooted feelings and their culture.[40] Thus Heine symbolized the same thing the big city symbolized: instability in the midst of the search for solidity.

Karl August Friedrich Albrecht Beyer (1847–1923) in his *Jüdischer Intellekt und Deutscher Glaube* (*Jewish Intellect and German Faith*, 1933) linked Heine and the big city in just this way.[41] Heine was for him, as for many of his predecessors, the "classic of modern Judaism." Just as the big cities held people of civilization but no culture, so Heine had substituted cleverness for feeling. This enabled him to make fun of what all held dear. In reality, he was driven by a quest for power. "Power has the same importance for the Jew that Germanism has for the German." The lust for power, the absence of ethical checks, left no room for a knowledge of what "powerful, good, and beautiful" meant. It knew only "more powerful, more beautiful, better."[42] This is another way of saying that with a Jew like Heine one never knew where one stood. Adolf Bartels crystallized this when he wrote that antisemites wanted to restore "old German settledness and solidity as opposed to Jewish cleverness."[43] Jews could never be people of culture—that was the crux of the matter. One National Socialist writer associated the Berlin salons of the beginning of the century with Heine—both attempted to "create culture," which to him was a contradiction in terms. Culture could not be "created"; it could only arise from true feeling.[44] Jewish cleverness sprang from Jewish rationalism and this, in turn, from the very nature of Judaism.

Nothing has been said hitherto in this analysis about racial ideas. Freytag, Raabe, and others like them did not subscribe to racism. A National Socialist study of the literature on Jewish emancipation from 1815 to 1820 noted all the accusations against the Jews which National Socialism was to perpetuate, but it also noted, with some surprise, the absence of a racial viewpoint.[45] Through much of the literature of the nineteenth century that absence can be traced. In one of the most significant early anti-Jewish pamphlets it was typically Judaism rather than race that provided the springboard for the image of the Jews. Carl Wilhelm Friedrich Grattenauer's (1773–1838) *Wider die Juden* (*Against the Jews*, 1803) has all the standard stereotypes, and the explanation given for them is this: Christianity believes in the unbelievable, the infinite, and is therefore divine; Judaism believes blindly in this world and is therefore a superstition.[46] This is the viewpoint that concerns us. One explanation for the absence of racial ideas is that anthropology, a prerequisite for racial thought, did not become popular until the end of the nineteenth century, a fact that is overlooked by many writers.

The denial of any possibility of Jewish assimilation, growing out of the fears of Jewish restlessness and cultural difference, already prepared the way for the intrusion of racial ideas into the concept of the Jew. Once all Jews were thought of as basically the same, the concept of race could be used to explain this sameness. However, the assimilated Jew was a figure of satire long before Jewish characteristics were dressed up in racial terms. Karl Barromäus Alexander Sessa's (1786–1813) play *Unser Verkehr* (*Our Visitors*, 1816), the first work of its kind, was merciless in its caricature of the assimilated Jew, but it had no racist base. The assimilated Jew, according to this work, could never become a Christian because he lacked culture, and his attempts to appear cultured are made the butt of satire. This character makes much of a composer whose name he pronounces "Mossart"—but this preoccupation comes from vanity, not from true feeling. Emphasis on the purity of the language was an integral part of the awakening German national consciousness, along with the glorification of the native soil as providing inspiration for the creativity of the *Volk*. The Jew had no place in the soil, nor could he have a true understanding, therefore, of the German language as the vehicle through which the *Volk* expressed itself.

The Jew's energy was directed wholly toward making money, and no assimilation could disguise this fact. Sessa's play was reprinted in the popular literary collection of *Reclam* and only eliminated from it after 1918; it unloosed a veritable flood of antisemitic caricatures.[47] Racist ideas were not prominent in Ernst Theodor Amadeus Hoffmann's (1776–1822) hate-filled *Brautwahl* (*Choice of a Bride*, 1821), either. Even the novelist Friedrich Spielhagen (1829–1911), writing later in the century, made the assimilationist Jew not a racist figure but a man filled with Jewish hate against Christians, all the more powerful because he lacks ethics.

It was after 1918 that the racial novel came into prominence. Jünger's *Volk in Danger* was such a novel. As we have indicated, his theme fitted in with the broader non-racial thought of the time. But now it was race which divided Jew and Gentile; Jacob Klosters believes in the Jewish race and the Mendelslohs come to believe in the Aryan racial myth. The characteristics which older writers had derived from their concept of Judaism were now presented in racial terms. Edith, Countess of Salburg (1868–1942), in her many novels of the 1920s and 1930s, tells us that Jewish greed and commercialism undermine the native roots of the people, a belief which was in full accord with the concept we have discussed of the consequences of Jewish rootlessness. She, too, thought that the Jews had no religion in the true sense of the word. But, she added, instead of religion the Jews are linked by blood, and this is a threat to all non-Jews.[48] That instability of which Heine was accused was now related to race. Carl Hauptmann (1858–1921), brother of the famous dramatist Gerhart Hauptmann (1862–1946), gives us an example. The principal character of his *Ismael Friedmann* (1913) lacks the virtue of solidity and steady application to work because he is of mixed race. His mother is the daughter of a Christian parson and his father is a wealthy Jew. He himself concludes that he will never have the rooted strength of the German because of this dividedness.[49] Beneath the preoccupation with race, there is here a continuation of an older theme.

Racism soon added its own contribution to the image of the Jew, however. Artur Dinter's (1876–1948) *Die Sünde gegen das Blut* (*Sin Against the Blood*, 1918) for the first time put racist ideas in the foreground of a novel.[50] It was here that this literature got its *outré* twist. Dinter's novel concerns intermarriage: however little Jewish blood is infused into a marriage, the children will always turn out to be Jewish stereotypes. A mother who does not know that she has Jewish blood but has had relations with a Jew commits suicide on seeing her baby, which, even in the cradle, looks "typically Jewish." And so it goes. This theme was continued in the

most blatant of the National Socialist novels—Tüdel Weller's *Rabauken!*
"Language and religion do not make a race; it is the blood which counts."
Here race was the determining factor; the Jewish religion was no longer
of primary importance in defining a Jew. This, however, did not keep
Weller from alluding to Freytag's *Debit and Credit* as fundamental to the
understanding of Jews. He also made the most of the Jews' alleged inabil-
ity to acquire a non-Jewish culture. They were unable to speak correct
German, for example, because it was not their "real" language. Heine
was mentioned once more as typically Jewish in his cleverness.[51] Weller
has already been quoted as saying that it is impossible to speak of ideals
when one speaks of Jews. In his novel he emphasized the dirtiness and the
ugliness of Jews. As we see, the older literary themes are carried into the
racial novel.

The creativity of culture was now transferred from its peasant and
bourgeois roots to the race as such. Almost to a man, these novels quoted
Benjamin Disraeli's (1804–1881) remark that "the racial question is the
key to world history."[52] The contribution that this racist element made to
the concept of the Jew was one of degree, not a change in the essence of
the concept. For the Jew there was now no escape from the Jewish stereotype; there were no more plans for Jewish assimilation. That avenue of
escape had been finally closed.

Eventually, even the religious history of the Jews was given a racist
tinge. Werner Jansen's (1890–1943) *Die Kinder Israel: Rasseroman (The
Children of Israel*, 1927) was hailed as the greatest racial novel of all
time.[53] The theme is the call of the blood which the assimilated Moses
hears at the court of the Pharaohs. Moses may be handsome and strong,
but his blood ties are to the boy Aaron, a stereotype Jew. The Egyptian
Jews live in a city that could be the ghetto of Prague. Moses leads these
outcasts from Egypt with the approval of the Pharaoh, who understands
that the call of the blood is stronger than the appeal of Moses' royal foster
parents. No Jew can ever renounce the heritage of his blood. The belief
in the racial unity of the Jews was always combined with a description of
their external features, which supposedly expressed their racial characteristics. Julius Streicher's (1885–1946) newspaper, *Der Stürmer*, summed
up this viewpoint neatly when it dismissed the question whether the Jews
were a religion or a race with the remark that the Jewish physiognomy
settled the point.[54]

The significance of racist thought is misunderstood if its absurdity and
bad taste are stressed and the continuation within it of an older, "respectable" trend ignored. Veitel Itzig is just as absurd as Dinter's characters,

and Raabe's Moses Freudenstein just as evil as Weller's Jews. It will not do to see the difference in the fact that Freytag and Raabe are undoubtedly more skillful writers. Their novels are just as schematic, their characters types rather than individuals—something that friendly contemporaries noted about Freytag's *Debit and Credit*.[55]

The racial characteristic of the Jews was still their lack of culture, their mere civilization. We must understand this basic carryover of themes and see this antisemitism—whether racial or not—as a part of the retreat into feeling which Spengler summarized in his interpretation of history in terms of culture versus civilization.

One last example will underline how respectable this older line of thought was and how its very respectability prepared the way for surrender to National Socialist racism. It is striking how a sensitive man such as the Swiss historian Jacob Burckhardt fits into this picture. He was frightened by the trend of the times, just as the writers mentioned here were frightened after 1848. He, too, wrote off the dream of progress and believed that something else had to take its place. "As the illusions of the 'progress' which had dominated since 1830 come to disappear, it is essential to have someone tell us all that belongs to the kingdom of illusions, and to give up our vain hopes in time." Burckhardt goes on to speak of the "merciless optimism" of the times, of the "terrible kingdom of this world."[56] These sentiments of 1875 were shared by many earlier writers; they led to the retreat into feeling and the glorification of provincial life. Burckhardt, too, had a distaste for large cities, a factor that made him reject the call to be Ranke's successor in Berlin. Provincial Basel was more to his taste. Large cities had destroyed the culture that had once existed in small centers of influence. "In large towns, however, artists, musicians and poets grow nervous."[57] This nervousness is equivalent to "not knowing where one is," to being blasé, as Burckhardt said of Heine—to lack a real sense of what is beautiful.[58]

It was fear which dominated Burckhardt. He blamed this, in the last resort, on the eighteenth-century idea of the goodness of humanity, which had become the idea of progress, "i.e., undisturbed money making and modern comforts, with philanthropy as a sop to conscience."[59] Once again, modern progress meant materialism, and the big city symbolized the "nervousness" that is the enemy of true art. Into this framework Burckhardt placed his bitter remarks about the Jews. They were the materialists, with their appanage the "venal" press.[60] Jews were not creative but imitative. Thus in Frankfurt "the wealthy Israelites build with Caryatids." These must show up to good advantage when "Kalle and Schickselchen and Papa with their famous noses, appear on the balcony between females from the Pandroseion."[61]

Are these merely lapses in taste on the part of a great historian? Burckhardt's image of the Jews fits in much too well with our previous analysis for such an explanation. The historian, living in his little room over the baker's shop, regulating his life with clockwork precision, was a man in search of security in a time when, as he put it, "all authority is disintegrating."[62] Burckhardt's withdrawal from a world that seemed to him in the process of dissolution took the form not of flight into aesthetics but of dedication to the study of history, which could help destroy modern illusions. Yet he believed that humanity had constantly before it a vision of an ideal and that this ideal could best be recaptured through the contemplation of the visual arts. Greek art expressed this ideal: "the hour at which our culture no longer sees beauty in the type represented by the Greek Gods will be the beginning of barbarism."[63] For Burckhardt, Kalle und Schickselchen were the antithesis of this "ideal type," the representatives of modern illusions. The "ideal type" put forward by the historian coincided with the ideal of beauty held by the entire völkisch movement, and both showed the profound Greek influence on Germanic culture. The "Jewish face," a popular term so listed in Campe's Dictionary in 1808, was opposed to the eternal ideal of beauty and typified the fact that Jews stood outside the culture that for Burckhardt was the "spiritual essence of the age."[64]

Burckhardt was no racist—he was not even personally close to the völkisch movement—and this lends some importance to the coincidence of his thought with völkisch conceptions. Burckhardt had earlier shown some understanding for the Jewish faith and the tragedy of Jewish life under persecution, but by the 1860s his views had changed. Modern Jews had lost their religion, were purely world-centered, and symbolized the commercialization of life that would destroy the culture of Europe.[65] The Jewish stereotype, and all that it meant, was passed on by some who were not closely associated with völkisch or racial thought but were profound and creative thinkers in their own fields of interest. But such authors also sought to destroy modernity and, like Burckhardt, they looked to the past in order to find eternally valid principles that might be used to renew the modern world. If such principles were found within an eternally valid cultural context, the Jews would very likely become the foils in the subsequent contrast between culture and civilization.

German antisemitism is a part of German intellectual history. It does not stand outside it. Above all, it became involved with the peculiar turn which German thought took after the first decade of the nineteenth century. German thought became at once provincial, in its search for roots, and idealistic, in its rejection of mere outward progress, in its belief in the irrationality of culture. Here the Jew was the outsider, and if he could at times gatecrash by assimilation in the nineteenth century, that did not fundamentally alter the emerging image of the Jew. Culture was closed to him, for he lacked the necessary spiritual foundations. This differentiation between culture and civilization, still part of the intellectual equipment of many Germans, is one of the clues to the Jewish tragedy of our times. National Socialism marked the victory of the Philistine, even if it was the Philistine with a soul who triumphed.

2

The Image of the Jew in German Popular Literature
Felix Dahn and Gustav Freytag

What was the route that rendered the Jews the storm center of modern events? Why was it, as Alan Bullock (1914–2004) has written, that "hatred of the Jews was perhaps the most sincere emotion" of which Adolf Hitler was capable?[1] Even at the turn of the century the most acute observer of his time, Friedrich Nietzsche, wrote in *Beyond Good and Evil*: "I have never yet met a German who was favourably inclined to the Jews . . ."[2] The causes of antisemitism have been examined many times, and it has been the consensus that hatred of the Jews was predominantly due to political and sociological factors. Hannah Arendt (1906–1975) sums it up when she writes that "anti-Jewish feeling acquires political relevance only when it can combine with a major political issue, or when Jewish group interests come into open conflict with those of a major class in society."[3]

Such analyses of the "Jewish problem" while correct as far as they go lack an important dimension: they do not include the image of the Jew as reflected in popular culture and therefore in the popular imagination outside any overt conflict or immediate political issue. If a movement or class turned to antisemitism, it could rely on evoking a certain image in the public mind whenever the word "Jew" was used. Hitler himself has told us how he became aware of the Jewish problem, not as a result of political or sociological reflections, but when one day he "chanced to be strolling through the inner city of Vienna." There he encountered a figure in black caftan, with "black curls," and looked into an "alien" face. Henceforth, he claimed, he could distinguish the "alien face" of the Jew from all other faces.[4] Hitler here reflects a stereotype of the Jew as it developed in the popular imagination, an important dimension of modern antisemitism.

43

How can we trace the growth of such an image in popular culture? We have one type of source material readily at hand in nineteenth-century German writing, for that century saw the rise of literature as a mass medium. There is, as we have recently learned, much information that the historian can derive from such popular literature: "the attitudes and preconceptions literature reveals—attitudes which, though they may be trivial in themselves, yet to the extent that they are widely shared, underlie and motivate basic historical changes."[5] This is especially true of the image of the Jew as found in German literature of the nineteenth century: we see the creation of a stereotype that in the end came to haunt Jews and Gentiles alike. Even before Hitler had his encounter in Vienna, a popular novel had "opened his eyes." To be sure, he made this statement in retrospect, but Wilhelm von Polenz's peasant novel *Der Büttnerbauer* (1895) may well have conditioned him for his discovery on the streets of Vienna. Von Polenz had fully developed the Jewish stereotype that Hitler was to find confirmed on his walk through the inner city.

There were two currents in German literature that fashioned the popular image of the Jew. One stemmed from romantic, völkisch preoccupations, and the other was concerned with integrating the newly powerful middle classes into the German nation. The first of these produced Felix Dahn's *Ein Kampf um Rom* (*Fight for Rome*, 1867), one of the most popular German novels of the century; and the second produced Gustav Freytag's *Debit and Credit* (1855), a novel of equal impact. Dahn's *Fight for Rome*, though not published until 1867, was planned in 1858 under the stimulus of the Italian Risorgimento, which provided a sharp contrast to the division of the German people. The novel was intended as a contribution to the movement for German unification. Its theme is the Gothic conquest of Italy in the early Middle Ages, and the eventual defeat of the Goths.

The hero of Dahn's novel is a whole people, the Germanic Goths, a tribe which is both honest and courageous and whose blond, manly exterior mirrors a purity of soul. It is when this purity becomes soiled that the Goths are betrayed. Thus, Theodoric's daughter becomes "Italianized" and turns against her own people. The contrast between the virtuous Germanic tribes and their adversaries is the theme of the entire novel. There is Cethegus, the Italian prefect of Rome, who typifies a rational, calculating cleverness that leads to his eventual downfall. There is Theodora, the wife of the Emperor Justinian, who combines in equal measure a ruthless will to power and love of intrigue.

It is Jochem the Jew who commits one of the most dastardly acts in this novel, when he betrays the impregnable stronghold of Naples to

Byzantium. He does so by leading the invaders into the fortress through the sewer system. Jochem is the Jewish stereotype: puny and cowardly, with a face bearing "all the calculating cunning of his race."[6] To underline the fact that he is of a foreign race, he is made to speak a mixture of Yiddish and German, the special "language" that Jews will speak throughout such popular literature.

This picture of the Jew is not in itself new. Léon Poliakov (1910–1997) has shown how such features as the long nose and the short body build first appeared in German caricatures of the fifteenth century.[7] With the controversy about Jewish emancipation in the late eighteenth century, the so-called characteristic physical features of the Jews entered polemical literature. "By his hair and physiognomy the Jew clearly shows how great the difference is between him and us . . . no less is also the spiritual distance which separates us."[8] By the middle of the nineteenth century these features were even more accentuated. They were presented as fact, separated from polemics or caricature, and this in writing designed for mass consumption. The stereotyped Jew now had ugly features both as an inherent characteristic of the race and as an outward sign of his soul. However, as we shall see, Dahn and other writers of that period believed that some Jews could shed the stereotype common to their people; but such Jews were in a small minority. After the Second World War, when a former National Socialist literary critic came to revise his literary history and to expunge the now discredited racism, he used an argument that shows the continuing force of this physical image of the Jew. Racist theories, he said, had not been proved because it was impossible to present factual evidence before the invention of photography.[9]

Dahn's novel is influenced by Romanticism. He employs Sir Walter Scott's (1771–1832) *Ivanhoe* (1820) motif. The beautiful maiden Miriam is in love with the handsomest of the Goths, the future King Totila. Her father, the patriarch Isaac, is an upright man, a loyal servant of the Goths. Miriam and Isaac further underline the contrast with Jochem. For Jochem's treachery is carried out not just for financial gain but to spite Miriam, with whom he is in love. However, it is made quite clear that Miriam and her father both despise Jochem, the typical Jew. Their association with the Goths has ennobled them and set them apart from their own people, and both die a glorious death for the German cause.

For all that, the Jewish stereotype emerges clearly. Jochem is "inherently" bad, without any redeeming qualities. His outward appearance mirrors the evil of his soul. Jochem's end is also typical: he is killed by Miriam's father as a traitor to the Goths. The stereotype Jew died a violent death in these novels: his type became a commonplace and introduced a significant element of cruelty into the picture, to which we will return.

Dahn's hero is a Germanic people; Gustav Freytag's hero is a Germanic merchant house. *Debit and Credit* exhorts the German nation to "honest work." Freytag here attempts to integrate the middle classes into the nation. The problem of integration was already a cause of concern in many German circles. What was involved can best be explained by referring to a much read work that posed the problem central to Freytag's novel: Wilhelm Heinrich Riehl's (1823–1897) *Die bürgerliche Gesellschaft* (*Bourgeois Society*, 1851).

The middle classes, Riehl tells us, are now in possession of an overwhelming material and moral power; but this very fact constituted a danger for the nation. Why was this so? Because, unlike the old peasantry or the aristocracy, the middle classes lived by "competition" and were thus in constant movement, in contrast to the land-bound conservatism of the older classes. The middle class ran the same danger of rootlessness and restlessness for which a Jew like Heinrich Heine was condemned, as we saw in the previous chapter.

For Riehl it was the peasant who represented the true historical German type; he was the best guardian of the roots of *Volk*. The nobility was a peasantry on a "higher level." What characterized this healthy force in the nation was the peasants' clinging to custom, which, for Riehl, represented the essence of morality; indeed, custom formed the crux of his sociology.[10] This glorification of the peasant is one of the constant factors in popular German literature of the nineteenth century, and the novel by von Polenz which opened Hitler's eyes was in that tradition. If the peasantry was the stable element, Riehl regarded the bourgeoisie and the proletariat as the forces making for social change, and opposed therefore to the stable and custom-bound life of the peasantry. Therein lay the danger to the unity of the German people. The problem, therefore, was to "settle down" these bourgeois classes, to curb their inherent, destructive radicalism.

Riehl thought this was possible for the "honest" bourgeoisie, and in this he was not alone. *Handel und Wandel* (*Trade and Change*, 1850), by Friedrich Wilhelm Hackländer (1816–1877), one of the first entirely bourgeois-centered novels to come out of Germany, pictured commercial life as honest, quiet, demanding steady work, rather than dominated by sudden accidents of speculation. Moreover, commercial life was bound to the locality. It was foreign travel which induced unsteadiness by stimulating the imagination. Here, then, was a settled middle class which was no danger to the *Volk*.

46

But the proletariat was a different matter. Riehl redefined the word "proletariat." Unlike Marx, he viewed this segment of the population as a rootless, unsettled, useless class which defied integration with the *Volk*. It included the migratory worker and also the journalist, the bureaucrat, and, above all, the Jew. The Jews were, in fact, the mainstay of the proletariat, whether they were "rootless" intellectuals or peddlers.

The accusation of rootlessness was the key to this antisemitism; it was on a par with the treachery of Jochem toward the Germanic Goths. This accusation seems to have been taken up at the popular level somewhat before the Jew as "international banker" came into vogue. The influence of the one image on the other needs further examination. That both Riehl and Freytag were concerned with the integration of the middle class in the nation does not mean that Freytag was directly influenced by Riehl's work. He reached the same conclusions by a slightly different path. Freytag was a scholar and believed that, just as scholarship has a stable base from which one cannot depart, so the state should reflect a similar stability. It was the national question that preoccupied Freytag, as it did Riehl. He looked at all foreign peoples as "books which were closed to him," and he deliberately avoided any connection with foreigners whom he might meet.[11]

It was Gustav Freytag who in *Debit and Credit* translated Riehl into popular terminology. The "hero" of the story is the merchant house of Schröter—because it is old and established, honest and "pure." The racial characteristics which Dahn assigned to the Goths have here been transferred to the German middle class. It is the aristocrat in the novel who provides the contrast on one level. He is a spendthrift and given to luxury. But he is, after all, also a German, and thus in the end his fortune and reputation are saved through the wise management of an honest merchant, of the house of Schröter. The Count of Rothsattel departs and settles on his eastern estates, saying in effect that it is the mission of the nobility to recapture its former strength and virility by colonizing among the Slavs. Here, at the outpost of Germanic culture, the nobleman finds his place. For Freytag did not want to do away with the nobility. On the contrary; every class had its set place in the nation. It was a mistake for the Count of Rothsattel to dabble in finance; that was the province of the "honest" bourgeoisie. Similarly, the merchant apprentice who is in love with the count's daughter is not allowed to marry her but marries the heiress of the house of Schröter instead. Everyone in his place. There must be no rootlessness, no "proletariat."

The real contrast in the novel is, therefore, not between a German merchant and a German nobleman but between the house of Schröter and the house of Ehrenthal. Here the stereotype emerges sharply at every level. The contrast is represented in part by the merchant apprentice Wohlfahrt on the one hand and the apprentice in Ehrenthal's house, Veitel Itzig, on the other. Veitel's appearance is described in great detail: he is puny, pale, has red curly hair, is poor and slovenly in dress.[12] But the contrast is even more broadly drawn. The very housing of the characters reflects it: Schröter's establishment is old, solid, clean as well as comfortable; Ehrenthal's is dirty, small, and cramped. From housing, we pass to family life. At the Schröters', all is love and *Gemütlichkeit*; at the Ehrenthals', all is hate and rootlessness.

That German critic who thought the novel especially rewarding for literary criticism because it was so schematic was right. Indeed, Itzig and Wohlfahrt represent opposite poles, as do Ehrenthal and Schröter.[13]

But here too the good Jew appears, though much more briefly than Dahn's loyal Miriam and Isaac. He is Ehrenthal's son, who despises his father's business and his way of life. In the words of one contemporary critic, he typifies those Jews who integrated their hearts and souls completely with the nation.[14] Once again, the salient trait of Bernhard Ehrenthal is his being as "un-Jewish" as possible. Realizing the nature of his parents and his co-religionists, he almost dies of shame. It is in fact his failure to convert his father to "decency" that provides the impetus for his death. Decency means honesty, straight dealing, and rejection of usury which was deemed essential to the German character. Just as in Dahn's books, these good Jews do not redeem the race—they fail in their efforts to do so—but rather they serve further to underline the contrast between the norm and the exception (we shall return to the importance of the "good Jew"). Here too the element of cruelty is e vident. Itzig is drowned in a dirty river, and Ehrenthal, ruined, his only son dead, goes mad. Once again, the stereotype is associated with a cruel end. It is "honest" labor which triumphs in the novel. Riehl's peddler goes on being a peddler, but on a larger scale. Rootlessness means dishonesty, dirt, and shiftlessness. The Jew is obviously used here as a warning to the middle classes against "dishonest labor," against the failure to "settle" and to become integrated with the nation.

It is surely not without significance that the work was greeted by a chorus of praise. One professor lecturing on Freytag remarked that there exists nothing closer to reality in all literature than the Jewish characters in this novel. For who had not known a Veitel Itzig, an Ehrenthal? His only criticism concerned Freytag's brief nod in the direction of such decent Jews as might exist, for this constituted a misrepresentation of true

Jewish family life. He is right to remind us that the novel was unique among German books in running through fifteen editions within a few years.[15] Moreover, Freytag had many imitators. Von Polenz, of whom Hitler spoke, was only one of this large number. His viewpoint was similar to Freytag's, except that his hero is a peasant whom the Jew dispossesses. Once again rootlessness is pitted against the "soil" and the "nation."

Neither Dahn nor Freytag shared the racial antisemitism of National Socialism. Freytag's case is of special interest in this connection, for he thought of himself as a liberal. A recent German article has emphasized that Freytag was a politician of the strict liberal school. Surely, by the standards of Western liberalism, *Debit and Credit* fails to meet any criterion of liberal judgment. But it was German liberalism which Freytag adhered to, a liberalism preoccupied with historical roots and with the national question. He shared in the search for "historically based security," in the concept that the more men open their minds to the laws and connections of the past, the more security they will feel in the present.[16] This historical-mindedness in the name of security meant for these liberals an emphasis on patriotism, and there Freytag typified what has been called the "tragedy of German liberalism": its stress on the historic nation rather than on historic freedom.

Thus Freytag could call the medieval German laws against the Jews a "shame of the nation" and yet in his book depict a Veitel Itzig. For his goal was the assimilation of the Jews into the historic nation. The high praise which Freytag had for his Jewish friend Jacob Kaufmann was that the "Bohemian Jew boy" became a German patriot of his own free will. It was the unassimilated Jews who were the "sick part of our people" and who must be kept from infecting the healthy.[17] The distinction between the good Jew and the bad Jew which we saw in Dahn's Isaac and in Ehrenthal's son becomes significant here. The good Jew is one who ceases to be a Jew. The bad Jew is the Jew per se, who refuses complete assimilation. Freytag built on the tradition of the Enlightenment. As we saw in the previous chapter, men like Christian Wilhelm von Dohm distinguished between Jews who refused to shed their "superstitions" and those who could be emancipated because they ceased to be Jews.

This led Freytag to raise an important question, and typically enough, in a reply to Richard Wagner's (1813–1883) antisemitic tract on the Jews in music. Freytag asked what is "typically" and "eternally" Jewish and what is not. Is it "inherent" in Jews to lack a sense of honor, to have too great a capacity for sophistry and dialectic? Here the "inherent" Jewish qualities are those of Veitel Itzig. But Freytag had hope that the Jews could raise themselves above the stereotype he himself had helped to create and could therefore respond to the liberating effects of German culture. Freytag's historical orientation enabled him to believe in this possibility, for who was to know what characteristics would turn out to be inherent and which were merely a result of unfavorable historical conditions?[18]

The limits of Freytag's liberalism are clear. But they help to shed light on another question which this analysis raises. Surely one can read Freytag or Dahn and remain unaffected, just as one reads Charles Dickens's (1812–1870) *Oliver Twist* (1838) without absorbing the antisemitic stereotype of Fagin. Indeed, one must already have a preconditioned frame of mind to retain the stereotype's influence. It could be readily proved, I believe, that such a frame of mind existed in Germany. Gustav Freytag's own conditioning is not difficult to ascertain for those who have read his memoirs. Living in Silesia, the border between Germany and Poland, he had come into contact with Polish Jews. It was their way of life and their way of making a living which he thought most typically "Jewish," an impression enhanced, no doubt, by a lawsuit which Freytag had to wage against some Polish Jews as the executor of the estate of a relative.[19] Just as, from his vantage point on the frontier of Germany, he derived this prejudice against Polish Jews, so he acquired also a general and equally strong prejudice against all Poles.

Felix Dahn shared Freytag's distinction between "good" and "bad" Jews. The author of *Fight for Rome* avoided membership in antisemitic parties and counted Jews among his friends. Dahn protested publicly when the conservative and antisemitic *Kreuzzeitung* attempted to link his name to the growing antisemitic movement. But the fact that the *Kreuzzeitung* (1892) could make such an assertion shows clearly how in such circles the distinction between Jews who could be assimilated and those who could not was devoid of meaning. The antisemitic mass movements condemned all Jews and refused to make the distinctions so dear to the Enlightenment, as well as to Freytag and Dahn.

It is surely significant that Felix Dahn also spent the major part of his life in the border regions between Germanic and Slavic civilizations, first at the University of Königsberg and then at Breslau in Silesia. Dahn accepted the call to a chair at Königsberg in preference to offers from the universities of Bonn and Marburg, which enjoyed more prestige, in order that he might continue to work at the outposts of German civilization.[20]

For Dahn and Freytag both, the "frontier" mentality played an important part in the image they conceived of the Jew, and it was the concentration of the masses of Jewry in Eastern Europe that influenced their thought. It was the Jews from Poland whom they regarded as typically "Jewish" and it was their way of life which they translated into a generalized picture. Such preconditioning was not new or unique. A contemporary historian remarked that the concentration of Jews in Eastern Europe was an important element in determining the views of eighteenth-century thinkers on the subject of Jews. The geographical factor in the shaping of modern antisemitism must not be ignored. Eighteenth-century attitudes toward Jewish emancipation were largely determined by the actual location of the Jews to whom attention was directed; in the nineteenth century this same factor shaped the image of the Jew for writers like Freytag and Dahn.[21] We discussed in the previous chapter the importance of the East European ghetto in forming the anti-Jewish stereotype. Freytag's attitude illustrates, once more, the clash between the Germanic culture and the way of life of the Jewish settlements at its borders.

This does not tell the whole story, however. These authors were patriots and their attitudes toward the Slavic and Jewish civilizations applied equally to all foreign civilizations. Felix Dahn, after the war of 1870, warned against the "regression into cosmopolitanism," for Germany had for too long been the anvil of history. The Prussian general staff must draw the boundary lines against France, and its judgment must not be questioned.[22] We have already seen how Freytag reacted negatively to all foreigners. The image of the Jew became a part of this general rejection of "foreigners," and increasingly so as Polish Jews emigrated to Germany in greater numbers. It must not be forgotten, however, that the most effective argument for the Jewish stereotype may well have been the fact that Freytag and Dahn both had a place for the "good Jew." By providing for his existence, they made the other—the "real" Jew—believable. In this way the very fact that Freytag was a liberal in the German sense may have helped to further the credibility of the Jewish stereotype he presented.

Freytag's close associate Julius Wilhelm Albert von Eckardt (1836–1908) underlines this point. Here was a journalist who openly deplored the "creeping antisemitism" of his time and who, in the same breath, praised Freytag for his tolerance and moderation. Yet, in Eckardt's own writing we find the same distinction between "bad" and "good" Jews. He found a difference between the Jews of Hamburg, who represented an extraordinarily industrious and useful element of the population, and the Jews of Berlin, who were cheeky, pushing, and unclean. This Berlin phenomenon he blamed on the "generation of the founders"; that is, on the unsettled condition of money-making times. Once again the accusation of rootlessness is basic. It was for this reason that Eckardt dated antisemitism (which he deplored) from 1870, ignoring the development of the Jewish stereotype in popular culture, as many historians have ignored it since.[23]

But we cannot afford to ignore the stereotype. Nothing illustrates this better than the attitude of the Jews themselves toward their image in the popular mind. There was scarcely a Jewish household in Germany in whose library Dahn's and Freytag's books could not be found.[24] The acceptance of this stereotype, and reading these popular authors, became a sign of Jewish assimilation. Here the distinction between the exceptional, "good" Jew and the ordinary Jew came to have a greatly magnified relevance. How was one to accept the stereotype of a Jochem or an Itzig and yet remain objectively detached from it? It would be out of place here to discuss the inner conflicts and frustrations into which this situation plunged generations of Jews. We shall be taking a closer look at this problem in the next chapter and we shall notice how Jewish youth toward the end of the century rejected their Jewish past, which they equated with life in the ghetto. Whether Zionist or assimilationist, they were apt to accept Germanic ideals of looks and behavior and many a Jew formed his personality in contrast to the stereotype. For some, the equation of the good Jew with complete assimilation, with Dahn's Isaac or Freytag's Bernhard pointed the way. Moreover, many German Jews applied the stereotype to the Eastern Jews once the latter's immigration into Germany had taken on large proportions—a transference which, while popular with some Jews, was unacceptable to most Gentiles. After all, Freytag had also begun with an awareness of Polish Jews, and now they were for him *the* "Jews," pure and simple. Complete assimilation was in his eyes the only possible answer for the "good" Jew, so that in a few generations Jews would lose their particular identity.[25] No history of the German Jews can be complete without considering these attitudes and these frustrations.

The strength of the popular image of the Jew can be further illustrated by tracing it through both liberal and socialist thought.[26] This is a task which remains to be done. More research is also needed into the way in which this image spread to other areas of popular culture apart from mass literature. The first caricature based on this stereotype dates from the fifteenth century, as we have seen, and derives from religious rather than racial prejudice. The Jew who dances in the thorns, in the Grimms' fairy tale, shows the stereotype combined with an attitude exemplifying the cruelty that such a stereotype arouses in people, but still within a religious context. Religious prejudice may have remained as strong as racial and national prejudice. What part does the rural priest, for example, who teaches the catechism and the crucifixion, play in the spreading of this image of the Jew? It would be my feeling that his influence may prove to be as central as that of Freytag or Dahn.

All in all, the stereotype Jew that emerged from this segment of popular culture provided one of the most important roots of German antisemitism. It was an ominous image, the more so as it was in all instances associated not only with contempt but with actual cruelty. It became a reality in the early days of National Socialism with the pictures of caftaned Eastern Jews sweeping the streets or having their beards pulled amid the hilarity of the mob.

This image of the Jew provided an escape valve from serious social and political problems. It is typical that Freytag never concerned himself with social problems; he believed the analysis of "material" interests to be beyond his scope. The image of the Jew was outside the range of serious political and social analysis, and that was its strength. In this way it provided the emotional basis for a totalitarian solution of these problems. There must have been many who, like Hitler, when faced with real problems, first awakened to the stereotype of the "Jew" and then built their ideology around it. To be sure, anti-Jewish feeling only acquires particular relevance when it is combined with political issues or when Jewish group interests conflict with other powerful interests, but none of this would be of significance in an age of mass politics without the support and preconditioning of popular culture. That is why we must direct our attention to cultural investigation. Only in this way will we be able to understand fully the continued influence of antisemitism, which, distressingly, seems to predate and to outlast its immediate political or social relevance.

3

The Influence of the Völkisch Idea on German Jewry

I

The title of this chapter may at first seem presumptuous, for the völkisch movement laid the groundwork for the Jewish catastrophe of our times. Thus it has been assumed, almost a priori, that the adherents of the völkisch ideology were, from the beginning, opposed to anything and everything Jewish, and that the Jews in turn found themselves confronted by a worldview that was in essence repugnant to all that Jews stood for. Consequently, German Jewish history has usually been described either as the failure of Jewish emancipation or as the story of a separate people living on German soil. The former view reads history backwards; the latter applies to German history a criterion taken from the quite different history of East European Jewry.

After the triumph of Hitler many of the younger generation, seeking to reject Europe and all that it stood for, sought a new and specifically Jewish ethos. But this had not always been the case; indeed, there was a period in which Jews sought to describe their own situation in the same terms as those used by their fellow Germans. Robert Weltsch, who played a major role in Zionism, has recently reminded us that early in the twentieth century his generation felt that "what was important . . . was not the farewell to Europe, but instead a greedy acceptance of all that Europe had to give us." Even more significantly, he adds that for a German Jew, even for a Zionist, "Europe inevitably meant Germanness."[1]

For many of that generation such "Germanness" was equivalent to an empathy with the völkisch longings which were capturing their non-Jewish German contemporaries. For the youth of the bourgeois classes the völkisch movement was primarily a revolt which, starting in the last decades of the nineteenth century, took the form of a deepened feeling toward the *Volk* of which they felt themselves a part. This was the response of many young people to the crisis of modernity. Racist ideas, which in retrospect immediately come to mind, were often but by no means inevitably an ingredient of such enthusiasm. This is especially true of the Youth Movement, which was völkisch but *not* overtly racist in the majority of its *Bünde*. This has a heightened significance for our theme, for it was this movement which affected Jewish youth more than any other.

The question we must ask is whether this general atmosphere penetrated into Jewish life as it did into German life, and if so, what special problems were involved and what differences can be noted. In posing such questions we come to grips with a German-Jewish history which is part of the history of German and Jew alike, however much we would want to deny such a connection today. Only by confronting this fact and the problems it raises can we ever begin to write the modern history of German Jewry.

The atmosphere of the *fin de siècle* is basic to an understanding of the völkisch movement and especially the part of it that had an influence on Jewish youth. All over Europe the young generation felt the urge to break with the bourgeois world, to revitalize a culture which seemed to have lost its vitality. The young Siegfried Bernfeld (1892–1953) echoed the general feeling of his time when in 1914 he called upon Jewish youth to build a new life for itself separate from the straitjackets of school and parents.[2] The Youth Movement had already attempted to do just that even as he wrote. The first journal edited by high-school students in defiance of adult supervision summed up the hope of the generation by calling itself *Der Anfang* ("The Beginning").

What sort of beginning was this to be? In Germany, the revolt by bourgeois youth against society turned into neo-romantic channels. The Youth Movement sought to express its freedom through contact with nature, defined as the landscape of the *Volk*. These students thought they had found in the unspoiled native countryside that genuineness which they missed in home and school. Moreover, the nature to whose tune their souls could "swing" (as they put it) was viewed as a historical landscape. Thus, not only woods and fields but also villages, small towns, and ancient castles were integrated into their concept of nature. The landscape stood not merely for an escape from hated modernity but also for a past which reminded them of the natural genuineness of their German roots. Frank Fischer (1884–1914), an important leader of the early Wandervögel (as the members of the Youth Movement were called), put it thus: "Can there exist a vital connection between the *Volk* and rambling? That which is formed in tune with nature, which has lasted of humanity's creations and which through its form still exemplifies that creativity, speaks to everyone who learns to listen. Not only churches and castles speak in this fashion, but also [small] towns, paths, landscapes . . . woods, and even rivers."[3] Thus youth sought to establish a connection between their own souls and the "genuineness" which the landscape embodied. Siegfried Copalle (1882–1957), a leading Wandervogel, wrote that "the demon money has not yet taken possession" of the inhabitants of a town which has retained its medieval form. "The new buildings do not jar, nor are they misplaced . . . the son does not yet want to rise higher than the father, the craftsman still enjoys the work of his hands."[4]

It must be stressed that this was far more than a mere "back to nature" movement, for youth was seeking a way to go forward. These students felt that their own strivings could be based on such genuineness and consequently transform their world. "We do not want to go back *à la* Rousseau, but to go forward to overcome the world. Become a man of the times, through rambling become an organic man."[5] Youth was seeking an end to the alienation produced by industrial society; it thirsted for firm ground from which such a change could be effected. In short, the revolt against society, parents, and school swelled into a revolt against the bourgeois age. Romanticism was used to bolster a nostalgia for preindustrial times, when in place of alienation from society there had been a fusion of the individual with nature, with the *Volk*, and with the *Bund*.

Such ideas were part of a general climate of opinion which was crystallized by the Youth Movement in the first decade of the twentieth century. This line of thought had special significance for young Jews growing to maturity within German culture. They also wanted to go forward into the future and, as we shall see, many of them wanted to find a new point of departure. The immediate past was the world of the ghetto, while the present represented the status quo within a society that painted Jews in terms of unflattering stereotypes. The turn of the century was marked by a new and deep-seated wave of antisemitism and Jewish exclusion, a reflection of the increased impetus of German völkisch thought. The stereotype of the Jew was presented as the antithesis of that genuineness for which Germans longed. Jews were described as intellectual, and therefore artificial. They lacked roots, and thus rejected nature. They were urban people, possessed of special aptitudes for expanding even more the hated capitalist society. Many Jews felt this was a just image, and many of the young people, especially, thought they saw it exemplified by their parents.

Out of this complex of ideas, sensitive Jews formulated their own doctrine of revolt, not so much out of self-hate but rather because the Jewish stereotype seemed to typify a character which all youth, Jewish and Gentile, despised. If one reads through the many analyses of the "sickness of Judaism" written by Jews at the turn of the century, the same themes recur. Judaism is sick because Jews have lost contact with the genuine realities of life. They have been cut off from the strength of nature, from the non-intellectual, non-competitive sides of human existence. Young Germans talked about the "New German"; young Jews spoke of the "New Jew" in exactly the same terms. Jews also wanted to opt out of bourgeois society, to escape from the alienation which industrialism had brought. At the same time, they wanted to be rid of any association with a stereotype that might link them with the very capitalist and urban society against which they were fighting.

In this growing revolt, materialism was painted as an evil by young Germans and young Jews alike. This held true for those young Jews who became socialists as well as for those whose revolt took on a völkisch direction. The Jews who joined the socialist movement wanted to infuse it with a new spirit of moral concern, a new humanism, which derived from Kant.[6] Both the young socialist Jews and those who followed a völkisch inspiration rejected materialism in favor of an emphasis on the spirit of man: his consciousness of his own true nature. They rediscovered the emotional base of human nature, though the consequences they drew from their discovery differed. Among non-socialist Jewish youth, the German Zionists pioneered the revolt against bourgeois society. As early as 1901, speakers at a Berlin Zionist meeting called upon Jews to "cut loose from Liberalism."[7] The liberal political parties of the bourgeoisie for which the masses of German Jews had cast and were casting their votes must be repudiated. The rationalism and materialism for which they stood must be rejected.

This is the leading theme of the volume *Vom Judentum* issued in 1913 by the Bar Kochba of Prague, a germinal group in the intellectual history of modern Jewry. The Jews of Prague were in the forefront of German cultural activity within that city, but for some of them the ever-present tension between German and Czech served to heighten their own Jewish self-awareness. The Bar Kochba circle of young people was Zionist and included among its members some of the best minds of the younger Jewish generation — indeed, Franz Kafka (1883–1924) himself was close to this group, for some intimate friends of his were among the members.

The book which the group published reiterates ideas that were general among such youth: the Enlightenment, as one contributor claimed, wanted to know the world, but what is important is to intuit and to re-form it. The introduction speaks of the excessive emphasis on individual-ism in all culture and calls its readers to battle against a mechanical, soulless utilitarianism.[8] In another context, Robert Weltsch wrote about the Jewish people sickening from a soul torn by rationalism and enslave-ment. Thus the Jews could not understand nationalism, which was not a mere program but the unfolding of life itself.[9] Members of the Bar Kochba circle, like the future philosopher Hugo Bergmann (1883–1975), made a sharp distinction between a formalized patriotism utilizing propaganda and centered in patriotic clubs, and a nationalism that would fashion a "New Man," would infuse the whole individual.[10] Here these men were in accord with the German Youth Movement, which rejected the saber-rattling patriotism of its elders and refused to attend the official anniver-sary celebration of the Battle of Nations (1913), meeting instead on the Meissner Mountain, where groups of the Youth Movement declared their love for truth and sincerity.

It should be stressed that in spite of its overt denial of politics, the Meissner declaration (as this came to be called) was meant to constitute a program, however vague. What was rejected were the rationalizations of patriots and political parties. Instead, this Youth Movement emphasized the more genuine links of intuition, nature, and *Bund*, the "Germanic faith" about which men like Paul de Lagarde (1827–1891) and Julius Langbehn (1851–1907) had written. This was indeed a faith which con-sciously rejected the need for a rationale, at least in the beginning. Moses Calvary (1876–1944), a leader of the new Jewish generation, called par-ticipation in the nature ramblings of the Youth Movement "a simple form of reaffirming our Judaism" (1916). Whether or not this was specifically "Jewish" he held to be beside the point.[11] Small wonder that at this junc-ture of his life Calvary rejected all religious orthodoxy, since "orthodoxy and rationalism climax in the Enlightenment."[12] He was not alone. Just as Germans accused religious orthodoxy of imprisoning the German spirit, so young Jews condemned Judaism as it had been traditionally practiced. Robert Weltsch has written in retrospect of how Judaism as an intellectual force had ceased to exist, how it meant only a fossilized tradi-tion for that young generation. He calls it an empirical Judaism, and for him it must have been a part of the Jewish "frivolity of materialism."[13] Jews and Germans regarded their received religious heritage in a similar light. So too their urge to substitute for it a more vital and genuine world-view must be regarded as a common cultural phenomenon.

Perhaps here again young Jews had been impressed by a stereotype of Judaism. Since the middle of the nineteenth century Judaism as a religion had been symbolized in the West by the Eastern European ghetto—a quarter which, as we have seen in two previous chapters of this book, was widely regarded as ritualized, fossilized, strange, and, what was just as important, urbanized. For the new Germanism and these young Jews, the city typified the essence of rationalism and lack of genuineness. A Zionist journal charged (1910) that Jews who lounged in city cafés typified the neurasthenia and lack of ideals which had served to create the Jewish stereotype. It must be emphasized that it was from prewar times that such feelings reached out into the postwar age. And during the First World War, when many Germans and Jews came into firsthand contact with the world of the ghetto in the German-occupied sections of Poland, this view of Jews and Judaism was intensified.[14] Zionists, moreover, had a special impetus for their rejection of the ghetto. Non-Zionist Jews, and they were the vast majority, accused them of seeking to push all Jews back to a ghetto civilization. The Zionists desired to accept German culture all the more because of this accusation. It was unwarranted in any case, for they opposed the recent Jewish past with as much vigor as any assimilationist Jew.

Against this background, Martin Buber, in close contact with the Bar Kochba circle, attempted to revitalize Judaism. In one sense he played the same role in the Jewish context of the *fin de siècle* that Paul de Lagarde played in the German context, but with a significant difference: whereas Lagarde exalted the specifically Germanic, Buber sought to transcend the specific *Volk* in order to bring into being an all-embracing humanism.

Yet the similarity between Buber's rediscovery of the Hasidim and the contemporary German revival of mystics like Meister Eckhart (ca. 1260–1328) and Jacob Böhme (1575–1624) is too striking to be ignored. Germans also wanted to go beyond "liberal" or "orthodox" Protestantism to an earlier heritage which seemed more dynamic because it was less rationalistic, less fossilized. A mystic like Böhme had posited a definitive and emotional starting point, rooted in nature, for the "overcoming" of the present world. Such German mystics seemed to intuit cosmic forces linked to the German *Volk* and to nature as well. The soul was seen as a bridge between these two regions, just as it formed the link between them in the ideology of the Youth Movement. Buber's Hasidim performed a similar function by embodying a Judaism which was not rationalized, not fossilized, and surely not quiescent. Moreover, the dynamic nature of the Hasidim arose from a mysticism linked to a revived love for the *Volk*. The

Hasidim represented a heritage with which modern Jews could forge a meaningful link.

This connection between the Hasidic heritage and modern Jews was of the utmost significance for Buber, for he believed that a peaceful and genuine relationship of the individual to the *Volk* could be maintained only if there were an unbroken growth of *Volk* feeling, in which the individual did not have to choose between his inner self and his environment. Buber's Hasidim provided a means by which Jews could identify with the past while at the same time they continued developing in their own unique way.

This formulation was strikingly similar to the attitudes which Germans manifested toward their mystics. For both Jew and German, such historic identification was meant to signal the end of the alienation of modern humanity. The modern Jew was to be "uprooted" only to become rooted again in a neo-romantic mysticism. This solution to the crisis of modernity was anchored in the contemporary ethos to such an extent that it is hardly surprising that Buber's doctoral thesis (1901) should deal with the thought of Jacob Böhme. For Buber, Böhme was relevant to the modern age, for he expressed the unity of all living matter in God. Humans long for a deeper link with the world in which they live, and they can find this by giving free play to their inner experience, "for everything grows outward from man's inner spirit." The soul has received an accurate picture of the world from God. The trees, birds, and stars are our brothers and sisters. Humanity, then, carries within itself a picture of the God-given harmony of the world, whose many-sided splendors it can grasp through such a mystical intuition. Buber summarized and fully approved the theology of the Silesian mystic; it penetrated deeply into his own religiosity and undoubtedly influenced his interpretation of the mystical sources of Judaism which are central to his thought.[15]

Buber expressed this mystical element through a definition of *Mythos* as an eternal function of the soul, through which concrete events are transformed by the soul into divine and absolute experiences. *Mythos* for Buber is an elemental state of being from which the soul surges forth in quest of unity beyond itself. This *Mythos* finds its outward expression in the account of legends which deal either with actions performed by God, or with the centrality of humanity's inner experiences. Hasidic literature concentrates upon such legends, which demonstrate an intuitive understanding of the unity of God and the world and, as a result of this understanding, a love for the world which Buber also saw reflected in Böhme's theology. The *Mythos* expresses a true religiosity, opposed to all organized religion, and gives a picture of human creativity which according to Buber Nietzsche had also glimpsed.[16]

Buber links the *Mythos* to mysticism, but mysticism can also express itself directly, without recourse to legend. Mystical experience can project itself directly in its moments of ecstasy when one's inner life of the soul emerges, for an instant, in its purest form. For Buber this was not a specifically Jewish phenomenon but common to all mystical experience. In his *Ekstatische Konfessionen* (*Ecstatic Confessions*, 1909) he collected the descriptions by past mystics of their own experiences. Christian mystics provided the majority of his examples; their souls, in this stage of tension, received the "grace of unity."

Buber's emphasis on this mysticism and his praise for the inner experience are closely linked to the contemporary revival of interest in German mystics. Just as the Germans attempted to root this mystical tradition in their national mystique, so Buber eventually attempted to embody this *Mythos* in the Jewish *Volk*, exemplified by the Hasidim. Their legends are a genuine expression of the spirit of the Jewish people in their relationship to God and the world. The Jews as a *Volk* are opposed to the superficial forces of traditional religion and politics so characteristic of the modern age.

Buber's use of *Mythos*, his mysticism, closely paralleled important German writers of his times. We shall see in the next chapter how the important German conservative, Arthur Moeller van den Bruck (1876–1925), used the concept of *Mythos* in the same manner, to express the organic unity of the German *Volk*. Eugen Diederichs (1867–1930)—a friend of Buber's and publisher of Arthur Bonus (1864–1941), whose idea of *Mythos* is again close to that of the Jewish philosopher—summarized the feeling so prevalent at the time: that the world picture must again be grasped by an intuition that is close to the sources of nature. From this, humanity's spirit must flow and bring its soul into unity with the community of its *Volk*.[17] Significantly, Meister Eckhardt typified this "new Romanticism" for Diederichs, who himself was not only an influential publisher, but also played an important role in developing both the völkisch and the Youth Movement.

Buber attempted to translate the emphasis on the irrational cosmos into Jewish terms by employing the concept of the individual soul's proximity to the shared inner experiences of the *Volk* as a vehicle for the transformation of modern humanity. However, he broadened this concept by making Yahweh, the national deity, into the God of "all," the God of humanity, the Lord of the soul. Indeed, Buber was always in quest of a community that was not bound by laws and regulations, but instead was based upon the affinity of kindred souls. Such a community was formed by that mystic bond which Buber called the "community of one's blood," expressed through the *Volk*. But in the last resort, the values which such a community represents transcend the individual *Volk*, for to sacrifice oneself on behalf of the *Volk* was an act of divine revelation—and a revelation not confined merely to one segment of humanity.[18] This longing for a true community runs through most of the thought discussed in this book; it is shared by Germans and Jews alike. Both sought to overcome a liberalism that seemed to stifle the humanity within the individual. In an approach that was typical of the Jewish interpretation of this ideology, the *Volk* becomes part of a larger entity which includes all humankind. Yet the similarities between Buber's thought and that of the advocates of a new German self-consciousness are so startling at this point that they imply a common root in the general völkisch surge of the times.

Small wonder that even the vocabulary of the völkisch renaissance made its appearance here. Buber was apt, in his early lectures (1909–1911), to equate the historically and intuitively centered growth of the *Volk* with the instincts of its "blood." But this rhetoric, as well as Robert Weltsch's call that every Jew must become a "little Fichte," can be misleading if viewed in terms of a narrow and aggressive nationalism.[19] Both Buber and Weltsch looked upon the *Volk* as a stepping stone to a general European culture. Only by first becoming a member of the *Volk* could the individual Jew truly become part of humanity. As one young Jew put it early in the century, every *Volk* is held together by a "national religion" (in Lagarde's mystical sense) but in the end all humankind flows together.[20]

Two problems arose from this ideology, and neither one of them was ever satisfactorily solved. How could one claim that there was something uniquely Jewish in this call to the *Volk*? What precisely was the European humanistic tradition within which all humankind would flow together? All these authors rejected the legacy of the Enlightenment; what could they offer in its stead? In Buber's case mysticism took the place of a rationalistic approach to the problem.

To be sure, Buber derived much of his inspiration from a tradition of Jewish literature and Jewish thought. It remains for scholars to disentangle the specific Jewish tradition of mysticism and neo-Romanticism from the German impetus within which he worked. Undoubtedly Jewish intellectuals of this tradition existed in Eastern Europe, and some did reach their conclusions independent of Germanic influence. Buber, though he spent most of his adult life in Germany, came from a background rooted in East

European Jewry. However, the parallelism between his interpretation of the Jewish tradition and the Germanic ideas we have discussed is difficult to deny, nor can we ignore his own overt acceptance of the German mystical and neo-romantic tradition. Moreover, the substitution of mysticism and intuition for the traditional context of the Jewish religion, his rejection of scholarship, did introduce a vagueness into the quest for Jewish identity which made it difficult to disentangle the Jewish from the German, indeed from a general concern with human individuality.

It was easier to use such mysticism to build a humanism embracing all humankind than to isolate its specifically Jewish component. How this mystical approach toward life could provide the basis for a general European humanism is effectively illustrated in the thought of Buber's close friend, Gustav Landauer (1870–1919). Typically, Landauer considered himself a Jew and was proud of his Jewish heritage. But he could not arrive at a concise and consistent definition of his Jewishness. His pride in his origins fused with the belief in a general revolutionary tradition which supposedly derived from Jewish prophecy and which made the Jew especially suited to transform existing reality. This most famous of German anarchists rejected all traditional nationalism: the state and society must be built up from below. Their foundation rested on the voluntary and spontaneous unity of people gathering in small communities. Landauer did not shirk the call to revolution to overthrow contemporary society. He was one of the leaders of the Bavarian Revolution of 1918–1919 and was finally murdered by counterrevolutionaries.

Buber was the executor of Landauer's will. Much earlier, Landauer had praised Buber's *Reden über das Judentum* (*Speeches on Judaism*, 1911) because they combined the call to freedom with great depth. By depth Landauer meant the reawakening of the human soul, which draws unto itself a picture of the living world. Pitting himself against attempts to explain the world and man by logical categories and concepts, he cited the medieval mystic Meister Eckhart: "The path to understanding lies inward." Here, in the secret and private recesses of his soul, the individual recaptures his "living past" — for he is merely a link in a long chain of ancestors and progeny that forms the community to which he belongs. The individual thus rediscovers the community to which he is linked through his blood and learns further that he is merely an "electric spark" within a larger unity. Clearly Landauer was here following Buber in postulating an emotional link between the individual and their ancestors: a living community which each person rediscovers by looking into their own individual soul.

This "genuine community" was contrasted with the pale and artificial community of state and society. Landauer believed that if the Jews would only follow Buber's advice, they could create such a "genuine community" and therefore become a truly "genuine" people, "magically united" through the depth of their souls. And, because by recapturing this ideal these people would also have received an image of the unity of the world in their souls, their deeds would be performed on behalf of humanity at large.[21]

The distinction between an artificial and a genuine community (*Gesellschaft* and *Gemeinschaft*) was a commonplace in German *fin de siècle* thought and was adopted by the Youth Movement as well. Buber the Zionist and Landauer the anarchist shared in this attitude. The *Volk* or the people were an integral part of this mystical thought, but unlike many Germans, these Jews did not end up in the bonds of a narrow nationalism, which they rejected. Landauer never became a Zionist but, for all that, he spoke before the Bar Kochba circle in Prague. He made it clear to these young Zionists that he regarded nationhood as merely a disposition, a readiness to work for causes that were not solely national but first and foremost those of humankind.[22] It was precisely on this point that Buber, though a Zionist and not an anarchist, agreed with Landauer. His disillusionment with the state of Israel, once it came about, is well known. The nationalism that prevailed in the new state seemed to negate the high goals that Buber had set for it. Yet, could a modern state, besieged on all sides, regard its nationalism as only a "disposition," as merely a stage in its progress toward eventual union with all humanity?

In fact, a large number of German Zionists continued to see no contradiction between Jewish nationhood and the flowing together of humankind by the means which Buber had put forward and which Landauer so well exemplified. Such ideas, dating back to the prewar years, penetrated into the 1920s. Then Robert Weltsch, in the important German-Zionist newspaper *Jüdische Rundschau*, exhorted his readers to regard the Zionist movement as centered on the inner development of the Jewish nation, on the awakening of the soul, so that the essence of the Jewish heritage might be once more recaptured. He conceived of this heritage in cultural terms, which he considered more important than political or economic factors. Such a Jewish culture was not exclusive; it was part of a living, eternal law. By living a national life based on this principle, Jews would attain a harmonious relationship with all the other peoples of the world. Weltsch accepted the definition of culture which Martin Buber reiterated when the shadows were closing in over Germany (1929). Culture cannot be "made"; it is part of the life process itself, rising up from life's very foundations. The essence of this process is the constant confrontation and struggle between God and humanity; its reality is always one of inward growth, not of outward power.[23]

Thus Robert Weltsch protested against the military pomp and circumstance with which the banners of the Maccabees were brought into a Jerusalem synagogue on the festival of Hanukkah (1925). Such demonstrations could lead to the same hollow, theatrical nationalism which dominated other nations, besides serving to alienate the Arab population.[24] This humanist nationalism remained alive in the postwar age and retained its similarity to the original national impetus that had dominated some of Germany's youth before the First World War.

But its days were numbered in Germany. Through the experience of the First World War an aggressive nationalism had come to dominate the German scene, and the postwar German Youth Movement largely accepted the change. By 1929 few voices in Germany took up the cry of one Zionist writer that nationalism, if it was to serve the common good, must be humanitarian, inner-directed, cultural, for only thus could all the diverse groupings of humanity attain harmony.[25]

The völkisch influence on German Zionism did not, in the end, transform the belief in a Jewish *Volk* into an aggressive, exclusive ideology. But the German völkisch movement did lead in this direction—providing a deep, long-lasting difference between Jewish and German thought. To be sure, the German Zionists were also becoming increasingly isolated within the Zionist movement itself, for there a more aggressive nationalism triumphed in response to the longings of the oppressed masses of Eastern European Jewry and the realities of the Palestinian situation. Not that German Zionism stood alone, for among some East European Zionists humanistic nationalism had also found its adherents. However, the peaceful coexistence of Arab and Jew in a binational state had informed the political direction of most of German Zionism, providing the concrete application of the harmony among all peoples toward which a genuine folkdom was destined to lead. But this was not to be. The problem of creating a humanistic nationalism has not been solved for Jews in Israel any more than it has been for any other modern nation.

What then was specifically "Jewish" about a nationalism which in its early stages was so closely related to völkisch influence? This proved a troublesome problem for many Jews of that generation, in spite of Martin Buber's attempt to offer a specific Jewish tradition that would crystallize the values of the *Volk* while at the same time rejecting the religious orthodoxy that, throughout history, had served to hold Jews together. Even

Buber's great influence could not reconcile the conflict between a Jewishness focused on the soil of Palestine and Germanism as an ideological force.

Moses Calvary told the Zionist leader, Kurt Blumenfeld (1884–1963), that "my dreams ripened among pines, not among palms." From the time of its founding (1912–1913), the Zionist Youth Movement Blau-Weiss (Blue and White), was faced with this problem. The Blau-Weiss was an offshoot of the German Youth Movement and shared its ideology as well as its action—the emphasis on nature rambling, on learning to live in nature and to "view it with one's soul." The hope, as one leader put it, was that this sharing of a foreign experience would lead to the realization of a Jewish goal. But was this possible? Gershom Scholem, destined to become one of the foremost Jewish scholars of his time, attempted to solve the problem by rejecting the Youth Movement aspect of the Blau-Weiss and calling for a renewed preoccupation with the Jewish religion and the Jewish heritage. He failed, for few were willing to discard the movement whose völkisch influences were shared by Jew and Gentile alike. Then, at one of its last meetings, the Blau-Weiss leadership confronted the problem once more (1924). They castigated the Jews' longing for Palestine, which they considered stemmed merely from externalized religious and historical feelings. A simple personal relationship to soil and earth could provide the only genuine sentiment for the necessary return to the homeland. But it was precisely this feeling for historical nature which the Youth Movement inculcated—a nature that included the people who dwelt within it, the ancient towns, as well as the forest and fields. The leaders of the Jewish Youth repeated a cardinal tenet of the German Youth Movement and went on to admit that such a return to nature had to take place for Jews "on German soil and in the German landscape." The discussion ended with the only possible conclusion: today the cultivating of a close relationship to nature would take place within the German landscape, but "next year in Jerusalem."[26]

It was easier to state the problem than to find a solution to it, and only vague hopes and pious wishes seem to emerge from these writings. Small wonder that Moses Calvary himself, as a leader of the Blau-Weiss, found his way back to the safe anchor of orthodox Judaism once he had emigrated to Palestine, as did others who in their youth had dreamed too German a dream. Moritz Goldstein (1880–1977), a writer on Jewish problems, informed the Bar Kochba that the Jewish *Volk*, through its own force, would overcome Nietzschean nihilism as well as discarding the image of Goethe and Kant. But he failed to specify the Jewish content which would take the place of such German thought and instead merely posited that the Jews were peculiarly suited to be the "*Volk* of the idea."[27] Robert Weltsch cited as a paradoxical formulation of those days the contention that preoccupation with Nietzsche or Friedrich Hölderlin (1770–1843) would make stronger Jews than "a forced return to a ritual in which we do not believe."[28] Some sidestepped this paradox by calling for "deeds, not cerebration," while others talked vaguely of the Jewish "urge toward higher things."[29] But what Weltsch calls a paradox is simply the result of the way this new Jewish consciousnesss emerged.

The idea of the *Volk*, centered on the irrational forces of nature, necessarily looked for its fulfillment to a specific historical landscape that would be a reminder of the past and an impetus for the glorious future it could call its own. "Because the nature which infused [the Wandervögel] was the nature of the German *Heimat*, thus from love of landscape grows love of *Volk* and fatherland, a national-German . . . background for all forms of culture and life."[30] For the Germans all this was "given," but for the Jews the desired transference of Germanism to a Jewish context presented an essentially insoluble dilemma. Jewish youths did not want to build on the foundations past generations had laid; rather they yearned for a cleared and empty space where they could construct a new edifice. But their wish was beyond granting, and thus the Germanic ideology moved in to supply foundations for them.

The dilemma was clearly manifest when Moses Calvary had to answer the accusation that the German heroic ideal had been simply and schematically grafted onto the Jewish heroes of old. His contention was that heroic figures like Siegfried had been romantically awakened for German youth only within the last decades and that Jewish youth could not but see their heroes under the same aspects if they were to be in tune with the age. For Calvary, young Jews had to fashion their Jewishness after the German model, and especially through the model of the Youth Movement. He saw Blau-Weiss in this light. For Calvary, given the Jewish situation, this imitation was a necessity. However, his ambivalence is clearly stated in a letter written to Martin Buber during the First World War (1916). There he criticized the philosopher Hermann Cohen (1842–1918) (about whom we shall have more to say in the last chapter of this book) as an "enraged German." Jews do not necessarily have to form a united front with Germanic thought, he felt.[31] However, he saw that the Blau-Weiss had adopted such thought in an attempt to recapture Jewish identity.

The Jewish Wandervogel believed that the feeling for the German landscape would be translated into a feeling for Palestine. Yet, as can be clearly seen, the definitions of Jewishness made from this context merely echoed the ideals of the German Youth Movement. An article entitled "An Outline of Our View of Man" in a volume issued by the Zionist group, the Habonim, in 1935 had this to say on the subject: what Jews needed was the immediacy of experience, a strong, non-questioning, unconscious life. This meant being close to nature, to the earth and the labor it entails, to the rhythmic changes of the seasons. Finally, there was the longing of the Jews for manual work, for land and community life. But what was specifically Jewish about all this? This is an excellent summary of the völkisch urge of German youth, and the praise the article accords Knut Hamsun (1859–1952) as "poet of the blessing of the soil" could be duplicated throughout the history of the völkisch movement.[32] It was easy enough to say in 1914 that "we want to transfer the healthy effect of the Wandervogel onto our own youth," but it was quite another matter rationally to sort out the Jewish component from the Germanic, especially against the background of a general revolt of youth against rationalism and industrial society.[33]

To be sure, a new emphasis on the Hebrew language solved the problem for some of these figures. But here again it was difficult to combine a literary emphasis with the new stress on a nature-bound anti-intellectualism. Nonetheless, Hebrew as the daily language certainly gave a heightened intensity to the revived Jewish consciousness. Just how far this changed the ideological content is open to question, however, since it was difficult to build a secular national consciousness for a people who had always sought such identity through their religion. Perhaps this is the crux of the matter; if so it still poses a major problem for modern Israel.

Hans Goslar (1889–1945), an active Zionist (who later became press secretary to the Prussian government in the Weimar Republic), attacked Buber, somewhat unjustly, for rejecting his religious heritage and calling for a revolt of youth without it (1918). "What we know is not solely the dark urgings of the blood."[34] Buber had tried to lay a religious foundation, but since this was itself stated in mystical terms, it seemed overwhelmed by what Moses Calvary called "the same call which also sounds for the peoples which surround us, the call for a more colorful and artistic modeling of life."[35] By the First World War, however, many youths had increasingly found the answer to their Jewishness through a deepening of the experience that bound them together, with their own age and kind, in a meaningful community: the *Bund*.

The *Bund* was no ordinary group, but a specific product of the German Youth Movement. It resolved the urge toward an organic, rather than an alienated person, by positing unity of soul, body, and spirit as the prime law. This law bound together individuals who had voluntarily entered the *Bund*: unity of soul and spirit was to be attained through shared experiences of nature and *Volk*, unity of the body through a shared Eros. For a good many Germans this became the nucleus from which all true states should have their beginning, and it constituted an alternative to existing, unsatisfactory political organizations. At times the Zionist Youth Movement Blau-Weiss took refuge in this principle of spontaneous and voluntary association, for "Judaism is difficult to define." The calendar issued by the Blau-Weiss for 1916 asserted that experiencing a living Jewish community through shared joys and shared roaming was enough in itself to define the "desire for Jewishness."[36] Admittedly, this was criticized in their journal as a mere "drifting within the stream of the German Youth Movement," but Heinz Kellermann, making a study of youth for the Berlin Jewish community, was nevertheless correct when he berated Jewish youth for being "stuck" in such a vague collective experience, unable to define their Jewishness in a more traditional or rational manner. He criticized young Jews for believing that the *Bund* as such sufficed to explain their Jewishness.[37] Once again one is struck by the common strivings of Jewish and German youth.

Indeed, the strong trend toward the *Bund* and *Orden* in German youth during the Weimar Republic had its parallel in the activities of Jewish youth. For example, the German-Jewish *Bund* of roamers, the Kameraden (Comrades), founded after the First World War, asserted in 1924 that the conscious will to be a member of the *Bund* was all the program called for; there was no need to work out specific goals toward which the organization should strive.[38] The Comrades illustrates the dangers involved in making the *Bund* simultaneously the organizational framework and the mystical unit that superseded all defined goals and programs. For the Comrades split up under the growing shadow of National Socialism. Some members now felt the need for a clearly worked-out program that would lead into a better future. The Werkleut (Craftsmen) split off from the Comrades in 1932 and adopted a Marxist program. Others left to found the Schwarzes Fähnlein (Black Flag), which desired to use the völkisch thought in order to assimilate its members into the German nation.

We have already noted that the large Zionist youth organization, Blau-Weiss, considered itself a *Bund* and refused to abandon the model of the German Youth Movement. They avoided a split in their ranks, very likely because of their specific general goal of settling in Palestine.[39] But the Blau-Weiss also discussed its *bündisch* nature in the pages of its journal, once again raising the problem of its own relationship to the dominant mood of articulate German youth.[40] Moses Calvary spoke for the majority: an abandonment of the *bündisch* nature of the organization would mean its end as a true community. The individual personality of each member, if left free to unfold itself, would destroy the meaningfulness of the shared experience. The Blau-Weiss followed this ideal. Calvary reiterated a general article of faith of the Youth Movement: the stronger the natural ties of the individual with the *Volk*, the more freely such an individual can develop without damaging the community.[41]

Strong leadership was equally important. In the words of a German Youth leader, community and leadership form a *Bund*. Both Zionist and anti-Zionist Jewish youth groups adopted this principle of strong leadership. In the *Schild*, the organ of the Jewish War Veterans which furthered *bündisch* organizations for non-Zionist Jewish youth, this ideal was defined both before and after Hitler came to power. In an article written at *Pessach* time in 1929, Moses was held up as such a leader, and his leadership attributes were exactly the same as those which the *Bünde* had consistently maintained. A leader must know the soul of his people, its true nature, and must be filled with love for the *Volk*. Movements and revolution are made by the *Volk*, but only the leader, "the soul of the *Volk*," can give them purpose. The task of the leader is therefore to understand the *Volk* in order to rule it with complete sovereignty (*beherrschen*).[42]

Not only the German and the Jewish Youth Movements but the völkisch movement as a whole subscribed to this view of the leader. After Hitler had come to power, the *Schild* wrote that the realization of the leadership concept was a positive step on the part of the national revolution. This fact, it went on, should not blind Jews to seeing its advantages as a system of government, not only for states but for all types of organization.[43] Here we can detect signs of progress from hitherto blindly held attitudes of mind to an acceptance of their possible political consequences.

German Zionist youth, especially the Blau-Weiss, were the first to test these concepts against reality when, in the 1920s, they went out to settle in Palestine, just as young Zionists had been the first to take up the völkisch ideas that had agitated German youth. The ideas to which these youths had paid homage in Germany did not survive the reality of settlement. The transference of Germanic ideals to a Jewish context had been beset with difficulties even in Germany; in the harsh reality of Palestine, the attempted symbiosis broke down at once. For all its anti-intellectualism, it had been too intellectual for the prosaic facts the immigrants faced. The Zionist adaptation of völkisch ideas broke down earlier than that of assimilationist groups within Germany. The latter's confrontation with reality did not come about until the Nazi seizure of power.

II

The influence of völkisch thought on German Jews has a further aspect which serves to heighten the dilemma of the link between German and Jew. After the First World War, and especially in the years preceding the Nazi seizure of power, those who desired a more complete integration of the Jews with the Germans turned to the völkisch ideas which were sweeping all before them. During an earlier period these ideas had been rejected by assimilationists in favor of a deeply held belief in liberal values. Such liberal values were retained to some degree and there was still a strong element of Jewish liberalism well into the Nazi period. However, this link with the past was ill-equipped to cope with the new realities, and at last the *C.V. Zeitung* (official organ of the "Central Organization of German Citizens of the Jewish Faith") found itself the sole spokesman for a liberalism which had been rejected by most Germans and many young Jews alike.

After the First World War, German nationalism gathered increasing momentum while liberal ideas fell into discredit. As a result, many of the younger Jews who wanted to be accepted as Germans turned to the völkisch ideology in order to find a basis for their arguments and attempted to use this ideology to deepen their German-Jewish identity, just as the young Zionists had used it earlier to provide a road toward Jewish identity. Such efforts reached a climax at the time of Hitler's triumph and their own incipient expulsion from the community. To be sure, these young Jews were in a minority, like the young Zionists before them. The vast majority of German Jews clung to the principles of liberalism with something like desperation. Nonetheless, the efforts of this minority are a part of the story of völkisch influence on German Jews; nor should they be judged too harshly in retrospect.

We must not be blinded here by what eventually happened, but seek rather to understand the situation as it existed among the nationalist groups with whom these Jews sought to come into contact. Even after their seizure of power in 1933, and into the next year, some Nazis showed a certain ambivalence in their attitude toward Jews. For example, as late as April 1934, a Nazi leader gave permission to the Jewish war-veterans organization for their youth groups to play German teams at football— provided the games were played in private and with the "necessary restraint."[44] There is evidence, some still hidden among private papers, that until 1934 there existed at least a possibility, however tenuous, for a

National Socialist–Jewish understanding. One Jewish youth leader who tried to bring it about believed that an accord could be reached with the Röhm group.[45] There is some semblance of truth there, for the "socialist" revolutionaries around Ernst Röhm (1887–1934) and Gregor Strasser (1892–1934) were less inflexible on the Jewish question, to the extent that they desired to bring about a truer social and economic revolution.

Against this background, some Jewish youth groups felt that integration with the new Germany was possible, and they bolstered their hopes by putting into practice essentially völkisch ideas rather than transmuting them into a new Jewish nationalism. The Black Flag sought to find a "path toward Germany" and in so doing adopted wholeheartedly the völkisch ideology. The German Jew should be a "soldierly and *bündisch*" man, they asserted, using the same slogan many of the youth groups in the nation used. Moreover, in accordance with the traditional beliefs of the Youth Movement, the "*bündisch* man" was defined as an aristocrat, one whose stance derived from his very being. In tune with all we have discussed, it was asserted that "not matters of reason, but vital forces" were basic and that these forces were fashioned by the human spirit. Once again the question arises: what was specifically Jewish about this *Bund*? Religion was overtly rejected, and instead a typically vague reference to Jewish history and Jewish tradition took its place.[46] The Black Flag, taking its origins from the Comrades, was preeminently a *Bund* and sought to transform the young Jew into a "New Man" on a parallel with such attempts by the German Youth Movement, now re-formed as the Bündische Jugend. In passing it should be stressed once again that these German *Bünde*, though völkisch, were not National Socialist, and indeed the majority of them opposed that movement.

In 1934 the Black Flag had only a thousand members yet, like all *Bünde*, this body had no desire to be a mass movement. But, as with the other *Bünde*, discipline proved difficult to impose on the whole national organization. In spite of the trappings which emphasized such discipline at public meetings—the solid phalanx carrying the flag, the military deportment and uniforms of the members—the local *Bünde* at times went their own way. For example, the Hamburg *Bund* of the Black Flag was influenced by the Deutsche Jungenschaft led by Tusk (Eberhard Köbel, 1807–1955), which combined mystic rites with allegiance to the Communist Party.[47]

Such local organizations, however, were not regarded with particular favor by the Reichsbund Jüdischer Frontsoldaten, the Jewish war-veterans organization, founded after the First World War, which numbered some

30,000 members. That organization provided the forum for the Jewish *Bünde* (to which we shall return), which desired to strengthen German-Jewish identity; both the leader of the Black Flag and Hans-Joachim Schoeps (1909–1980), who had founded his own *Bund*, the Vortrupp, made national speaking tours under its auspices. It is not surprising that a veterans organization should have sympathized with the ideal of *bündisch* and soldierly comportment, or that its members, having risked their lives for the nation, should have felt a special need for ideological identification with Germanic thought. Long before the Nazi revolution, the Reichbund had consistently called for a return of Jews to the soil. The Jew as peasant and craftsman formed a necessary reservoir of Jewish strength, because, in the eyes of the Reichsbund, urbanism was sapping the very roots of Jewish existence through a process of proletarianization.[48] Defined in accordance with völkisch ideology, proletarianization was not a "class" term, but, as Wilhelm Heinrich Riehl had used it in the nineteenth century, denoted uprootedness.

Riehl had directed this word especially against the uprooted and urbanized Jews. From the end of the nineteenth century onward, however, a Jewish settlement movement attempted to transform Jews into farmers in Germany. Significantly, the organization to further Jewish settlement, which the Reichsbund superseded, was founded in 1897 at the same moment that the Germans began to step up their efforts to "return the *Volk* to the land."

Such attitudes were heightened under Nazi pressure, for Jews were now forced to leave the so-called "free professions," the doors to which were barred to them. The leader of the Reichsbund called once more for "work on the land, which makes man healthy, strong, and free," as well as, typically, "uncomplicated."[49] Statements like these must be read against the darkening horizon of the times, but clearly they were a continuation of a tradition that was shared by Germans and Jews. Moreover, among the German Jews themselves the Zionists, with their attacks on Jews who lounged in city cafés, shared identical attitudes with the assimilationists, though they despised each other.

The adoption of völkisch ideas undoubtedly facilitated the reassertion of Germanism deemed necessary and desirable by the leaders of the Reichsbund. In keeping with the ideology, the *Schild* ran a series focusing on heroic figures of the Jewish tribe within Germany, all military leaders or inventors, and pointed with pride several times to the Jews who had fought in the Free Corps.[50] These attitudes reached the limits of good taste when the Reichsbund in October 1933 sent the new Nazi government a declaration affirming its stand along with the German fatherland, for Germany's *Lebensraum* and honor were at stake. The German Reichsbund was not unique in its reaction to rightist and antisemitic pressure. For example, in the 1930s a league of French Jewish war veterans reacted in much the same manner to the rising tide of anti-Jewish feeling in that country. Just as the Patriotic Union of French Jews stressed their deep roots in France and advocated "French" courage and morality (in contrast to the Bolsheviks and East European Jewish immigrants), so the assertions of the Reichsbund must be viewed as a militant Germanism in the face of Nazi contentions. Throughout history and in every nation, veterans' organizations tend to become rightist pressure groups.[51] Jewish veterans' organizations shared this tendency, now heightened by the attempts to exclude them from the national scene.

Hans-Joachim Schoeps was right when he wrote, in 1934, that the Reichsbund had established itself as the organization of German-conscious Jews. The front-line experience of the First World War which that organization sought to reflect in its attitudes had a definite affinity to the events that were taking place in contemporary Germany.[52] Indeed, the Nazis exploited the "spirit of the front lines" which supposedly had existed during the war. Perhaps therein lay the hope for a better understanding? At any rate, the veterans' organization served to provide a mass audience for German-Jewish symbiosis, which was based on völkisch ideology.

In this connection, Hans-Joachim Schoeps's Vortrupp is of special interest. This small Jewish *Bund* regarded itself as a continuation of the German Youth Movement, which the Nazis were by that time destroying. Like the Youth Movement in general, these people saw themselves as a "Third Force" opposed to both Bolshevism and Western democracy. We are back with the theme that reappears so many times in this book. Moreover, though the Vortrupp disapproved of Nazi racial ideas, it approved of movements fighting against both Bolshevism and the corrupting influences of modern liberalism. Within the Jewish scene it sought to provide a "third alternative" to the Zionist movement and to the liberalism of sections of the official Jewish establishment such as the C.V.[53] Jews were considered to be one of the German tribes (*"Stamm"*) who, like the Saxons or the Bavarians, had lived for centuries on German soil. There was nothing unusual about this specific view of the place of the Jew in the nation. Most of those dedicated to assimilation, including the Reichsbund, shared it. Schoeps, a conservative, felt that the Jewish claim to Germanism was based on history, order, and law. His definition of Germanism was colored by his own profound experience of the Youth Movement, and he predictably opposed liberalism, materialism, and the Enlightenment. Further, he was dedicated to the maintenance of a *bündisch* aristocracy of youth on the same idealistic basis that the Youth Movement had proclaimed.

Schoeps is a Jewish theologian, however, and a religious historian of great power and importance, and it was to be expected that he would introduce a specifically Jewish element into this ideology. Unlike Martin Buber (whom he accused of having more in common with Meister Eckhart than with Abraham, Moses, or Job), Schoeps's conception of Judaism was not necessarily linked to the emergence of a Jewish *Volk*.[54] Indeed, Schoeps's religious ideal was removed from this world and its politics. Being a Jew meant participating in a historical relationship to God, who stood in the very center of his faith. This was an individual relationship and, unlike Buber's, did not express itself through any collectivity. Schoeps was greatly influenced by Søren Kierkegaard (1813–1855) and Martin Luther (1483–1546). The essence of his faith was "comforted despair," and in 1934 he wrote that Luther's cry "I believe, God help my unbelief" was the only true testimony a Jew could give.[55]

This Judaism did not conflict with the specifically Germanic posture of the *Bund*; young Jews could be dedicated to a völkisch Germany and still hold to this existential Judaism. Schoeps was the antipode of Buber's Zionism, though both shared an emphasis on the inwardness of faith. They differed sharply on how this faith expressed itself in history: Schoeps, in rejecting the idea of the Jewish *Volk*, believing as he did in a fusion of German and Jew, accused Buber of standing outside history and its necessity.[56] However, neither was able to solve the problem of how to relate the Jewish faith to the German environment, how to accomplish the transfer from völkisch-oriented Germanism to Judaism. Schoeps of course did not want such a transfer. He wanted Judaism to be an essential element of the Germanic ideals of his group. He called the Zionists the true assimilationists because they accepted a foreign nationalism as their own, yet it is hard to see how his Judaism offered much on earth beyond an essentially Germanic worldview.[57]

For all these groups, and others like them, the form life took was all-important, and this vital question was invariably linked to the völkisch ideology. They, like the Zionists earlier, were battling against the Jewish stereotype, and when this image was elevated to an article of national faith, the battle took on added impetus. Their image of the ideal Jew was not significantly different from the ideal of the earlier Zionist generation. Here we can see clearly the common völkisch base which the assimilationist groups shared with the young Zionists, if to a different purpose. The ideal Jew was aristocratic, rooted in the genuineness of the landscape, anti-urban, soldierly, and bound to his fellows by the *Bund* of a shared spiritual experience. Moreover, he was tough, sinewy, and well formed in body. This emphasis on physical form was a further feature of the German movement.

Form was defined as the forming of life (*Lebensgestaltung*) and as such had been a basic ingredient not only of the Youth Movement but of the whole *fin de siècle* revolt against bourgeois society. It is no coincidence that long before the emergence of the German-Jewish *Bünde*, the organization of Jewish "Turners" (gymnasts) was founded, advocating the "bodily renaissance of the Jews" and linking this with the beginning of a Jewish consciousness of peoplehood.[58] In time, the belief in the regenerating effects of nature was combined with the concept of nature as strengthening the body through struggle. Once again the ideal was similar to that of the völkisch movement. "The German must learn to have form, to want to be beautiful," and Jewish youth—Zionist or assimilationist—echoed this sentiment. This meant pleasure in strength of body and in sport.[59] Sport itself was never endowed with a purpose of its own, such as sheer enjoyment, but was always integrated with ideological concerns. It had been so for the Jewish Turners and it remained so for the Jewish *Bünde* and the Reichsbund, which emphasized sport as vital for the moral and physical health of Jewish youth. Moreover, it is no coincidence that from the Zionist side Robert Weltsch wrote some of his early articles on the nature of Jewish nationalism for the *Jüdische Monatshefte für Turnen und Sport* (*Jewish Monthly of Sports and Gymnastics*), a publication specifically linked to a German tradition that, since the beginning of the nineteenth century, had held that gymnastics and sport had a definite, overriding national purpose.

What, then, was the uniquely Jewish component of this thought? This question was a constant preoccupation of both the Zionists and the advocates of German-Jewish symbiosis. Siegfried Bernfeld summed it up concisely in 1915: Jewish youth as a *Bund* differed from German youth because its members were consciously Jews and their cultural drives were for the most part taken from the past and present of the Jewish *Volk*. Being a Zionist, he added that the orientation of these Jews was toward an autonomous Jewish culture in Palestine. Otherwise, he contended, the young Jewish community was much the same as the German. Like the Germans, they strove toward higher things, rejecting school and parents. Bernfeld wrote with great sincerity, but he too illustrates a dilemma that existed before and after him. For he not only denied a concern with Hebrew and

Yiddish and a specifically Jewish culture; he also dismissed the question of religious affiliation.[60] The vagueness of the Jewish past and present, the lack of specific ways in which it differed from German history, suggested a romanticism difficult to distinguish from that of the host country.

Nothing has been said here about the concept of race. It was never predominant in the Youth Movement or in the völkisch tradition to which young Jews tried to relate. Moreover, for Jewish youth the acceptance of this ideology never quite obliterated that belief in humanity which their liberal parents held so ardently. Those who played an important role in the Zionist aspect of this ideology, like Buber and Weltsch, became the principal spokesmen for a binational, Jewish–Arab state of Israel. Fichte and *Volk* were part of a specifically German culture which was assimilated, but humankind as a whole was never lost from sight. Racial ideas had no place here.

It is significant that even those Jews who seemed to accept racism changed the concept so as to deprive it of that exclusiveness essential to racist thought. Max Naumann (1875–1939), the leader of the Verband nationaldeutscher Juden (Association of German National Jews)—an extreme assimilationist group which was politically conservative—provides a good example of this ambivalence toward a racism which, at first glance, he seemed to accept. Writing in 1920, he asserted that Jews belonged to a race characterized by a distinctive body build, idiosyncratic facial expression, and peculiarities of language and physical movement. This stigmatization could surely have come straight from any major racist, Hans Friedrich Karl Günther (1891–1968), for example; it was a bald reaffirmation of the stereotype, justified on supposedly racial grounds.

Naumann, the assimilationist, would not admit, however, that such considerations would call for Jews to turn away from Germany and seek separate identity. He suggested that a solution to the problem lay in the fact that Jews "feel" German and that "our German feeling overcomes the blood"; this was the inward orientation of the völkisch ideology.[61] The German racists felt that there was an inherent difference between their own soul and the Jewish soul, and this disparity determined the differences in physical appearance. Naumann denied the validity of this hypothesis: though the rest of his bodily make-up might give a different impression, the soul of the Jew is German, he said. In this context Naumann qualified his racism still further by dissociating the Eastern Jew from it. In his view, Eastern Jews were physically different from and spiritually foreign to German Jews.[62] Thus the Jewish race becomes a German-Jewish race. Later (in 1933) he maintained that racism was the product of a justified

German anger against Jewish abuses of Germanism, especially as practiced by the liberals of the *C. V.* Once the anger passed, he contended that
the nationaldeutscher Juden would be ready to join the German *Volk*, for
they loved Germany with a passion that was self-justifying.[63]

Naumann's ideas are worth mentioning, for they show how difficult
it was for any Jew to accept racism, even when he could come to grips
with that school of thought which built a racist structure on völkisch
foundations.

Naumann perished at the hands of the Nazis. Nothing that has been
written here is meant to apportion praise or blame before the gates of
history. It is far more important to understand the historical context out
of which the ideological correspondence sprang; those who were involved
could not see into the future. Moreover, the very absence of racism from
that part of the völkisch ideology which these Jews accepted, and from
their own ideology, should put this discussion into its proper light. None
of the men and women we are here considering lived in enforced or even
self-enforced isolation. Rejecting the Jewish past as it had evolved during the centuries, Jews partook in a culture which in a very real sense was
theirs as much as it was the Germans'. Why it was the völkisch culture
which attracted some Jews so strongly is easily understood. Jewish youth
was a youth in revolt, and that meant revolt against the bourgeois society
of their parents, a society imbued with liberal and rational ideals. To be
sure, the revolt of many young Jews and Germans became leftist and took
a Marxist direction, but for the majority of bourgeois youth this step
seemed merely a substitution of one materialism with another. They saw
conventions enforced in their own homes and in their schools in the name
of what seemed to be a shallow, materialistic society, and they became passionately concerned with creativity, with the inward person, with a spiritual dynamic which could reach far beyond the dreariness of industrial
civilization. German youth could build on a German romantic tradition,
and the Youth Movement in fact revived the spirit of the Wartburg. Young
Jews had no such traditions, and consequently they adopted those of the
culture into which they were born.

For these Jews this meant in addition an escape from the atrophy of
their own past. They saw their religion as shallow and empirical; they
saw it in association with urbanism and the ghetto. The völkisch ideology
offered a path toward the achievement of a Jewish consciousness which
they thought could be transferred from German to Jewish concerns. This
transference never quite succeeded, for it tended to cloud the uniquely
Jewish component of their national awakening. Later, others saw in this

transference a chance for an even closer German-Jewish symbiosis. But that failed also, for the very awakening of the new German völkisch self-consciousness called for a "clean separation" and not for unity. The failure of German-Jewish unity on this level has its tragic aspect. A common revolt of youth based on the same ideological grounds could not overcome the inherent problems faced by the Jew who wanted to revitalize his *Volk* or by the Jew who wanted to become one with Germanism.

From a wider historical perspective, this analysis throws some light on the depth and penetration of völkisch ideology. Even some of those against whom it was potentially directed came to share many of its presuppositions. For even where völkisch thought was not overtly racial, it tended to separate Germans and Jews and thus worked for the exclusion of Jews from German life. Völkisch thought was one response to a world which Robert Musil (1880–1942) has well described: "A world has come into being in which the realm of objects [*Eigenschaften*] exists apart from man."[64] Jews and Germans wanted to blot out this alienation. Since it was the youth who desired this, the revolt was directed against their elders, who were pictured as prisoners of a liberal, rationalist age.

The men and women we have been discussing were a minority in Jewish life, but they constituted a significant minority. They tried to cast off the political attitudes which had dominated German Jewry since its emancipation.[65] They felt at one with the change in public opinion that was taking place all round them: the new völkisch nationalism and the inner-directedness of all human experience. The problems which their experience raises are much more important than the mere numbers involved. The end was tragic, but the questions they tried to solve still haunt our own times. For who among us has yet found a way to end alienation? Who has bridged the gap between materialism and human creativity? Who has succeeded in infusing modern nationalism with the belief that genuine culture is more important than outward, aggressive power?

4

The Corporate State and the Conservative Revolution in Weimar Germany

I

During the nineteenth century the history of representative institutions was viewed in terms of the development of parliaments. It seemed as if this form of popular representation was triumphing everywhere. German and French scholars joined their English colleagues in tracing the rise of parliamentary government as tantamount to the development of democracy. The twentieth century, on the other hand, may well go down in history as the century which decisively challenged this connection between democracy and parliamentary representation. When the German constitutional theorist and lawyer Carl Schmitt (1888–1985) wrote that parliament as a bourgeois institution of the nineteenth century lacked a basis in the age of mass industrial democracy (1926), he was summing up a widely held point of view.[1] There was a turning away from what the previous generation had regarded as the bulwark of democratic progress. Was this simply a flight into Caesarism? Can we say that if the nineteenth century saw a trend toward parliamentary democracy, our own century has seen an equally strong trend toward government by dictatorship?

It would be misreading the history of anti-parliamentarianism to regard this trend merely as a heightening of the anti-democratic forces which have always played an important role in Western history. Rather, this was essentially a search for the new forms that popular representation might take, a quest for a different kind of democratic expression. Few wanted to do away with popular participation in government: the majority believed that parliamentary institutions were, in fact, inhibiting such participation. Schmitt gave the principal reason for this: parliament had become a class institution, a weapon in the hands of the bourgeoisie. Spengler had called such government the continuation of private business by other means.[2] The parliamentary institution was no longer representative of the whole nation; instead, the true nation should be an expression of the *Volk*—a mystical entity above, apart from, and outside social class or political party. The *Volk* constituted an organic whole which could not possibly be represented through a system based, as it seemed, on the selfishness of private interests.

While this rejection of parliamentary government could be analyzed for the whole of Europe, Germany provides a particularly significant example. In the political and economic chaos of the 1920s, the search for alternate forms of democracy had room to grow. More important and symptomatic, this search came to presuppose a general effort to do away with the bourgeois age. This was so for those who took their inspiration from the Bolshevik Revolution, but it was also the aim of those who wanted no part of Bolshevism. This search for new democratic forms could take place within a socialist framework that rejected both communism and the bourgeois society. We shall analyze this search for a different kind of socialist democracy when dealing with the German left-wing intellectuals in the last chapter of this book. However, for the most part those who desired such a "Third Force" came from the right, rejecting all forms of Marxist socialism as well as bourgeois forms of political representation. Their attempt has special significance in modern history: it raised the question whether a rejection of parliamentary government in anti-bourgeois terms could find a firm basis that would lead neither to communism nor to some form of dictatorship. We must not see this quest simply in terms of the National Socialist triumph or of its eventual failure. Both these factors served to narrow the possibilities, until parliamentary government seemed once more the only means of true political participation, and dictatorship or communism the sole alternatives.

The term "conservative revolution" has been applied to this attempted "Third Force": conservative because it based itself on the organic unity of the *Volk*, founded on history and tradition; revolutionary because it opposed bourgeois society and, for the most part, the capitalist system as well.[3] This revolutionary conservatism, through its concern with the *Volk*, was a part of the völkisch movement in Germany. To be sure, it placed a greater emphasis on the necessity for revolutionary action and the importance of the corporate state than the rest of the movement, but this should not obscure its essential orientation. Revolutionary conservatism can be described as the left wing of the völkisch movement. In this discussion, however, we shall use the term "conservatives," which is what these individuals called themselves.

81

Among the advocates of the "conservative revolution" there was much talk of a "socialist state"—by which many of these conservatives meant something akin to National Socialism. But this must not be confused with either Hitlerian policies or Oswald Spengler's "Prussianism and Socialism," both of which were rejected: Hitlerian ideas because they seemed a thinly disguised acceptance of bourgeois society, playing the parliament game; Spengler's because in his praise for the Prussian aristocracy he seemed to deny that every member of the *Volk* should participate in the nation's destiny.[4] Moeller van den Bruck, the most influential conservative theorist, made the point about Spengler. For Moeller van den Bruck, socialism meant the ideological unity of the *Volk* as opposed to the divisiveness of parliaments and political parties.[5] He wanted the nationalization of production as part of this organic unity—the common *Mythos* which had once held the people together.[6] Moeller van den Bruck looked back at this past unity and fused its aim with a desire for strong corporate organization.[7] Corporate ideas were an essential part of a state "beyond Marxism and Capitalism." *Das dritte Reich*, to use the title of Moeller van den Bruck's most famous work (*The Third Reich*, 1923), symbolized this attitude for many revolutionary conservatives, though not for Adolf Hitler. It is significant that Moeller van den Bruck at first titled his famous book *Die dritte Kraft* (*The Third Force*).

One historian has called this conservatism a flight into the past, and the corporative ideas a part of this flight.[8] Certainly, the corporatism which provided the structure for the corporate state was understood by many conservatives to be a return to the medieval guilds. Groupings by occupation were considered the essence of a structured society, for here the worker would get his "rights" side by side with his employers. Such corporatism, however, must be superimposed on a true community, which constituted the basis of the state. Indeed, for most revolutionary conservatives the "true community" became the true corporate unit, displacing the occupational chambers. We shall therefore have to consider the ideal of the group, or *Bund*, which is essential to this concept at some length later. Some of the people involved, however, did not go back to past examples but saw this corporatism embodied in the soldiers' and workers' councils (*Räte*) which had come into being at the beginning of the 1918 revolution. Unlike the left, however, they saw these councils not as an instrument of the workers to obtain sole control over the state but as an example of self-government by special-interest groups, an element which has always been considered of prime importance in conservative ideology.[9] But those who thought along these lines were the exception rather than the rule.

Did the emphasis on a true community reflect the vague romantic unity of the *Volk* rather than a well-worked-out economic theory? The völkisch thought of these conservatives, the mystical basis of their view of the *Volk*, is clear in Moeller van den Bruck's description of how the new order was to come about: "The state must be renewed through a worldview [*Weltanschauung*]."[10] Their thought tended always to stress the ideological rather than concrete and pragmatic solutions to the problems confronting Germany. These individuals and groups maintained their conservatism in this manner, combining it with a backward look at history.

Yet the past was more of an inspiration than an example to be imitated by the present. Revolutionary conservatives wanted to go forward "into history." The symbiosis between conservatism and revolution was in their terms to be more revolutionary than conservative, directed to the fundamental change and even overthrow of existing society. That is why they stand at the left wing of the völkisch movement. The past was a weapon against bourgeois society and through a corporate structuring of society provided the memory of a congenial political and economic form. Those taken with this thought talked constantly of the "new Germany."

It was the ideological weight that was to drag the movement down, the precedence given to the fact—as Moeller van den Bruck put it—that Germany was now without an "idea" and that it had better get one. Moeller van den Bruck's emphasis on the importance of a worldview was meant to lead toward anti-rational conclusions, for such a view must be rooted within the mystical entity of the *Volk*. Typically enough, he praises *Mythos* rather than history, for *Mythos* expresses the drive of the *Volk* soul. Moeller van den Bruck's use of *Mythos* matches that of Martin Buber discussed in the previous chapter. For both these men this concept expressed the organic unity between the individual and the *Volk*, as well as the nature of the *Volk* as a living organism. The *Mythos* of a people, their legends and superstitions, are closer to the realities of life than any product of historical scholarship.[11] The organic unity of the *Volk* must be restored. "The nature of democracy consists in this: that the *Volk* must emerge as a political (organic) whole."[12] The *Volk* was viewed in typical völkisch fashion in terms of a common *Weltanschauung* and the solid Marxist fusion of ideology and economic theory condemned as "superficial." As a result, revolutionary conservatism became bogged down in a search for the "genuine," for "roots," and for a social harmony achieved through racial rather than economic theory. The revolutionary conservatives had few ideas about economics, as we shall see, but ideological considerations were always uppermost in their minds. The roots of failure must be sought here, but that does not lessen the importance of the effort.

Moeller van den Bruck wrote that liberalism, with its parliamentary form of representation, was the expression of a society, not of a community.[13] It was artificial inasmuch as the government was divorced from the community as a whole and had lost contact with the real longings of the people. Previously, people of all political persuasions who criticized Wilhelminian Germany had made this very point, and this gave further impetus to the revolutionary conservatives' theories. Writers of lasting influence such as Paul de Lagarde and Julius Langbehn had sought to unify the people and their government through a mystical idea of the *Volk*. Such ideological unity would lead both to greater individual fulfillment and to genuine representative government. Langbehn had already advocated the form of the corporate state as best suited to those aims, but neither of these men thought in terms of revolution against bourgeois society.[14] It was the Youth Movement, arising in the new century, that gave these ideas a sharper edge against the existing order. Revolutionary conservatism was a conscious rebellion against its environment, though it did not always find a coherent expression of its aims. Where it did so, both Marxism and parliamentary government were rejected in favor of a more genuine unity of the *Volk*. By the 1920s the largest group in that movement, the Bündische Jugend, provided some of the most important theoretical expressions of the "Third Force."

A concern for *Individualität* (individualism) stood in the forefront of the Youth Movement and this was true also of revolutionary conservatives in general. Marxism, a youth leader wrote, "is nothing more than the acceptance of mechanization [of life]. From this, no salvation can come for the individuality of each person."[15] Parliamentary government, with its political parties, atomized the individual, divided him from his rulers, and produced a ceaseless conflict between the individual and the masses.[16] The leader of the important *Freischar* demanded that state and people be reunited once more. The state must be an expression of the community, the *Volk*. He went on to suggest a corporately structured *Volk* as the antithesis to the present "anonymous" state.[17]

This was a quest for a new kind of democracy. What seemed to be needed was a "new concept of the community," and for this the Youth Movement before and after the war could draw on its own experiences.[18] The movement consisted of several well-defined groups, each with a conscious spirit of its own. Through common activities, such as hiking through the countryside, these groups acquired common experiences which rendered them cohesive units. Unity of body, soul, and spirit was the primary law of their community.[19] Such empathy provided genuine unity within the group and, through the group, with the *Volk*.[20] This was the true *Bund*, and it was opposed to bourgeois artificiality; that is, to the society they found dominant. A certain activism was part of their make-up: "living the common experience" took precedence over thinking about it.[21] The war experience and a glorification of life lived dangerously heightened this drive for action on the part of the Bündische Jugend. Even after the war, in the face of the problems of the German Republic, some of the groups never formulated a coherent ideology. Yet all of them thought of themselves as cells for the renewal of the nation, and the poet Stefan George's (1868–1933) ideas of a "secret Germany" that would redeem the nation played some part in their literature.

Many of these groups never progressed beyond a kind of *Volk* mysticism based on the "taking in" of nature, but some were more specific about how a group should be structured, how it could become a true *Bund*. The automatic equality of all members was rejected as a mechanical, abstract idea and therefore not "genuine." The existing unity of the group implied a structured, hierarchical society, in which every individual had their place according to their individual merits. This hierarchy was built on both the corporative and the leadership principles. The leader of the *Freischar* envisaged a society in which the leader confronted the diverse special interests organized corporatively.[22] Within the *Bund* itself the leadership principle was the important one. The leader of the Bund Deutscher Neupfadfinder (New Scouts) held that the foundations for the life of the individual were provided by the community and the leadership.[23]

Important from our point of view is the fact that these groups thought of themselves as independent units dedicated to a specific way of life. This was the cell from which "all states had their origin."[24] What was more logical than that they should envisage the ideal nation as consisting of such self-contained groups? In this manner the existing schism between the people and their government would be organically bridged. For example, the political manifesto of the Jungdeutsche Orden, a political movement which was sparked by war veterans independently of the Youth Movement (1929), advocated a constitution in which the state was to be made up of groups, not individuals. These ideas also took hold in all the Bündische Jugend.[25] They were in the very air and were, moreover, projected outside the nation itself. Their emphasis on the *Volk* was neither exclusive nor aggressive, for they held that the individual *Volk* was a self-contained group within an international community composed of many different groups of peoples.[26] One youth leader summed up the general feeling among the *Bünde*: the nineteenth-century state was in the process of transformation. The new basis for the state was to be the rediscovery of the group—the community to which the individual had a direct relationship and in which he belonged. "Where the *Bund* exists, a new Germany starts." Martin Voelkel (1884–1950), the leader of the New Scouts, added that although capitalism devoured its own children, the idea of the proletariat was equally unconvincing; it had betrayed German socialism to the enemies of the nation. The *Bund* of men was the only true reality.[27] Similarly, the Jungdeutscher Orden called for a true community (*Sozialer Volksstaat*) cemented by the ideological ties of the *Bund* as opposed to a parliamentary state that equated the bourgeois and the nation.[28]

These ideas were basic to the concept of the corporate state which we find in the 1920s among the conservative revolutionaries. The new Germany was to be based on individual groupings, called *Bünde*, and these various units would constitute the nation. Corporate structure was envisaged in these terms; after all, the medieval guilds also had been bound by shared experience (the worship of a particular saint, etc.) which differentiated them from groups based only on special economic interests. Indeed, corporatism would prevent the institutionalization of special interests, as the Jungdeutscher Orden put it, and substitute the "ideological ties" of the *Bund* as the source of true association among men. In the Jungdeutscher Orden occupational corporate chambers would have a separate existence confined to economic life but not representing the nation as a whole.[29] This then was the political thought that for these conservatives typified the real negation of the parliamentary bourgeois state.

These ideas influenced important völkisch organizations such as the north German wing of the National Socialist Party. Albert Krebs (1899–1974)—closely associated with Gregor Strasser, who until 1929 was second only to Hitler within the Party organization—wrote in 1928: "What is the state? Its germinal cell is the *Bund* of men which gathers around a leader."[30] Friedrich Hielscher (1902–1990), a leading conservative revolutionary, defended the student corps on the grounds that the law of the *Bund* was more important to them than the law of the state itself. The spirit of the *Bund* was weightier than the profit motive of the bourgeoisie.[31] It was widely held that a state based on such groups would restore the organic unity of the nation and at the same time free the state from involvement with capitalist private interests.[32]

This was an important point for those who believed that parliamentary government meant merely carrying on private business by other means.

A state made up of self-governing organic units would change all that. Krebs, active in a white-collar labor organization, believed that the social struggle would then be fought out within the corporate units and thus the state would be freed from the pull of divisive forces.[33] He himself fused the *Bünde* and the occupational groups into one corporate structure. For Krebs too it was the ideological cement of a true *Bund* which held such units together and this was where they found their origin. Such an organization of the state would deprive political parties of their power. A grouping of corporations was envisaged by some as a "first chamber," and did not exclude an elected parliament. Somewhat confusedly, however, this setup was supposed to eliminate the political party system.[34]

The *Bund*, then, was to be the corporate cell out of which the national structure would grow. Essentially this was an aristocratic concept: the *Bünde* of the Youth Movement considered themselves an elite "order." The transformation of this idea of association into a general principle at the basis of all political life seemed to modify in an important respect the idea of the elite. Yet the concept of the *Bund* could also be applied to the leadership group within the corporate state. This was done, for example, by Hans Zehrer (1899–1966), the moving spirit of the influential Tat Kreis (a group of intellectuals gathered around *Die Tat*, a journal originally founded by Diederichs). The leaders, a minority group, must form a *Bund* among themselves in the spirit of the Youth Movement. Through this *Bund* they would lead a corporately structured state—for Zehrer, the only way to bring discipline to Germany. The entire nation would then be held together by an ideology that for him was derived from a Lutheran and Protestant inspiration.[35] Once again the ideological factor asserted itself as basic to the *bündisch* and corporate state. The concept of a binding ideology was so important to the cohesiveness of the *Bund* and therefore of the state that economic theory was submerged beneath it. A state based on such groups would automatically solve all problems, and so the literature on economic theory often does not go beyond a condemnation of the international capitalist conspiracy. Here we have in a heightened form the dilemma that plagued the whole movement. The formula "Neither capitalism nor Marxism" sought implementation through a corporate structuring of society and economics, but in the last resort it was bolstered by a romantic notion of the historic unity of the *Volk*. Historians have stressed the "political aestheticism" of the Youth Movement in particular, by which they mean that concrete political programs became lost in the almost ecstatic worship of the new Reich as the true democracy of the *Volk*.

Moreover, the concepts, on the one hand, of strong leadership within the group and, on the other, of corporate representation were bound to conflict and to introduce a dichotomy into this political thought. Within most of the groups, the leader was thought to be representative of the whole, but if this system were to be applied to the national scene, the corporative structure would lose its meaning. This dilemma was solved for a great many people outside the Youth Movement through the Italian example. Carl Schmitt attempted to resolve the conflict between leadership and democracy by saying that society should be divided into corporate bodies economically as well as politically, by treating the local governments as corporate entities. But—and here he parallels ideas already discussed in the Youth Movement—this must all be rooted in the *Volk*, which shares the same ideology and longings. And here the *Volk* is based on a common Aryan race. The leader, the corporations, indeed the whole *Volk* share this mystical tie; their attitudes toward life are therefore identical. It follows that no real differences between the leader and the corporations can arise. The *Führerprinzip* (leadership principle) is able to permeate the *Volk* as a whole, dominating the diverse corporations.[36] A similar relationship developed in Italy between Il Duce and the Chamber of Corporations. There is a significant point of contact here between the ideas of the conservative revolutionaries in Germany and the fascists, which calls for further study.

Although the group of conservative revolutionaries as a whole never emphasized economic problems, the men who stood squarely in the middle of the political struggles of the 1920s did attempt to put a greater emphasis on reality. The conservative revolution (like the völkisch movement in general), through its attempted closeness to nature, tended toward the ideal of a society of peasants and craftsmen. However, the industrial worker could not be ignored. August Winnig (1878–1956) made a major contribution toward facing this problem. He had been a Social Democrat and subsequently moved closer to the kind of conservatism we have been discussing. As chief administrative officer of East Prussia he became involved in the Kapp Putsch (1920) directed against the Weimar Republic, lost his position, and thereafter devoted himself to theoretical questions, chiefly that of the relationship of the worker to the state. As part of the confusion that accompanied the growth of big cities, the worker had lost all their rights. They were no longer a true citizen but had been depressed into proletarian status. The once free German worker had now lost their freedom and it was the prime duty of the state to restore it to them.[37] It seems clear that, like all those associated with this movement, Winnig

88

thought of the workers in terms of craftsmen, without himself denying the necessity of an industrial society.

What, then, was to be done? Once again the concept of a hierarchically structured society came to the fore. The proclamation that all are equal would not better the lot of the workers, August Winnig said, for such equality was in direct opposition to nature itself: "Nature has many aspects, except one: equality." Doctrines of equality were, therefore, artificial— as artificial and divorced from the "genuine" in humanity as was all parliamentary representative government. Only humanity estranged from nature could believe in such a fraud.[38] Rather, there must be a revival of the organic state, which meant that everyone must be coordinated in the service of the *Volk*. At the same time the overweening financial advantage of the employers must be curbed: because of their unrestrained capitalism, the wages of the workers were constantly shrinking.[39] A corporative organization of occupational chambers must be set up. Laborers and employers working together would have specific rights and duties toward one another. Once again, a strong concept of leadership would give direction to economic endeavor and the ideology of the *Volk*; the organic, natural principle would cement the whole organization.

Winnig was a moderate; his economic policy took scant advantage of what Gregor Strasser called the "anti-capitalist longings" of the people. It is typical that his ideas were shared to a large extent by a man such as Paul Bang (1879–1945), who was also involved in the Kapp Putsch and subsequently became principal economic advisor to Alfred Hugenberg, the head of the Deutschnationale Volkspartei (German National Party). He too sought to lead the economic system back to what he called the "principle of personality," as opposed to the goals of capitalism. Even more moderate than Winnig, he proposed to make every worker a small proprietor and he saw the road to this goal in much the same kind of worker-employer collaboration that Winnig had advocated.[40] Bang cannot be called a conservative revolutionary, and Winnig can claim such a designation only in a very limited way. Their corporative ideas sought social justice without advocating the abolition of the present capitalist system, however much its excesses were deplored. Here the organic principle was made a substitute for economic change. The capitalist system was to remain intact, integrated with the ideology of the *Volk* and expressed through corporate organization.

"True socialism is the community of the *Volk*."[41] This phrase sums up the basic attitude of the revolutionary conservatives. For most of them— the author of this phrase, for instance—this socialism was combined with opposition to existing capitalist society. Paul Krannhals (1883–1943), a writer of some influence, believed that the principal task of any economic system was to allow the free development of individual personality. Against this stood the enslavement of humanity through money and credit. Just as the state had been separated from the *Volk* by parliamentary government, so the economic system had been detached too, because money had become a value in itself and for itself alone. "Money and blood [the *Volk*] are contrasting elements which could not be in greater opposition."[42] Capitalist finance must be abolished and money again made a reward for real work. Credit was the essence of unproductive capital—so thought the conservative revolutionaries. They were attracted by the clause in the first program of the National Socialist Party which called for emancipation from the "slavery of interest charges." Once this had been accomplished, Krannhals believed, trust between workers and employers could be restored as they collaborated in the interests of the *Volk* through corporate chambers.[43]

In essence, these ideas were not new. The early English socialists, for example, had put forward a similar opposition to the workings of capitalist finance. In Germany, however, the ideological basis of the *Volk* was always in the foreground and now was increasingly coupled with racial ideas. The true community on which the state must be built was said to be Aryan in nature, and because this was essential for the proper working of politics and economics, it had to be defended against all enemies. Traditionally the Jew had been cast in the role of enemy. Thus the action necessary to implement true socialism was not a revolution as such but, rather, the elimination of the Jews, who came to represent the slavery of interest and the domination of unearned capital. Not merely the ideological predelictions of the *Volk*, but also the "respectable" economic theories of Werner Sombart (1863–1941), distracted these revolutionaries from attacking bourgeois society as a whole directly and effectively. For Sombart, the Jews, through their "rationalism" and their "impersonal commercialism," played the principal role in building modern capitalist society. Conservative revolutionaries were increasingly driven to racial thought as a substitute for the "overthrow of society" which many of them sincerely desired. Krannhals summed up the general position: "With Jewry stands or falls the mechanistic and materialistic concept of the economic system."[44] These thinkers increasingly envisaged their revolution as directed against the Jews and not against the employer class; with the overthrow of the Jews, they believed, the fetters of capitalist finance would fall to the ground. However, this antisemitic, racial focus must not be allowed to obscure the urge toward change and toward a "new Germany" which inspired the movement.

At its extreme, this urge called for decisive action against existing society. This was best illustrated by the brothers Otto (1897–1974) and Gregor Strasser. They worked in the industrial north of Germany and first attempted to turn the National Socialist Party in the direction of such action. When this attempt failed, Otto Strasser tried to carry on with a movement of his own. "Movement" in this case is too limiting a word, however, for the Strasser program managed to capture the hopes and imaginations of a wide variety of people who flowed in and out of all sorts of radical groupings without allowing firm organizational forms to take root. It was a constant coming and going that may well have been due to the nihilistic components which, as Otto-Ernst Schüddekopf (1912–1984) has pointed out, existed in all the social revolutionary groups. For Strasser was not alone. Many National Bolsheviks as well as some youth groups shared his ideas.[45] They all wanted to abolish the existing system, and despite their frantic opposition to the communists there was an element among them not averse to collaboration with this enemy: "every opposition to the system must be furthered."[46] A very different, radical attitude predominated here to that found in the other men and groupings discussed: it was the revolutionary overthrow of society as a whole that was desired; the capitalist system had to undergo a fundamental change.

For all this, once the ideas and plans of the Strassers are analyzed, we are back to the main theme of this chapter. The *Fourteen Theses of the German Revolution* put forward by Otto Strasser when he left the National Socialist Party (1929) advocated the overthrow of capitalism. This was the *sine qua non* of the revolution's success. Yet the specific economic reforms proposed were scarcely geared to the kind of overthrow of which the program spoke so enthusiastically. According to one of Otto Strasser's formulations, German socialism entailed the sharing by the workers of 49 percent of all industry. This would have left working control in the hands of the managers.[47] Land was to be nationalized and those who "held" it were to be responsible to the state. Yet they would still be regarded as "proprietors." Each individual's share of property and profit in the economic system was to be directly related to his work or responsibilities to the state. That state was once more defined as an organic community based on a common race. In turn, this meant a "living" (i.e., genuine) structuring of society formalized in occupational and corporate, as opposed to parliamentary, groupings.[48] Here the emphasis is again on the *Volk* and on a corporate system that will cater to the needs of the nation rather than to the profit motive. Later, Otto Strasser added that the corporate state with its occupational groupings was the true "Germanic democracy," because it was in tune with the aristocratic principle of government. His corporate state would be built by national representation from occupational groups in the localities. Strasser contrasted this with the Italian model, in which the official party was predominant over the self-government of the working population.[49] His racism, however, gave his structure the ideological and dictatorial unity which, as we have seen, was explicit in all this thought. Here too the Jews represented the evils of capitalism, while the Aryan ideal provided the basis for a cohesive society.

Corporatism would allow for unity of planning and of personal development, as well as for initiative on the part of the leaders of the economy. Equality as such was not advocated. Society would be structured through a leadership hierarchy within each corporate unit. Albert Krebs who, like Otto Strasser, eventually left the National Socialist Party, made a familiar point when he discussed the kind of corporate society that this socialism would bring about. Through it, he maintained, the state would be removed from the play of private interests, whose battles would be fought within the corporate groupings themselves, supervised, however, by the state. In view of this last idea, it is difficult to understand Albert Krebs's opposition to Italian Fascism. To be sure, as Krebs wrote, Il Duce and his followers had no real appreciation of the racial ideas that were necessary to give ideological unity to the structure as a whole.[50] Krebs accused some of his fellow revolutionaries of a vital mistake in downgrading *Volk* and race.[51] Despite the emphasis on the overthrow of the capitalist system, such ideological considerations were of great importance. Even in the case of avowed revolutionaries, opposition to materialism led in a neo-romantic direction, and in turn this caught up the revolutionary impetus.

It is difficult to assess the true political potential of such revolutionary conservatism and with it the chance of transforming Germany in a corporative direction. National Socialism may have offered such an opportunity, and if Gregor Strasser had been a man of greater personal decisiveness, he might well have won his battle against Adolf Hitler and the "Munich clique." As it was, he fell into obscurity and was assassinated on 30 June 1934. His brother Otto's Black Front suffered from organizational instability, a common failing of all these small social revolutionary groups. Indeed, with the rapid radicalization of the German masses to the left and right, many a Strasser follower wandered off into the communist camp.[52] The failure of the radicals did not benefit the more moderate advocates of corporatism. The Youth Movement never pushed through to really effective political action, and men like August Winnig were, for all their influence, isolated figures. Hope might have lain in another direction, that of the white-collar unions, the largest of which was the Deutschnationale Handlungsgehilfen-Verband (Nationalist Union of Commercial Apprentices). Krebs was an important official in that organization and Max Habermann (1885–1944), one of its most important leaders, also believed that the corporate structuring of the nation provided the most "natural" political and economic organization.[53] However, the union shared only antisemitism and a belief in the *Volk* as general principles and its members never formed a coherent political force. Yet at one point this large union (some 450,000 strong) could have been politically effective. In 1928, one of its leaders made contact with the Catholic Christian trade-union movement. The idea behind this was for some sort of concerted action to eliminate political parties and replace them with "organic democracy." A corporate state might well have been the eventual outcome.[54] But this attempt at change from below never gained ground and led, instead, to the founding of another political splinter party.

The only real political chance to create the "new Germany" seemed to present itself with the short-lived 1932 government of General Kurt von Schleicher (1882–1934). Gregor Strasser at this point called von Schleicher's proposed government (in which he was to be a member) the "cabinet of anti-capitalist longing."[55] It is more probable that von Schleicher was merely using Strasser's differences with Hitler in an attempt to split the National Socialist Party and that he never really sympathized with Gregor Strasser's kind of National Socialism. At any rate, von Schleicher soon fell from power and Hitler, who was anti-Strasser, became the next Chancellor. The final collapse of revolutionary conservatism was not brought about solely by the triumph of Hitler; it was foreshadowed by the basic weakness we have discussed. The society "beyond capitalism and Marxism" was basically a society held together not by an explicit social or economic aim, but by a romantic ideology. It was in those terms that Franz von Papen (1879–1969), having failed in his attempt to govern Germany, tried to revive the corporate ideal once more at the time that the National Socialists were forming a coalition government with conservative forces. The group to which von Papen belonged was close to high finance and scarcely sympathetic to revolutionary conservatism. Von Papen, therefore, tempered the idea of the corporate state with the statement that "all true revolutions are revolutions of the spirit against the mechanization [of man]."[56]

Von Papen said nothing about economic change, though he referred to the medieval concept of the guilds and to Catholic corporate thought. There was no mention of a society, capitalist or Marxist; nor of a "new

Germany" going forward "into history," Von Papen's theorist, Edgar Jung (1894–1934), held that the "new Reich" was indeed the "new Middle Ages"—a model of the organic *Volk* of the future.[57] The emphasis on the "spirit" so prominent here was also that part of the revolutionaries' philosophy that most endangered their avowed objective of overthrowing the present system. National Socialism retained this emphasis, but it rejected ideas of corporate society as out of place in a Führerstaat. The party program envisaged the creation of occupational chambers, but these were to be economic units only, without wider significance. An official party commentary on corporatism rejected this type of organization as fostering a spiritual attitude that favored an aristocratic way of life rather than a mechanism for the better representation of the *Volk*. Thus Nazism, which called itself democratic, rejected the political concept that Mussolini wanted to put into effect in his fascist state.[58]

National Socialism cut through the problem of the relationship between the group and the leader by stressing personal relationships through the leadership principle. National Socialism seemed to revive the past in forging pseudofeudal ties between the individuals in the leadership hierarchy. The loyalties that cemented the structure of the group, however, consisted of a web of reciprocal duties among the leadership itself. The only parallel with a corporate society was in the personal groupings which these feudal leaders built up around their persons and which constituted the leader's *Hausmacht* (personal following).[59] In effect, the National Socialist state was a network of such groupings, but there was no concept of a corporate organization of the community as a whole.

Von Papen's reference to Catholic corporate thought leads to the possible connection of the ideas we have been analyzing and the Catholic corporate ideology which influenced all Europe. At certain points the influence of Catholic corporatism led to ideas vaguely similar to those held by the conservative revolutionaries. Othmar Spann (1878–1950), an influential professor at the University of Vienna, provides a good example of this trend.[60] Spann, resorting to the conservative and Catholic theorists of the nineteenth century, believed that a return to a feudal order would restore the personal relationship between ruler and ruled which had been lost in the impersonal modern state. The medieval estates should be revived, each having a say in its own sphere of influence. Thus, the cobblers would direct shoemaking; the teachers, education; the generals, the army— but the king or the nobility would control national politics, which was their province. These estates ran counter to the unity of the *Bund* in which

94

so many conservative revolutionaries believed and which did not permit a sharp division between politics and professional life: the *Bund* and its spirit included all facets of human existence.

Moreover, the corporate ideas with which we have been concerned in fact developed from different sources. The emphasis on the group, the *Bund*, cannot really be linked to Catholic thought, and it was not from this source that these corporate ideas derived. To be sure, the medieval example cannot be discounted. However, guilds provided an inspiration to the revolutionary conservatives, not in a purely restorative sense, but as a reminder of a type of organization that could be adapted to the new Germany. The link with Catholicism faces a further difficulty. The revolutionary conservatives were not only antisemitic but also anti-Catholic, equating Catholicism with anti-national ultramontanism. Thus they overtly rejected any Catholic influence. This animosity also played a part in their hostile attitude toward Italian Fascism. The Italian experiment with corporate forms was never seriously discussed. But Fascism was analyzed in terms of its link with the Papacy: to these men it was another "Roman" thing. Hitler was constantly accused of imitating Italian Fascism, and the link with the Papacy in that movement seemed to be paralleled by the Führer's brief flirtation with the Catholic Center Party. Neither Italian nor Catholic ideas seemed to have any measurable influence on the revolutionary conservatives.

The long-range preparation for revolutionary-conservative thought lay rather in the *Genossenschaftslehre* (Theory of Associations) of the nineteenth century, the idea that the state must be constituted through associations: whether guilds, estates, classes, or local communities. The people, considered as individuals, were merely an amorphous mass. For Hegel, a corporate structure had been the intermediary between the state and society.[61] This concept was very similar to the attempt to free the state from involvement with special interests. Instead, special interests should be reconciled within the corporate group. Otto Friedrich von Gierke's (1841–1921) concept of the corporation as a "morally free being" growing up organically out of and through free individuals has many points of contact with the ideas we have been discussing. Moreover, von Gierke—one of the most influential German political thinkers of the nineteenth century—in contradistinction to Roman Law allowed a corporation to have greater independence from the state: it could speak directly through its own organs and did not have to be represented by others.[62] This is reminiscent of the ideal of the group or the *Bund*, the cell through which the corporate state was to grow. Such ideas, rather than Catholic or Italian corporatism, were apparently the historical background for the political and economic form which revolutionary conservatism was to take.

The immediate roots of this "German Revolution," as Strasser called it, must be sought in the revolt against Wilhelminian Germany. The "Revolution" was directed against the kind of bourgeois and capitalist society which Germany seemed to represent. For it a true democracy of the *Volk* must be substituted. Hermann Burte (1879–1960), in one of the most popular novels of the age, *Wiltfeber, der ewige Deutsche* (*Wiltfeber, the Eternal German*, 1912), says of his Germanic hero that he sought and found the *Volk*, not the bourgeoisie.[63] A contrast between *Volk* and bourgeoisie has been implicit in all that we have discussed. The concept of the "masses," the "proletariat," was also rejected. Burte's hero seeks typically to "destroy the masses for the sake of the *Volk*."[64] The emphasis on the *Volk* in antithesis to the bourgeois and the masses—to parliamentary capitalist government and Marxist theory—was bound to lead to a romanticizing of the nation. This overwhelmed and frustrated the revolutionary impetus implicit in such völkisch thought. Strasser's *Fourteen Theses of the German Revolution*, for all its emphasis on the overthrow of the existing order, goes on to discuss the German "soul."[65] The purity of the German soul and its genuineness became the base on which the revolutionary-conservative concept of society rested.

Small wonder that this political thought led to an overemphasis on racial theory. We have seen how left-wing völkisch thought could slide over into racism; the examples we gave earlier do not stand in isolation. The predominance of the irrational and the absence of specific economic and social programs inevitably led many advocates of this conservatism to adopt racial theories: racism not only would provide coherence for the *Bund* but also would automatically solve the complex problems of the times in opposition to the existing order. In the opinion of the official journal of the German fraternities, the corporate organization of national life would free the state from involvement with special interests, leaving it to devote itself solely to its own true task. This was to further the race, through racial hygiene and foreign as well as domestic policies. The journal concludes its discussion with the statement: "Not economics but race determines the fate of a people."[66] At its extreme this led to the coining of the phrase "biological socialism" to replace the term "German socialism." Erwin Guido Kolbenheyer (1878–1962) defined this in contrast to "demagogic socialism," by which he meant the concept of the equality of individuals. Biological socialism rested rather on a hierarchy of merit determined by the biological make-up of the individual. Not collectivism but corporate groups based on this principle must constitute the state, for it determined the kind of work and position to which individuals could attain. Biological structures were inherited, and thus Kolbenheyer's socialism became an extreme conservatism based on a biological group system which he saw in racial terms.[67]

The "spirit" came to dominate the conservative revolution, and social change degenerated into a changing of the people's soul. The enemy became not the employer, not even the bourgeois, but anyone who opposed the racial policy necessary for the new Germany. The antisemitism always latent in the conservative revolution was the crux of the matter. The Jew was the enemy; a conspiracy kept the revolution from succeeding. This theory, the panacea of second-rate intellectuals, was substituted for an analysis based on the realities of the situation in which Germany found itself. As Strasser's program put it: together with the Freemasons and the ultramontanes, the Jews destroy the soul of the people.[68] For Otto Strasser this may have been secondary to his other theories of change, but in the economic hypotheses of the movement such delusions played a leading part. Antisemitism fused with the racial approach to identify the enemy who stood in the way of the new Germany.

There is an interesting parallel here with the Christlich-Soziale Partei (Christian Social Party) founded by Adolf Stoecker in the 1870s. He also started out as a social reformer interested in bettering the lot of the working class within the framework of a national socialism. In his case too, the substitution of a corporate state for a parliamentary system became a political goal.[69] Soon, however, antisemitism predominated and his call for reform (including the abolition of the Stock Exchange) made its appeal to the lower bourgeois and the displaced intellectual. Similarly, the revolutionary conservatives came to attract these classes of the population, for their theories envisaged a structured society based on a hierarchy which did not allow for economic success in the granting of status.

The Youth Movement had not managed to transcend the bourgeois origins against which it was in revolt; neither were revolutionary conservatives able to find a theory that would effectively eliminate bourgeois capitalism. Instead, their ideas became a panacea for uprooted intellectuals and displaced bourgeois, of whom there was no lack in the Weimar Republic. The "anti-capitalist longings" reflected the desires of these people rather than of the workers, and the corporate state as we have defined it became their ideal. The dream of a nation "beyond capitalism and Marxism" collapsed in January 1933. Its advocates soon found themselves not only excluded from participation in power but imprisoned or exiled. Adolf Hitler did not want their kind of German revolution.

Yet the attempt at a "Third Force" had been made, and this very fact lends the movement an interest beyond any political relevance it might have attained in the Weimar Republic. Conservatism, it has been said, is anything from "high-minded inspiration to frustrated revolution, from religious revivalism to Babbitry and inertia."[70] In this case it was an attempt at revolutionizing the existing order. Much has been written about left-wing revolutions; little about right-wing revolutions, for conservatism is usually associated with a quest for stability and the status quo. Nevertheless, there were in this German movement very real revolutionary forces which wanted to overthrow both bourgeois society and capitalism as they defined it. Hitler availed himself of this impetus, only to betray it in the end. The quest for a democracy that was neither parliamentarian nor communist was over by 1933, betrayed and bogged down in its own ideological weakness. It seems doubtful whether this ideal of a corporate state will ever again be associated with the desire for a fundamental change in society. The future of such a system of government may lie with those Catholic corporatist ideas that preceded and paralleled the conservative revolution, although in Germany, at least, going forward "into history" has often meant returning to the romanticized traditions of the past.

5

Fascism and the Intellectuals

The history of fascism is finally coming into its own as a field of scholarly study, some twenty years after the movement's collapse. We need no longer look upon fascism through a window clouded with the accumulated experience of the Second World War. Historians have increasingly come to analyze fascism within its own frame of reference and are starting to disentangle the complex historical reality on which fascism wrote its message and from which it drew its appeal. It used to be thought by a good many historians that fascism, unlike socialist movements, was imposed by a willful minority upon a confused majority, that it was a movement opposed to intellectualizing. Such a "revolution of nihilism" could not be expected to capture the true enthusiasms and dreams of humanity. Benedetto Croce (1866–1952), for example, regarded fascism as a childish "adventure," a drunken activism, whose very nature placed the movement outside the mainstream of history.[1] Fascism seen as an aberration from the dominant current of European history and thought—the interpretation continues to the present day.

This view is relevant to the problem of "fascism and the intellectuals," for if fascism were merely a pragmatic, activist response to the immediate historical situation, the intellectual would have no real place either among the duped masses or in the cynical political leadership. If prestigious intellectuals like Ezra Pound (1885–1972) and Giovanni Gentile (1875–1944) became fascists, this could not be explained by their intellectual heritage or position but rather as another aberration—in Pound's case, insanity.

The refusal to consider seriously the fascist commitment of a good many intellectuals calls for a definition not only of "fascism" but also of "intellectual." If, with André Malraux (1901–1976), we define an intellectual simply as one who traffics in ideas, then a pragmatic, activist fascism would exclude such a person. The functional definition of an intellectual as the guardian of ultimate values within society would also make his fusion with fascism difficult, for that movement was supposedly devoid of the values which intellectuals prized. Above all, the tendency to define intellectuals as wedded to the ultimate values of rationalism, individual freedom, and Kantian morality has stood in the way of understanding the involvement of intellectuals with fascism. Croce is not atypical in having realized the menace to individual freedom which fascism represented, without ever having understood the movement itself.

The intellectuals with whom we are concerned fit into a broad definition: they regarded themselves as guardians of ultimate values in society and saw in fascism a means to realize these values. They defined their own task as primarily educational, at the same time being conscious of their importance as an intellectual "class" in confronting the problems of the age. Moreover, they did not lack a sense of history but saw in fascism a movement that recaptured the values of a past they prized: not of the bourgeois age of the last century but of Greco-Roman times—or more genuine spiritual values. It is typical that a young antifascist intellectual like Carlo Rosselli (1899–1937) understood fascism and fascist intellectuals far better than Benedetto Croce, the liberal of an older generation. Rosselli regarded materialist socialism as dead and advocated a new socialism representing "innate ideas" of liberty and justice. The intellectual must come to the masses with the truth, through ideas truly held.[2] Mussolini, he wrote, sensed the death of the older materialism, but his dishonesty rendered him a mere adventurer.[3] Rosselli shares with the fascist intellectuals his call for spiritual unity and his admiration for classical values. But the socialist anti-fascists and his enemies had still more in common: the call for a national revival on the basis of a spiritual impetus, the rejection of politics of pragmatism and compromise, and the concept of intellectuals as heralds of a new, non-materialistic age. The socialism of Rosselli, which was duplicated in other European nations, reflected the same concern that informed the fascist intellectuals: the more rationally ordered society became, the more non-rational became the needs of the individual in that society.

The trend toward irrationality was heightened by the nature of the historical reality within which the fascist commitment of these intellectuals was set. Liberal-democratic society was, in fact, working badly or not at all in nations like Italy and Germany. Political stalemate was added to economic crises: parliaments were ineffective in the face of rising unemployment and poverty. It is important to bear these facts in mind; for individuals of anarcho-syndicalist background like Massimo Rocca (1884–1973) or Dino Grandi (1895–1988) in Italy, the actual situation in which the country found itself was crucial in determining their allegiance to fascism—whatever additional reasons they gave for such a commitment.

The interplay between ideology and the historical fact is difficult to assess for each individual case. However, it seems clear that most intellectuals' commitment to fascism was based on a very real dilemma: after 1918 the society in which they lived did not seem to function well or even to function at all; its political and economic instability (which seemed to verge on collapse) had to be transcended. The figures we are discussing fled into an ideology which promised to restore culture as well as society; as intellectuals they judged the totality of society and refused to break it down into its constituent parts. This totality was symbolized by the temper of cultural activity—if the arts were restored, then society as a whole would be able to transcend the present. Idealism formed the core of their outlook and kept them from joining with Marxism, while the Marxist protagonists did their best to hold these intellectuals at arm's length.

Ezra Pound, the self-styled fascist, felt that poetry had an important part to play in society, and the Belgian fascist leader Léon Degrelle called leaders like Mussolini "poets of revolution."[4] When José Antonio Primo de Rivera (1903–1936) spoke of the Falange as a "poetic movement," he was not merely echoing Belgium's Degrelle or the Flemish fascist leader Joris Van Severen (1894–1940); he reflected a tendency of all fascism.[5] The role of poetry in the development of modern nationalism is well known and needs no elaboration here. Poetry, music, and art played an important part in the fascist movement as expressions of the non-rational needs of humanity, which must be satisfied if all were to achieve the necessary spiritual unity and take up the activism that would overcome the bourgeois age.

Economic and political reality did concern the intellectuals, but they believed that their idealism would solve the problems which plagued their times. To be sure, in Italy many intellectuals who came to fascism started with a pragmatic attitude toward the movement, for here ideological debates did not arise until well after the seizure of power. But even in Italy, Fascism held that the creative individual, because of his attitude of mind, would solve the specific problems facing the nation. In Germany the retreat into mystique in order to transcend the present had deeper roots. But all fascists believed that, in the last resort, the spiritual unity of the nation would resolve all difficulties. Most fascist intellectuals defined this spiritual unity as a resurgence of creativity viewed in aesthetic terms: the dawn of a new world of beauty and of aesthetic form. The shift from "aesthetic politics" to the idea of the state as the motivator of aesthetic rejuvenation distinguished fascist from antifascist intellectuals; in other respects, the worldview of the anti-fascists was close to fascist idealism.

Fascism itself was apt to describe the nation in aesthetic terms. Consequently, cultural matters played a large part in the literature of the movement. No doubt this view of the nation as a repository of culture attracted the allegiance of many intellectuals. The young French fascist Robert Brasillach was typical in his opinion that a great political movement must also be an aesthetic one, with a "lifestyle" appropriate to its ideology. Brasillach praised the culture of the court of Louis XIV (1638–1715, r. 1643–1715), the Soviet cinema, and, especially, the Nazi mass meetings and their liturgy, "the most remarkable of modern times." Brasillach, in common with fascist intellectuals of other nations, saw in this fusion of mass politics and aesthetic form a "collective beauty" analogous to the spectacles of the Middle Ages or of ancient Greece. Within such a context, the Third French Republic was an anti-aesthetic regime whose art and culture were part of fragmented reality.[6]

Not only in France, but in Germany and other nations as well, the organic unity of life and politics which fascist movements stressed included an emphasis upon cultural forms. This catered to the preoccupation of intellectuals with such matters while, at the same time, providing them with a rationale for their place in the movement. Moreover, this new world of beauty and aesthetic form was directed by the nation, which gave it a harmony and unity for which such humanity longed. The national state was the ultimate expression of all human desires, so it seemed to both the philosopher Gentile in Italy and the poet Gottfried Benn (1886–1956) in Germany, because fascism transformed the nation into an aesthetic as well as an ethical state. This belief glorified the state as the embodiment of human creativity and human idealism. It is important to stress that the attraction of fascism for intellectuals took place within the context of nationalism: a state that drew together into one spiritual unity the creative souls of its citizens—not the drab state of *raison d'état*, but a state whose very nature was identical with the cultural expression for which these men yearned.

Fascism and the Intellectuals

Fascism at first was linked with artistic movements which were not necessarily conservative or sentimental. Some factions of National Socialism sympathized with the Expressionist "chaos of the soul"; Mussolini's regard for Filippo Tommaso Marinetti (1876–1944) and the Futurists needs no documentation. The obvious attraction which fascism exercised on creative intellectuals is often overlooked. It gave them a place in the movement and made it possible for them to combine their creativity with a desire to infuse society with their concept of ultimate values.

To sum up: many intellectuals in post–World War I Europe believed that the liberal and bourgeois age had collapsed and that the misery which followed the war was the result of that collapse. Moreover, because of the development of liberal-bourgeois society, poetry (by which they meant all creativity) had fallen into a shallow materialism and sentimentality, and this decline was part and parcel of the corruption of society as a whole. Since creativity was at the roots of the unfolding of the human personality, the elimination of the present must stress the restoration of cultural values. These intellectuals found their answer in fascism and its national mystique. Though the postwar world brought the crisis of liberal-bourgeois society to a head, the position of the fascist intellectuals must also be seen in the context of a prewar literary tradition and as influenced by the contemporary development of Marxism. The fact that the intellectuals were a part of these historical developments must have made their entry into fascism a great deal easier.

The literary tradition of the *fin de siècle* had stressed the irrational, the problems of the individual in a restrictive society. Fascism claimed to reestablish the true creativity of man which had been stifled, just as an earlier generation of intellectuals had searched for the genuine beneath the façade of bourgeois society. The fascist contention that human creativity could only stem from the depths of a spiritual impetus symbolized by the nation appealed to such longings and, at the same time, to the longing for authority.

The role of socialism in rejecting the intellectual is equally important. Initially, many artists and writers supported the socialist labor movement, but this movement repudiated the intellectuals and alienated them, as a growing orthodoxy became increasingly suspicious of their allegiance to a working class to which they could not claim to belong.

Marx himself had been hostile to intellectuals and that feeling grew to ever greater proportions within the socialist movement. The beginning of the twentieth century witnessed a veritable persecution of intellectuals in the German Social Democratic Party and the collapse of the enterprises with which they had been associated. Socialist parties in other West European nations also seemed wedded to a materialism which repudiated the intellectuals.[7] Art was regarded as a social "product" and, in consequence, realism of subject matter was bound to triumph over the creative imagination. Writing about the future of poetry in 1937, Christopher Caudwell (1907–1937) asserted that there was no neutral world of art free from determining causes. These causes were the conditions prevailing in the real world in which the artist must live and whose tensions he must accurately reflect. The artist must not leave his soul in the past.[8] But intellectuals wanted to be more than a mirror for social and economic determinism; they might reflect the tensions of society, but they also wanted to transcend them through their own creativity. There was no room for their poetry within traditional socialism. Rather than work to introduce an idealist element into Marxism as Rosselli and others attempted, many intellectuals turned instead to the literary and aesthetic appeal of the fascist movement.

Fascism seemed to combine this appeal with a critique of bourgeois society which socialism had already presented. The word "decadent" best characterized the postwar present for these individuals. Here, once more, an already traditional critique fused with the literary tradition of the *fin de siècle*. At that time also the outwardly prosperous establishment seemed merely a disguise for inward decay. For many fascist intellectuals the supposed decadence of the present provided the springboard for their commitment to the fascist Utopia. A society in which spiritual unity replaced both the class struggle and human isolation, in which order was reconciled with the irrational mainsprings of creativity, presented a world in which ultimate values would surely triumph. Giovanni Gentile believed fascism to be a personal interpretation of the new spirit striving toward the ethical state.[9]

The disillusionment and despair of decadent reality haunted these intellectuals. Louis-Ferdinand Céline's (1894–1961) *Voyage au bout de la nuit* (*Journey to the End of the Night*, 1932) is typical of this mood. Wherever his travels led the hero of the novel, from fighting in the First World War to Africa, to the United States, and back to France, the picture never changes. The world is not what one thought it to be in one's idealistic youth, nor is it what it seems to be, for underneath all the hypocrisy it is devoid of compassion and love. Naked struggle, human selfishness, and lust for material gain are the only realities. Typically, Céline's famous novel centered on the fate of the poor in such a society: "The poor man has two fine ways of dying in this world, either through the complete indifference of his fellow men in time of peace or by the homicidal fury of these same fellow men when war comes."[10] Decadent materialism was responsible for this state of affairs. His half-crazed *Bagatelles pour un massacre* (*Trifles for a Massacre*, 1937) is filled with the images of putrefaction with which fascism in general was obsessed in the face of its enemies. Marxism was closed to him. Why, he asks, is there no communist work of literary excellence? Communism cannot produce any great works because it has no soul, but is devoted to bourgeois ideals.[11] The root of all evil, however, is capitalism, which has even managed to overcome the movements aimed at eliminating it—and capitalism is the handiwork of the Jews.

Ezra Pound reached the same conclusion in his "Usura Canto"; capitalism was introduced by Jews and "thereafter art thickened. Thereafter design went to hell . . ."[12] The search for clarity of form became a search for the "genuine," the genuine outside decadent society. Céline wrote that at least Hitler did not lie like the Jews; he was no hypocrite. The Führer tells me, Céline continued, that "might makes right" and I know where I am: there is no "syrup" as with the Jews—no general "indefinite wobble," as Pound would have called it.[13]

Before the Second World War Céline was loath to join any political movement. He believed in the inevitable triumph of the impotent, the megalomaniacs, and the decadent, all of which were symbolized by the Jew. His *École des cadavres* (*School for Corpses*, 1938) ends by affirming the necessity of racism but, at the same time, asserts that the Aryans were too cowardly and lazy to get rid of the Jews. However, after the defeat of France, Céline's attitude changed and he now took advantage of the Nazi victory to attempt to translate his racism into reality. In 1941 he called for the formation of a political party (*parti unique*) which would unite all racists and antisemites. Two years later he threw his support to Jacques Doriot (1898–1945), who accused the Vichy government of proceeding too slowly in constructing a fascist France. Finally, in 1944, when the deportation and murder of Jews was in full swing, he reprinted a part of the *Bagatelles* which held that pogroms were fully justified; "they are a blessing of heaven." The Nazis realized his worth, and together with some others appointed him as expert on the Jewish question to the army of occupation.[14]

Céline was not merely a collaborator with the occupying power, he was genuinely involved in using the occupation in order to bring about an end to that degeneracy which before the Nazi triumph he had thought to be inevitable. The Jews were his foil: a near-paranoiac, he believed in the Jewish world conspiracy against the Gentiles. Céline heaped praise upon the *Protocols of the Elders of Zion*, and in the *Bagatelles pour un massacre* left little doubt that he accepted the genuineness of this clumsy forgery. In his hands (to use Norman Cohn's, 1915–2007, phrase) the *Protocols* became a warrant for genocide, not merely by means of the printed word but also by attempted political action. Intellectuals like Ezra Pound or Gottfried Benn also turned to the Jew as contrasted with the Aryan in order to work off their own paranoid tendencies. Many an intellectual found their way to fascism because it seemed to provide a weapon against the conspiratorial menace of modernity. The fascists did not merely make use of Céline's theories; he himself joined the cause, though his proposed antisemitic and racist party never materialized. Toward the end of the war, and afterward, he again withdrew into his earlier pessimism and fatalism about the future of France. Céline's politics, his attitudes, grew out of despair with decadent reality. This despair, the opposition to bourgeois hypocrisy, and the search for sincerity, were all common to intellectuals who came to fascism and to many anti-fascist intellectuals as well. André Gide (1869–1951), no fascist or antisemite, praised the *Bagatelles pour un massacre* for its bluntness and rejection of polite formulations.[15] Gide failed to see that Céline's work would lead him directly into fascist political action.

The German poet Gottfried Benn, like Céline a physician by trade, found ultimate fulfillment in his commitment to National Socialism. His earlier works were filled with imagery of a disease-ridden and decadent civilization—much like Céline's, whom, by the way, he regarded highly. Benn's personal and artistic development traversed many stages and both Futurism and Expressionism played their part. What seems to have remained constant, at least until 1933, was a theoretical nihilism which denied the possibility of metaphysical truth. At times Benn sang Dionysian hymns to the cult of the ego (Nietzsche exercised a considerable influence on his thought), while directly after the First World War he defended the Berlin Dadaists when they were accused of bringing contempt upon the armed forces and distributing indecent publications.[16] Surely not an auspicious beginning for a future follower of National Socialism. But his attitudes had changed by the time of the National Socialist seizure of power, and in a famous speech on "The New State and the Intellectuals" (1933) he praised history as the absolute value which had put forth a new biological type in order to do battle against the decadent age. Humanity's inner struggles were waged not to maintain the consciousness of the ego (as he had held in 1920) but on behalf of an absolute: the Aryan had been sent by history to play a messianic role.[17] National Socialism produced "a new world of the soul, deeply exciting in determining the expression of man's inner self."[18]

Benn's evolution toward National Socialism explains one element in fascism's attraction for some intellectuals. It involved not only the longing for the genuine (Benn was seeking the great barbarians of the twentieth century) and the desire to eliminate decadence, but also the restfulness which the movement promised to a troubled soul. The intellectuals who fell prey to the appeal of fascism were not content to remain on the fringes of society or politics, to be united with those "rootless intellectuals" who had made and were making the greatest contributions to European thought. They abhorred rootlessness, and the fascist emphasis on the rootedness of the creative individual in the national soul made a strong appeal to them. National Socialism provided Benn both with excitement and with a firm intellectual *point d'appui* which he had hitherto lacked. "There are moments when this whole tortured life sinks into nothingness, when only the horizon seems to exist, its infinity, the seasons, the earth, in simple words— *Volk*."[19] The very discipline of a firm, simple, and organic ideology fulfilled a need not only for Gottfried Benn but also for a poet like Ezra Pound who had not passed through Expressionism. Yet there may well be some truth in Ladislao Mittner's (1902–1975) contention that the feeling of impotence in Expressionism led to dreams of violence, to a tyrant conceived in the imagination.[20] Certainly a good many intellectuals who had been Expressionists followed National Socialism in Germany and Benn only provides the most famous example.

The desire for discipline was always combined with a vision of creativity as springing from humanity's irrational nature. The cultural elitism which Camillo Pellizzi (1896–1979) saw in the "*gruppi di competenza*" shared such ideas; while Céline put the emphasis on humanity's "soul" and Benn heaped scorn on a "rationally thought-out culture."[21] Aesthetic principles replaced devotion to conventional morality. Such attitudes led to a love for the extreme, the direct, and the primitive; degenerate and corrupt society had to be transcended. But, in the end, these writers and poets called a halt to their adventure; they, like most individuals, longed for an authority to which they could relate themselves and they found it not only in an emphasis upon strictness of literary form but also in the arms of fascism.

The Marxist road was barred, and the simple fascist explanation for the supposed decadence of the age had its appeal. Capitalism was symbolic of the rationalization of life, and these intellectuals wanted to opt out. Pierre Eugène Drieu La Rochelle (1893–1945), perhaps the most interesting French fascist, believed that art had become scientific because it could no longer be artistic in a decadent world.[22] Like their predecessors in the nineteenth century, and many anti-fascist intellectuals, these men sought for the genuine beneath the surface rationalizing of life. They found this genuine element within their own souls and in a closeness to nature—once more, hardly new discoveries. Walter Benjamin (1892–1940) has given a good characterization of the attitudes toward which they were brought by their analysis of present society. These figures attempted to solve the dichotomy between "genuine" nature and modern technology in immediate and mystical ways. They were not content to take the more circuitous route of attempting to fashion better human institutions.[23] Intellectuals were led by their hatred of society and its institutions to a retreat into the supposed inner life of the spirit. Fascism as a political movement could benefit from this mystical and therefore ill-defined approach by making the appropriate compromises with existing institutions on its way to power. The intellectuals, however, built this contempt into a system of absolute values which transcended reality.

The search for the "genuine" was not supposed to be a return to Romanticism, however. The decadence of the age, wrote Drieu La Rochelle (1939), means that sentimentality has taken the place of the creative drive.[24] John R. Harrison was undoubtedly right in asserting that the literary leaders of the English world who sympathized with fascism wanted more austere, more direct forms, and a hard intellectual approach. William Butler Yeats (1865–1939), Ezra Pound, Wyndham Lewis (1882–1957), and T. S. Eliot (1888–1965) all opposed Romanticism in the name of the classical tradition.[25] Like Charles Maurras (1868–1952) before them, they plucked out the identity of beauty and order from the ancient heritage: a reassurance that culture would not be debased through democracy. Order meant authoritarian rule, and this would correspond in the political world to the strictness of form which they desired in literary style; for example Gottfried Benn, in 1934, praised strictness of form in contrast to pristine and unformed nature. An absolutism was needed which would exclude all chaos in art and lead to unwavering moral decisions. These decisions had to be in favor of harshness, struggle, and leadership, opposed to compromises and prevarication in art as well as in politics. A dictatorial leadership was required to give shape to the amorphous mass of democracy symbolic of decadent society—"sensitivity without direction," as Ezra Pound characterized that form of government and society.[26] Drieu La Rochelle, in his novel *Gilles* (1939), described a democratic French politician as a man who showed as much indulgence toward you as you did toward him; who reassured rather than led. The typical bourgeois politician believed in liberty and justice in the same way that a merchant treasured his rents and property.[27]

The longing for a *point d'appui*, for form and direction, led such intellectuals into advocating dictatorship. The French fascist Lucien Rebatet (1903–1972) put the case with admirable succinctness: "We have suffered a deep disquiet ever since the [French] Revolution, for we no longer know a leader [*chef*] . . . I aspire to a dictatorship, a strict and aristocratic regime."[28] Gottfried Benn could have written this passage, and so could Ezra Pound. Elitist ideas came into play here, were in fact basic to an understanding of the fascist intellectuals. Fascism had little of the proletarian vocabulary of Marxism, and many fascist leaders openly stressed the elitist nature of the movement. Their self-conscious concept of intellectuals as guardians of ultimate values made such writers and artists inherently sympathetic to such ideas. Moreover, their concept of culture and form was already elitist in nature: they were the most creative individuals and they knew the prized ancient traditions. Elitism combined in their ideology with the call for strong leadership.

True leadership must be committed to the unflinching implementation of spiritual values. Whether it be the classical values (defined by Wyndham Lewis in his fascist period as simple, rational, and aloof) or the living cosmos of a precivilized age (as seen by D. H. Lawrence, 1885–1930, at times sympathetic to fascism), the leadership of a chosen few was essential to lead humankind into the golden age.[29] The longing for authority of intellectuals in modern society is a common enough phenomenon. In fascism, as they analyzed the movement, this authority would be based on the ultimate values to which they were committed and which, indeed, they were already advocating through the written and spoken word.

The open-endedness of much of European fascism, its ideological fluidity under authoritarian leadership strengthened its attraction. German National Socialism was an exception here, for it was built on a more clearly defined ideological base. German idealism and völkisch thought had long histories behind them, and many German intellectuals must have found this ideological orientation familiar, even traditional.[30] However, the specific German tradition (in which Austria must be included) gave to this fascism a provincial cast which contrasts with fascism in Italy. In the West, at any rate, the fascist movements, and the intellectuals who were involved, looked to Italy rather than to Central Europe for inspiration. It is therefore dangerous to extend the ideological foundations of the German fascist experience to other countries.

Typical of the difference between fascism in Central and in Western Europe is the assertion of the leading German National Socialist philosopher Alfred Baeumler (1887–1968) that with the Nazi seizure of power the period of Hegelian striving was at an end. Hitler had transformed Hegel's "idea" into reality.[31] In Italy even Gentile, the philosophical idealist, called for a continual progression of the "new spirit" (meaning fascism), which should not be allowed to harden into a credo or a system of dogma.[32] Camillo Pelizzi argued that "the fascist state is more than a state, a dynamo" (1924).[33] French fascist intellectuals were apt to reject Hegelianism itself as blurring and reconciling differences in a bourgeois fashion, opting instead for a simple Nietzschean dynamic. Yet, even among the French fascist intellectuals, we find the longing for a *point d'appui*, though it is muted in comparison with other European fascisms. For example, the young fascist Robert Brasillach in his *Le marchand d'oiseaux* (*The Bird Merchant*, 1936) praises the binding force of nature and the peasant as contrasted with the vagabonds in the city.

This difference between Western and Central European fascism is important in our context, for it explains how some intellectuals could seek in the movement a repudiation of Germanic Romanticism and sentimentality and infuse it with a diversity of spiritual values, instead of seeing in fascism a single-minded concentration on the ideals of blood and soil. As far as some of them were concerned, race played a lesser part in producing the leadership than did a vision of Plato's philosopher king. We must not forget that racism and antisemitism until the late 1930s played a minor role in taming the "dynamo" of West European fascism.

Yet there existed an incipient conflict between the intellectuals' longing for authority and their equal love for the dynamic that would end the degeneration of their time. Drieu La Rochelle's fictional hero Gilles, not untypical for French fascism, finds mental peace in fighting on Francisco Franco's (1892–1975) side in the Spanish Civil War. There Gilles discovers that gods fall and are reborn, a process which can only take place through the shedding of blood.[34] For many intellectuals, fascism released an ever-present urge for action that could now find full play. This often became a commitment to brutality in the name of the spiritual values that must be realized. Gentile justified the brutality of teachers toward students: it would force students to affirm their own personalities.[35] Gentile associated the necessity for brutality with the quest for spiritual unity, which was all that really mattered.

Among these intellectuals is found a joy in immediate action rather than in long-range planning, in immediate decisions rather than in judgments *sub specie aeternitatis*. Because Charles Maurras refused to act during the fascist and war-veteran-inspired Paris riots of February 1934, many French fascist intellectuals broke with the *Action Française*. This predilection for the immediate could be documented in other nations as well. Such a desire formed an obvious contrast to the politics of compromise which characterized decadent democratic society. Julien Benda (1867–1956), understanding this tendency among the intellectuals of his time, characterized as "treasonable" the attempt to confer moral sanction on physical force.[36] This represents, of course, a treason not confined to fascist intellectuals; but the moral power which they lent to the activist struggle was regarded not merely as an unfortunate necessity but as an integral part of the system of absolute values. Such activist ideals could also serve to deepen the allegiance to authoritarianism, for leadership was necessary to win the battle.

However, the yearning for leadership must always be connected with the quest for the genuine of which we have already spoken. The Greek ideal of an ordered society was specified, side by side with a new paganism. The influence of Nietzsche received full play, for he had already praised the Greeks and the barbarians as the prototypes of the superman. This primitivism was rendered still more appealing through the experience of war, which had led a whole generation of European writers into ecstatic praise of naked brutality and the shedding of blood. Here indeed, in their view, was a Nietzschean reflection of life as it truly existed, and not as the bourgeoisie thought it to be. Writers such as Ernst Jünger (1895–1998) transposed the warrior to peacetime society: a new type had emerged who, as the "worker," would make a *révolution sans phrase*, and for whom freedom and obedience were identical concepts.[37]

The preoccupation of the fascist movement with the war attracted intellectuals who had found the "genuine" life experience in that catastrophe. Oswald Spengler's vision of the barbarians roaming the countryside is symptomatic as the expression both of an age which was finished and of the seeds of a new culture to come. For Drieu La Rochelle, the modern was characterized by barbaric simplicity and brutality, while Gottfried Benn was attracted to all that was primitive and archaic—only a return of this kind could produce the necessary will to power.[38] Robert Brasillach, writing about Alfred Rosenberg in Germany and his own French fascists, eulogized the "teachers of violence in France and the teacher of violence in Germany": both shared the wish to destroy a society built on bad ideas, and a respect for the heroes to come.[39]

The longing for primitivism dissolved into hero worship. This truly resolved the conflict between the love of activism and violence, on the one hand, and the longing for security and authority on the other. The nineteenth-century tradition of heroes and hero worship gave a respectable intellectual background to such a longing. The hero symbolized the "new type" of leader who would change the world. As Gottfried Benn put it: "History sent a new biological type to the front."[40] The "New Man" whom fascism put into the foreground of its efforts was infused with a Nietzschean will. Jünger conceived this type as a group, a leadership elite; in fact, a new "people." But others saw him as an individual symbolic of what other individuals could become. The hero, in this case, resolved not only the conflict between violence and authority but also the dichotomy between individualism and leadership. For creative intellectuals this was important.

Fascism, unlike socialist orthodoxy, did not exclude the cult of the individual, provided that the individual could be seen as the executor of some organic national force. The "New Man" whom fascism wished to create symbolized the new society. He had released within himself the creative forces of his own soul and through strength of will would usher in a new world. Intellectuals had a special mission in transforming the old into the New Man, for education played a vital part in this process and education was a traditional field of activity for intellectuals.

In all this, it is important to keep the chronological factor in mind. The intellectuals were attracted to a fascism which seemed open-ended and whose ideology, within its organic framework, gave it a "superb openness to artistic creativity." The "anti-idealist" congress of young fascist intellectuals in Italy (1933) was typical of this feeling. They opposed the Hegelian idealism of Gentile in favor of Nietzschean ideas. These young Italians were at one with equally young French fascists in their belief that Hegelianism blunted the necessary dynamic and led to a pedestrian, economic view of the state, from which "it is absolutely impossible to aim at fascism."[41] This heroic dynamic, as they saw it, seemed present in Italian Fascism until the early 1930s and in Germany until 1934. Then Hitler outlawed Expressionism and began to suppress all forms of creativity which did not conform to the tradition of völkisch art and literature. Even so, some intellectuals who had joined the Nazi movement, as well as members of the SS—dedicated to a "silent revolution in permanence"—opposed the fossilization of dogma and specific programs.

They dreamed instead of a real revolution, a true uprising of the German people, which would lead to fundamental change within the nation. Typically, such a commitment to revolution was used by an Expressionist writer like Arnolt Bronnen (1895–1959) to justify his conversion to National Socialism. He greatly admired a faction of the SA (the Sturmabteilung, a para-military Nazi organization) for wanting a revolution, though this longing was little more than a desire to release a pent-up dynamic. Bronnen lost his innocence soon after Hitler attained power. His reaction to this disillusionment was typical of that of many other intellectuals who had joined the Nazis for similar reasons: halfhearted gestures, pathetic in their futility against the "revolution betrayed."[42] The attitude of men like Bronnen toward Hitler remained ambivalent throughout the Third Reich. The hero of earlier days was not easily deposed in their confused minds. In Germany, unlike Italy, there was no real protest against the movement in power in favor of the "true movement" as it had existed earlier.

National Socialism, as we have seen, never emphasized the thrust toward revolution which Italian Fascism inscribed on its banners after the First World War. Mussolini himself may not have taken this radical vocabulary seriously, but the dynamic "open-endedness" which many earlier fascists had prized was more deeply embedded in the Italian than in the German movement. In Italy the protest of young intellectuals in the name of a fascist dynamic against a fascism grown old in power can be seen in at least two youth journals.[43] Marinetti, the Futurist, did not turn on Mussolini but instead in 1937 denounced Hitler for having condemned Futurism, Impressionism, Dadaism, and Cubism in favor of a "photographic static"—an unimaginative realism which sanctified the status quo.[44] However, for both the great fascist powers the dynamo which Camillo Pellizzi had praised had come to a standstill by the end of the 1930s.

This did not occur in the fascisms that remained out of power. Especially in France, where the splintered movement was largely in the hands of a Paris coterie of intellectuals, the problem of the fossilization of dogma never arose at all. Small wonder that these Frenchmen misread National Socialism and were disappointed when the German movement refused to carry through their kind of pseudo-Nietzschean revolution. Marc Augier ("Saint-Loup," 1908–1990) was one of the founders of the fascist-collaborationist journal *La Gerbe*. He joined the SS and felt that the Germans had reached the ultimate stage of Nietzschean thought and were standing on the threshold of a new and grandiose world. But Augier left the SS. Hitler turned out to be too exclusively German for this French fascist and did not have the vision to lead an anti-capitalist crusade to free the masses.[45] The "teacher of violence in Germany" could not, as Brasillach had thought, stand on an equal footing with the "teachers of violence in France." The eternal truth that National Socialism was supposed to exemplify was rooted in an unchanging history and race, which tamed the appetite for destruction and served to stifle any open-ended dynamic.

Hans Naumann (1886–1951) in Germany spoke of making sacred once again the eternal "holy bonds" which had cemented human relationships of old: the shared native countryside, the family, and the common ties of blood.[46] Mussolini at times equated reason of state, the traditional and unchanging needs of power politics, with the idealism of the fascists.[47] All this was far removed from the barbarians roaming the countryside, or the "New Man" some fascists wished to create who, at least in Germany, could degenerate into that sentimental nationalism which most of these intellectuals condemned. The restfulness of a coherent ideology for which thinkers like Benn longed had become separated from the excitement these intellectuals craved.

More seriously, the intellectuals' ideal of culture came into conflict with the fascist concept of hierarchy, which they misunderstood, and with the needs of fascism as a mass movement. Fascism believed in a hierarchy of function and not of status: potentially all members of the nation were equal. The elite stood out because of its service to the nation, not because of any intellectual superiority. The masses were not the enemies of culture, for they could be lifted into the category of "New Men" (although privately fascist leaders like Mussolini expressed cynicism about the masses). To be sure, intellectuals could become part of the functional elite as educators, but even then they were still faced with the needs of fascism as a mass movement.

This meant that the cultural ideals for which these intellectuals stood were compromised by reality: the bourgeois life which they despised was in fact integrated into the fascist mystique. All these intellectuals might have agreed with Matthew Arnold's (1822–1888) judgment on middle-class culture: "Can life be imagined more hideous, more dismal, more unenviable?"[48] The mass meetings which for Brasillach had symbolized aesthetic politics continued, but the cultural thrust of the movement took on a decidedly bourgeois cast. Fascism was annexing the tradition of middle-class reading and art, emphasizing the sweetly sentimental and conservative as the true products of human creativity. Italy did so perhaps to a lesser extent than Central Europe, but even French fascism sometimes lapsed into the despised genre. As a political mass movement, fascism had to appeal to the prejudices and predilections of its constituents, whatever ideals the intellectuals attempted to put into the movement. Here they were caught: on the one hand, they wanted the security and thrill of participating in a mass movement; on the other, such a mass movement tended to compromise with the cultural ideals of people deeply bound by bourgeois tastes and morals.

Fascism in Western and Central Europe made the middle classes the base of its power and appeal. The traditionalism which became part of fascist ideology praised precisely that sentimentality which many fascist intellectuals had condemned as bourgeois degeneracy. This development is most obvious in National Socialism's rejection of cultural experimentation. National Socialism felt that it could rely on popular taste in its battle against modernity in art and literature. Hitler wanted to substitute "eternal art" for modern art, and this meant that art must not create anything new but must instead reflect the general life of the people, which sought artistic expression. The people came first, so art must reflect their soul and thus appeal to them. When Goebbels abolished art criticism and substituted mere art reporting, he did so because the public had to be given a chance to make its own judgments, to form an opinion about artistic matters through its own feeling.[49]

The result was culture defined in terms of the popular taste of the non-intellectual classes. Sentimentality triumphed over strictness of literary form and Romanticism over the classical tradition. The intellectuals found themselves part of an organic worldview which had tamed their activism and which defined the genuine in terms of popular artistic tastes. Some, like Ernst Jünger, turned their backs on the movement, but most maintained their allegiance to fascism, though it had lost its élan.

In fact, fascism now repudiated the intellectuals, as the socialist movement had repudiated them earlier. For the fascists, artistic creativity was now defined as merely a reflection of reality, and the results of fascist artistic endeavor moved closer to socialist realism. Hitler's emphasis on "clarity and simplicity" had not meant a preference for strictness of form but rather a belief in an art and literature simple enough to call for the support of the populace. This tendency had always existed in fascism, but the intellectuals had chosen to ignore it, believing that it would vanish in the mystique of a national spiritual unity. But that very mystique led to a renewal of the old bourgeois culture. This fact became obvious only as fascism developed into the 1930s. Fascist professions of faith before this time might easily have led to a misunderstanding. It has, in fact, been claimed that in Italy the repudiation of the intellectuals was a conscious move of the Fascist Party to consolidate its power.[50] The peasant who provided fascism's heroic prototype proved to be not the Nietzschean Prometheus but a comfortable bourgeois.

In analyzing the relationship between fascism and the intellectuals, it is important to see the ideological commitment of the intellectuals within the diversity of fascism as it developed. The basic ideological presuppositions of the movement existed from the beginning in most fascisms, but they changed in emphasis and direction. Those fascist movements which came to power had to show political flexibility and find a solid base of support in one part of the population. Fascist intellectuals ignored the pressures of existing reality on fascism, thinking that the fascist revolution would break sharply with the corrupt present but remain uncontaminated by its imperatives. But fascism's own mystique was merely a profession of faith and, as it turned out, gave the movement flexibility in making alliances within an existing reality which the intellectuals deplored. Fascists came to believe that theirs was a spiritual revolution, which through a new type of human would renew the nation and the world; in reality, this revolution became enmeshed in the very middle-class values it was supposed to fight. The acceptance of the century-old tradition of popular taste—conservative and opposed to all art and literature which it could not understand—spelled an end to meaningful participation by the intellectuals in the movement.

The attempt to ignore realities in favor of some higher value which brooks no compromise is not confined to fascist intellectuals. The neo-Kantian socialists suffered from the same failing; their idealism had put an end to a meaningful participation in or alliance with the existing socialist parties. Drieu La Rochelle's hero had called for unity between young communists freed from Russian influence and young bourgeois freed from the trammels of liberalism. A "Third Force" would be created: a victorious fascism.[51] Instead, fascism became a mass political party, which stifled creativity in the name of its truth and showed a willingness to assimilate the values of the bourgeois age which those advocating a "Third Force" could not readily accept. Drieu La Rochelle himself found it difficult to join such a political party. At first (in 1936) he played an important role in the fascist party of Jacques Doriot (Parti populaire français, PPF), only to leave it again two years later and rejoin it once more after the fall of France. The suicide of Drieu La Rochelle at the end of the Second World War was not merely the result of despair in the face of the Allied victory, but to a still greater extent despair at what fascism had made of itself.

6

Left-Wing Intellectuals in the Weimar Republic

In 1926 Carl von Ossietzky (1889–1938), the famous pacifist, argued that Weimar, because of its *"triste juste milieu"* and the *"embourgeoisement"* for which it stood, was indeed the "impossible Republic."[1] Von Ossietzky's sentiments aptly reflect the relationship which grew up between the left-wing intellectuals and the democratic Republic they had so ardently desired. This attitude bears a haunting similarity to that held by Weimar's völkisch critics, a similarity which is all the more striking since these intellectuals called themselves socialists. The kind of socialism which they advocated is of great importance, not only in defining their attitude toward the Republic but also because it became the "socialism of the intellectuals" — and not just in Germany.

Neither the thought of such intellectuals nor the socialism for which they stood has yet received the kind of analysis it deserves. These intellectuals formed part of the attempt to liberate the Marxist heritage from the dogmatism and materialism of socialist parties, and the urge toward building a renewed socialism preoccupied many of them in the 1920s. The revival of the Hegelian element in Marxism provided one approach toward this goal. The philosopher Karl Korsch (1886–1961), who can serve as one example, stressed the link between human consciousness and material reality: Marxism constituted a total view of life and society which could not be reduced to a clumsy materialism. Moreover, as a theory of proletarian revolution, Marxism was concerned with constant dialectical change and must not be transformed into party dogmatism. Korsch was the Marxist teacher of the playwright Bertolt Brecht (1898–1956); but despite his pupil's fame, another approach toward socialist renewal became even more popular among intellectuals. It was the revival of Kantian philosophy in opposition to the Hegelian heritage that enabled many intellectuals to renew and redefine their ideal of socialism.

We are concerned with those men and women who attempted to fuse their socialist commitment with Kant rather than Hegel, though much more is involved in their attitude toward society than the mere rooting of socialism in a single predetermined philosophical base. These left-wing intellectuals represented very diverse opinions at a time when complete intellectual freedom reigned in Germany. It seems best to approach them via one of their many groupings, one which is fairly well defined. By means of this one group we can come to understand problems and dilemmas which were in fact common to a much wider spectrum of intellectuals.

The group which concerns us attained a certain cohesion through the journals it made its own: the *Weltbühne* and, to a somewhat lesser extent, the *Tagebuch*. These weeklies, which came to symbolize the political journalism of these intellectuals, were read and debated among the whole range of the intelligentsia, which in Germany was much more coherent and centralized than it is in the vast continent of the United States. Circulation figures do not tell the whole tale of their influence: together both journals had about 16,000 subscribers. This is not as inconsiderable as it might seem at first glance, for in a Germany surfeited with newspapers even a large-circulation daily was doing well if it sold 200,000 copies.[2] No doubt the circulations of the *Weltbühne* and the *Tagebuch* overlapped, but what mattered in the final analysis was the recognized role of these journals as the organs of an intelligentsia whose influence radiated far beyond the actual group which wrote and edited them. Thus they lend themselves particularly well to an analysis of the relationship between the left-wing intellectuals and the troubled Republic.

The term "intellectual" has too often been applied to all those whose primary function is the traffic in ideas. Scholars, publicists, and even coffee-house poets have all been called intellectuals. Surely such a definition is much too broad to be useful—scholars are at times distinguished by the very absence and suspicion of ideas—and something more concrete is needed.

The term itself is intimately connected with nineteenth-century social protest, as, for example, in the Dreyfusard "Manifesto of the Intellectuals," which supported the army captain against the rightist forces in France. Because of this alliance between intellectuals and protest, many have come to associate the term "intellectual" with the political left. But intellectuals of the right have also been involved in protests against existing society, whether one recalls Charles Maurras in France or, indeed, the völkisch thinkers in Germany. It is this common element of protest which made the individuals around the *Weltbühne* concede "honesty" to their völkisch opponents, and the *Tagebuch* lament that "elemental movements" of protest should get mired in German *Gemütlichkeit*, and at one point treat Hitler as an idealist who believed his own "stories of cops and robbers."[3] But protest is not the sole ingredient of the kind of intellectual with whom we are concerned. Joseph Schumpeter's (1883–1950) definition of intellectuals is helpful here. He called "intellectual" those people who wielded the power of the spoken and written word rather than relying chiefly on experience.[4] In addition, such intellectuals, especially in Germany, were concerned with absolutes. They sought actively to make society correspond to a preconceived image of humanity and the world. The left-wing intellectuals of the 1920s not only were deeply rooted in the tradition of German idealism but also focused on the Kantian categorical imperative. This attitude was, further, combined with contempt for the politics of parliamentary compromise.

Kurt Hiller (1885–1972), a most important ideologue of the *Weltbühne*, summed this up nicely. Pragmatism, he wrote, is the substitution of fact-collecting for speculation. It is the shirking of thought dressed up as a doctrine. Political Philistines, he continued, are concerned with goals which can be achieved tomorrow, whereas the true politician works for a goal beyond the limits of their own life and perhaps even their own century.[5]

What were these goals? Hiller and his group called themselves "socialists," but within a non-Hegelian idealist context. The historical dialectic and the class struggle were deemphasized in favor of a neo-Kantian ethical imperative. This socialism had already caused considerable controversy among Marxists during the last three decades of the nineteenth century, long before the left-wing intellectuals took it up during the Weimar Republic. It is difficult to summarize, in short compass, the socialism to which they were committed, for they remained Marxists only in a general way. "Left-wing" seems a better phrase to describe their attitudes, however vaguely. Yet, if we place this socialism in a historical context and analyze the background out of which it came, the concept acquires a more precise meaning. Moreover, the importance of that socialism which haunted the relationship of the left-wing intellectuals to the Republic also emerges in much sharper relief.

The Weimar intellectuals were the heirs of the dispute within socialism which centered on the problem of whether historical materialism should be complemented by an ethic which derived from Kant. Engels had taken a firm stand against this in the 1870s, castigating the introduction into Marxism of "timeless" or "eternal" verities.[6] However, others felt that Marx and Engels had submitted to Hegelian influence because they lived at a time when Kant was scarcely known, and that it was necessary to complement the consequent philosophical lacunae in their thought. By 1909, Franz Mehring saw a greater danger to Marxism in forces like Kantianism than in the revisionism advocated by Eduard Bernstein (1850–1932).[7]

The Marburg philosopher Hermann Cohen decisively influenced the attempt to link Kant to socialist thought. Many left-wing intellectuals were later to follow in his footsteps. During the last three decades of the nineteenth century, Cohen stressed human rationality as the only possible foundation for the comprehension of reality and of the world. The roots of comprehension lay not in the senses or in feeling but in human judgment, and such judgment must exclude reliance on transcendental factors. For Kant the world of appearances was also the world of reality, but Cohen held that only concrete reality mattered and that its nature depended upon how people organized the world of their experiences. Reality was still defined through the human mind but it must be closely connected to the external world.[8]

Here was an emphasis upon the organic relationship between the mind and external reality of which socialists could approve. However, Cohen rejected Marxist historical materialism. The rational mind stood in the forefront; how it decided to organize reality would determine the course of reality itself. Economic or social conditions did not, themselves, determine a person's consciousness as Marx had believed. Cohen held that logic exercised in connection with the progress of the exact sciences would guide humanity in fusing their own rational judgment with the world of facts.[9] What, then, of the "thing in itself," the ethical imperative? Cohen's definition was taken up by the left-wing intellectuals: The individual is an autonomous being within all of humanity; they must never be used as the means to an end; they can only be an end in themself.[10]

This definition of the categorical imperative excluded the use of tactics or force in the relationship among people. Cohen held this ethical ideal to be eternal, uniting all humankind, just as the possibility of rational judgment is not dependent upon the evolution of history. Freedom consists in the rise of the individual to an autonomous entity. But the categorical imperative, so defined, must have a close relationship to reality and cannot (as with Kant himself) simply stand transcendent behind the actual reality. Cohen believed that the law, founded on correct ethical premises, must keep the categorical imperative from sliding into mere subjectivity.

The law is the anchor of ethics. The task of all must therefore consist in making over their laws into this image.[11]

But the law operates within the framework of the state. In consequence, Cohen stressed the importance of giving the state an ethical base in conformity with the categorical imperative. The state provides the framework of his political thought, and the just state is the goal toward which his neo-Kantianism aims. Typically, Cohen praised the Social Democratic Party—provided it lost its materialist, anarchist components. Belief in the basic equality of humanity went hand in hand with respect for the law and the state. Praise for the Socialist Party was combined with equal praise for Bismarck's supposed advocacy of universal military service and universal suffrage. Such developments would lead inevitably to a more ethical and just society: "The idealist worldview does not consist in the vague hope that everything will come about as it should, but in the knowledge that everything must come out right."[12] Belief in reason and the state was combined with an unquenchable optimism—a certainty of the inevitability of progress—which was close both to liberalism and to accepted socialist doctrine.

Cohen on the one hand emphasized the permanence of the rationality which binds all human generations together and on the other held that the state through law must keep the categorical imperative from becoming merely subjective. The fixed law of the state must anchor the unchanging categorical imperative in present reality. Moreover, the idealism intrinsic in this neo-Kantian thought made the proper ethical consciousness, as embodied in law, the prerequisite for all economic and social change. If this had any direct connection with Marx, then it was Marx stood on his head.

Socialists could approve of the all-encompassing rationality of Cohen's thought and of the close organic connection between the human mind and reality. Moreover, Cohen had called for greater equality among humanity and had castigated capitalist society for degrading economic activity into an impersonal task. People's work was treated like the goods at a sale, and this made human beings a means rather than the end of all striving as the categorical imperative demanded.[13] Cohen's emphasis on action as springing out of rational human judgment became for these intellectuals an urge to act in society, since judgment from which decision springs must be closely connected to reality.

Judgment, the ethical imperative, precedes any action to change society, and the economic or social necessities for such action take second place. This was reassuring to intellectuals. It meant that the philosophic mind which they possessed was the prerequisite for the liquidation of capitalism. The elitist ideas of the left-wing intellectuals were part of this neo-Kantianism, and so was their emphasis on the importance of educating humanity's reason and thereby his judgment.

Marx's concept that every social order (however defined) has forms of consciousness peculiar to it was denied in favor of an eternally true ethical imperative eternally acting on people and society. Cohen posited a close connection between the human mind and reality, but in contrast to Hegel's philosophy, the real and the ideal were not fused but separated. The ideal was the model and the state merely the framework out of which the ideal must grow. History, therefore, was not an empirical reality but only a hypothesis which was infused with the perfect, infinite, and universal end: the just and ethical society.[14] This was in the custodianship of the intellectuals until such a time as the people themselves came to see the light. Moreover, the custodians of the ethical ideal were forbidden to use strategy or tactics even for the sake of revolution—for the use of such evil methods would nullify the very ideal which made meaningful changes in society possible.

The attraction of Hermann Cohen's neo-Kantianism did not reflect the powerlessness of the bourgeoisie, as a recent communist attack on the philosopher would have us believe, or the dream of a reactionary, as Vladimir Lenin (1870–1924) held in his polemics against the Marburg philosopher.[15] Rather, it reflected the political frustration of intellectuals who were confined to the spoken and written word instead of making their mark as organizers of mass movements in industrial society. The growing isolation of the intellectuals within the socialist movement must not be forgotten; it was not the least important factor which rendered such ideas attractive.

This isolation had increased before 1914, and after the war both the communists and the Social Democrats were deeply suspicious of the intellectuals in their midst. In 1925, the Social Democratic leadership prevented the formation of a "society of intellectuals" within the SPD (Social Democratic Party): it would only arouse suspicion among the workers. Such a society was founded as an unofficial organ of the party but it lasted only a few years.[16] The intellectuals were increasingly alienated by the organized socialist movement, and neo-Kantianism came to their rescue; it called for leadership on their part and restored their self-respect. However, by linking themselves to this tradition, they seemingly left Marxism ever further behind—although at first they did attempt to retain the historical emphasis of traditional Marxism together with the neo-Kantian insights.

Kurt Eisner (1867–1919) in a famous essay on Kant (1904) held that Kant's ethic provided the living content which filled the form of human action within the flow of history. It was typical that most of these intellectuals did not deny the historical dialectic. For them, as Eisner put it, the ethic stood above all concrete forms of society and provided the standards by which such forms must be measured.[17] The mind must organize the experiences of reality according to ethical principles, and when this has been done, the world will be changed. As Eisner wrote in an article celebrating the seventieth birthday of Hermann Cohen: Marx created a social physics, the natural surroundings within which, initially, the social ethic must unfold.[18] This was an attempt to link the ethic to reality, something Hermann Cohen had also believed was possible (even if for him this was not a reality determined by the historical dialectic). Yet the accompanying idealism contributed a tension which, by the 1920s, was to snap the link that bound the ethical imperative to social action springing out of social reality. In the last resort, socialism was defined as being in tune with this ethic, providing a moral imperative for each individual, rather than arising from the present state of society.

It was the task of the intellectual to present this socialist vision to the people, who, once having grasped it, would actualize the socialist society. Eisner discovered firsthand the shortcomings of the belief in categorical imperatives as he unsuccessfully attempted to avoid violence when leading the Bavarian Revolution of 1918–19. But the left-wing intellectuals of the Weimar period continued to elaborate this socialist thought.

Kurt Eisner had been close to Hermann Cohen and praised him as the only man who ever influenced him to the very core of his being. Leonard Nelson (1882–1927)—an important figure in this socialist tradition, to be discussed later—had also learned the importance of the Kantian tradition from the Marburg philosopher.[19] But Cohen's influence went far beyond his contact with individuals. Even if his works were too technical to attain a large readership, the popular *Geschichte des Materialismus und Kritik seiner Bedeutung in der Gegenwart* (*History of Materialism*, 1866), which reflected Cohen's influence, served to spread his ideas.[20] Neo-Kantian thought will follow us throughout our analysis of left-wing intellectuals—at times combined with Marx's historical emphasis, though stripped, to be sure, of most of the dialectic and pushed into the background of revolutionary theory.

For the intellectuals of the twenties, the demand for a just social order was combined with an ever-present vision of a society that stands outside the actual course of history. This vision of justice called for the abolition of capitalism and an end to the bourgeois society built on exploitation. The original manifesto of the *Weltbühne* (1918) contained such a demand for economic change, but the eternal imperative of freedom and justice was held to be primary, even as economic and social change was taking place.[21] Freedom was described in individual, indeed liberal, terms: the human being, not a soulless dialectical materialism, must be kept always in view. The neo-Kantian definition of the categorical imperative which called for autonomous humans led intellectuals to sympathize with part of the liberal heritage which orthodox Marxists scorned. Hiller called socialism the "true liberalism" because by abolishing exploitation it led to freedom of the individual. "Liberalism has a double face: the front, the cultural, we must love and nourish; the rear face, the economic, we must abolish."[22]

Leonard Nelson, philosopher and educator, himself both a leading neo-Kantian and a socialist, rejected historical and economic determinism in a manner typical of the left-wing intellectuals, many of whom were his admirers and considered him their philosophical master. The historical situation was held to be not primary (as orthodox Hegelians and Marxists insisted) but secondary to the strength of the individual will in effecting that law of reason which is common to all people.[23] The appeal to economic necessity or dialectical determinism made the individual's struggle for justice unnecessary, and if this struggle was thought to be solely the business of one class, then the individual did not even have to make the effort. The individual must stand at the center of the road to socialism. Nelson rejected the "materialistic theory" that powers independent of humanity determine the course and outcome of the battle. An "objective law" which is not of human invention prescribes the goal, but individual will makes sure that that goal is reached.[24]

Nelson's thought was in the tradition of the neo-Kantian socialists, but in order to strengthen the socialist content of his ideology he went back beyond Hermann Cohen, to Kant's student Jakob Friedrich Fries (1773–1843). Fries had taken an active part in the German revolutionary movement after the Congress of Vienna and had been dismissed from his academic post. Hegel himself had attacked Fries in the preface to his *Grundlinien der Philosophie des Rechts* (*Philosophy of Right*, 1820): the philosopher—so Hegel felt—had demonstrated his stupidity by expecting political and public life to be guided from below, by the people themselves.[25] What Hegel condemned made Fries important to Nelson. It enabled him to reject Kant's own liberalist definition of freedom in favor of freedom interpreted as true political and economic equality among all.

Such must be the goal of the ethical will and through this use of the will the weak would triumph over the strong.[26]

Nelson went further than Cohen had done in his stress on equality and in his rejection of freedom as purely individualistic or embodied in law. The concept of the ethical will is parallel to the concept of judgments made on rational grounds, but for Nelson reason itself was defined in terms of instinctual values. Cohen's attempt to fix rationalism in reality, through science or law, gave way to a greater idealism. This was typical for most of the left-wing intellectuals: increasing idealism in the definition of reason went hand in hand with an emphasis on the strength of the ethical will, which would overcome their isolation and lack of political power. Nelson had experienced both this isolation and the lack of political power in the First World War and in the revolution which followed.

Hiller likened the use of reason to the highest efforts of humanity — but not to be confused with the intellect. His phrase was the "mysticism of the ratio," which in turn demanded ethical justification of all actions in order that the lost paradise of humanity might be recaptured.[27] Looking at the rise of National Socialism, Hiller hazarded that something exists in humanity which seeks to reach beyond the confines of its reason toward limitless vistas, and that this must be taken into account.[28] Leonard Nelson put this in a more neo-Kantian context: what should be is more important than what is — the striving upward counts most. Ratio dissolves itself into the human will, and Kurt Hiller wrote that from rationalism the will rises, liberated from the shackles that intellectualism has fastened upon it.[29] At the end of this striving comes the good society, the classless society in which economics will no longer be the chief consideration. Marx's end was accepted, but his analysis of how this end should come about was rejected.

In transforming Kant's *Ding an sich* (a thing-in-itself) into a dynamic, eternal essence of things which strives ever upward, the left-wing intellectuals moved toward the völkisch thinkers, especially Houston Stewart Chamberlain (1855–1927). He too had detached the categorical imperative from the course of history and infused it with the limitless vision of the Germanic soul. Both inveighed against the sterile materialism of Marxist orthodoxy.[30]

The content of this eternal essence of things was, of course, quite different in each case: for Chamberlain it was the German race; for the left-wing intellectuals it was a classless society, the elimination of injustice and war. They were pacifists, not believers in imperial or aggressive policies. Moreover, they retained an emphasis on human reason while searching always for a middle ground between such rationalism and the *Geist*.[31]

The categorical imperative had fused with the *Geist*, the true eternal spiritual imperative; it is important to stress that these intellectuals and their enemies shared a common German idealist tradition.

The German left-wing intellectuals were not alone in their familiarity with the tradition of idealism. We find the same development toward the "mysticism of the ratio" in the thought of the significant Italian left-wing intellectual, Carlo Rosselli. Rosselli too condemned the materialism of Marxist orthodoxy and accused the socialists of ignoring the irrational and the passions. The moral imperative which led to the overthrow of capitalism and to the good society was a passion.[32] Rosselli's separation of the categorical imperative from rationalism has been ascribed to the Mazzinian tradition in Italy, which was not unrelated to German idealism.[33] Thus, this socialism was set in a larger European framework, a fact to which we shall have occasion to return.

The parallelism between the Italians and the Germans might also lead to the conclusion that the rejection of the Marxist historical foundations, the hostility to materialism, entailed an ever-increasing idealism which overwhelmed the categorical imperative itself. As for the German left-wing intellectuals, it is typical that, in this connection, both the *Weltbühne* and the *Tagebuch* placed the emphasis on the young Marx rather than on what the *Tagebuch* called "Marx's theories during his exile"—that is, after 1847. The "humanist Marx" was contrasted favorably with communist doctrine and especially with Engels's determinism.[34]

The *Tagebuch* in particular believed that once Marx left Germany he had lost contact with the people of that country, and that therefore orthodox Marxism could never really apply to the important concerns which dominated Germany after 1918.[35] Here too it was condemned to sterility. But how could these intellectuals themselves have a bearing on the issues which preoccupied the German people? The power of the ethical will must be used to transform society. Their activism sought concrete results, and it seemed obvious that the people themselves were not ready for the message and that a strong leadership was therefore essential. Under the Republic the people were becoming *verpöbelt* ("homogenized"), as Kurt Tucholsky (1890–1935) wrote; depressed into one mediocre mass.[36] The *Tagebuch* was constant in its admiration of leadership types who stood out from the masses and in themselves realized the ideal of ethical, autonomous individual.[37] Its pages castigated the "megalomania" of the proletarians, which had deprived the Communist Party of all real leadership.[38] But, unlike the *Weltbühne*, the *Tagebuch*'s search for leadership never became a full-fledged theory, though both shared the same attitudes.

The Manifesto of the *Weltbühne* in 1918 called for a "Council of the Wise," which would not be elected but instead would renew itself through its own inner law and by its own right. This would function as an upper house of parliament, with both initiating and veto powers.[39] The Wise were the intellectuals, those who had the right kind of ethical power of will. For Leonard Nelson, the "cultured" were the "true invisible Church" which must help society, for their viewpoint was not vitiated by allegiance to private interests.[40] Kurt Hiller in 1920 defined the people who should constitute this elite: the publicists, the "literati" who made things happen through their use of words. The mere person of wisdom lacked the drive to perform deeds, the artist was devoid of ethical sense (and logical thought), while the scholar was without the necessary universalism.[41] Surely this shows a touching faith in the power of the word and in those who used it.

This faith was shared in turn by Adolf Hitler, who in *Mein Kampf* gave preeminent place to words as instruments of political activism. But the use of words by these intellectuals was focused on the *Geist* and not on the "magic" of mass propaganda. The wave of the future, Hiller believed, was a revolution paced by the intellectual elite, and such a revolution was not friendly to "unleashed masses."[42] Their tradition was that of the feuilletonists, and they did not reflect the interest in controlling and manipulating the crowd of which Gustave Le Bon (1841–1931) had written so eloquently. Typical of the difference of approach between Hitler and the left-wing intellectuals was the fact that whereas the future Führer emphasized the importance of the spoken over the written word, the intellectuals did just the opposite. They were interested not in the technique of the mass meeting but in a sophisticated and literate analysis that would prepare the way for individual spontaneity and strength of will. The elite would set the example, and the people, with the right guidance, would inevitably follow. Their approach to humanity and the masses was doomed to failure. The feuilletonist has never been a revolutionary activist but is rather a critic and popularizer. Hiller called on the true publicists to give up the feuilletonist's use of words for the sake of words and to become more than just the purveyors of other people's ideas.[43] But it was all in vain. Pressed by their failure to realize this elitist ideal, the litterateurs became once again feuilletonists of an older tradition. This concept of the elite was one more factor in the unreality which increasingly engulfed these socialists.

As might be imagined, references to Plato abounded in the discussions of elitist rule. Kurt Hiller summed up the ideal of the elite in his plan for Germany's rule after the Nazis were defeated: "It is not majorities that represent a nation; its best people represent it. To ascertain what is right from the standpoint of ethics and what is intelligent from the standpoint of the intellect is a task for a just and intelligent person and not for the majority."[44]

This ideal of an elite led the *Weltbühne* and the *Tagebuch* to admire the electoral system of the Catholic Church, in which otherwise they saw a great and powerful enemy. Leonard Nelson, who rejected all institutionalized religion, attributed the success of the Catholic Church to its leadership principle. The *Tagebuch* summarized the reason for this: papal elections represent a combination of democracy and aristocracy; everyone is eligible but there are no popular pressures in the choice of leadership.[45] It seemed the ideal "mixed government" of Aristotle—neither pure aristocracy nor pure democracy.

Given the absolute to which all this was related, freedom of criticism must be guaranteed to all people at all times under the rule of the elite. Leonard Nelson's faith in free discussion is reminiscent of John Stuart Mill's (1806–1873).[46] This leadership was not to be a new despotism. Kurt Hiller founded his journal *Das Ziel* (*The Goal*) as a call to activate the *Geist* (1916). Its pages contain contributions by a wide range of intellectuals, from Heinrich Mann (1871–1950) and Franz Werfel (1890–1945) to the literary critic Alfred Kerr (1867–1948) and Hans Blüher (1888–1955), the philosopher, who praised the Youth Movement in its pages. What gives some unity to their diverse articles is a protest against the bourgeois society that restrains the *Geist*. Hiller contributed criticism of the work of the other contributors, stressing that the *Geist* exists independent of both capitalistic and anti-capitalistic ideas. However, a social revolution was necessary to pull down the artificial barriers that had been erected against a natural aristocracy of intellectuals, which can only gain by the addition of fresh proletarian blood.[47]

II

The Republic did not bring such a social revolution, but at its beginning the *Weltbühne* and the *Tagebuch*, new journals then, attempted to translate theory into fact. The earlier neo-Kantian socialism laid the foundations for an activism that was derived from rational human judgment. The two new journals now moved closer to the Unabhängige Sozialistische Deutsche Partei (USDP, Independent Socialists). It was only logical for a man like Kurt Hiller to call upon his fellow citizens to support the party to which Kurt Eisner had belonged. But this party fused with the communists, for whom little sympathy was felt among the left-wing intellectuals, not only because the communists had become a bureaucratized political party but also because of the rapid disillusionment with the Soviet Union which permeated intellectual circles, a disillusionment that was due to Lenin's supposed sacrifice of principles to expediency.[48] Meanwhile, the intellectuals had attempted to take political action on their own.

Kurt Hiller initiated the Council of Intellectual Workers (*Rat der Geistigen Arbeiter*) in November 1918. This council, held in Berlin, was not supposed to represent a political party but an intellectual elite summoned to demand democratic and socialist political action. Beside Hiller, the novelist Heinrich Mann played a leading part in the council, giving an address at its first meeting in which he called for a new kind of democratic Republic. The formation of such councils or soviets was a general feature of the German Revolution of 1918, and another Council of Intellectual Workers met in Munich that same year. However, once it became known that a similar council existed in Berlin, the Munich council adjourned without ever meeting again. The Berlin council was a disappointment from the start, though its delegates appeared at workers' mass meetings and three representatives were sent to the constitutional assembly at Weimar. The economic program of the council called not for abolition of all private property but for the nationalization of certain industries, the division of large landholdings, and the confiscation of fortunes of a certain size.[49] The council soon achieved independence from the direction leaders like Hiller wished the intellectual leadership to take. In *Das Ziel*, Hiller criticized the 1919 Congress of Intellectual Workers (or "activists," as they had taken to calling themselves). Already they had begun to assimilate orthodox Marxism, stressing the narrow concept of class struggle—egalitarianism—and concentrating almost exclusively on the need for economic liberation. Hiller now demanded that the council should return to its principal demands of 1918: pacifism, socialism, and intellectual aristocracy. A call should go forth for the permanent institution, within the nation, of both a cultural and an economic council.[50]

The congress of intellectuals, clearly, had moved further toward orthodox Marxism than Hiller and his friends desired. Within the framework of the revolutionary situation of 1919, it threatened to support a change which would lead to a new imprisonment of the *Geist* and also to a violence which these intellectuals, who were pacifists, abhorred.[51] Hiller believed that the intellectuals on the council should reach the masses by setting an elevating example, spreading the *Geist* through debates and through the printed word. Leadership meant the education of the masses, not violence or the revolutionary tactics that were bound to accompany a sudden and fundamental change in the established order.

All these efforts came to naught. They are of small importance politically and interesting only in the context of our discussion of the socialism of the intellectuals. Established socialist and communist parties triumphed and in their triumph rejected these intellectuals and their ideas. No wonder that the *Tagebuch* complained by 1930 that access to the masses had been cut off, so far as intellectuals were concerned.[52]

Yet this was not quite true. Leonard Nelson proved the most active of these intellectuals in attempting to project himself onto the political scene, and he died (1927) before his own failure had become manifest. During the revolutionary days of 1917–18 he, like Kurt Hiller, founded a new group—the Internationaler Jugendbund (International Youth League)—in some ways not unlike Hiller's organization, though much more effective. The IJB was not to exist in isolation: here youth educated in the ethical will would work in all the leftist parties and gain leadership. The first declaration of the IJB, addressed to the "free youth of all classes and peoples," stressed the primacy of pure reason over selfish interests and party dogmatism. The structure of the organization rejected what Nelson called "formalistic democracy" in favor of the ideal of a Council of the Wise.[53] The members of the IJB worked within the SPD (Social Democratic Party) but increasing conflict due to fundamental differences in outlook led to the expulsion of the IJB from that party.

Nelson refused to give up. He agreed with Cohen that the judgments formed by the rational mind could be organized only through the world of real experience. Fries too had emphasized that the means by which the true ethical human society can be activated must derive from the actual experience of reality. Acting upon such premises, Nelson founded a new organization destined to replace the IJB, the Internationaler Sozialistischer Kampfbund (International League of Militant Socialists), the ISK, which lasted from 1926 into the postwar world. It was organized on the leadership principle and as a party of revolutionary cadres. As the crisis of the Republic deepened, the concept of a Council of the Wise was combined with Leninist ideas which supposedly symbolized both the need for fundamental change and the determination to avoid any entanglement with the existing order. But Leninism was misunderstood—ethical rather than materialist or historical considerations were given continuous prominence: "the material foundations of society are dependent upon the spiritual superstructure."[54]

The IJB and ISK which replaced it stressed practical work and education. For the IJB, practical work consisted in the unsuccessful attempt to infiltrate the SPD; for the ISK, in a rapprochement with the communists and in the call for a united workers' front against fascism. The educational aspect was primary, however, in these elitist organizations. For Nelson, as for Fries and Cohen before him, the human will must be led from darkness and lack of clarity to the ethical imperative which exists in all humanity.[55] Such training was essential for any correct political action. Along with the IJB, a philosophical-political academy was established, and later every ISK member was required to take part in regular training courses.[56] Leonard Nelson also established a boarding school, the Walkermühle, partly for the sake of ISK party members but also to put into practice a genuine program of socialist education on which the future would depend.

The goal of the school was to bring reason into the consciousness of the students and to instill among them a will to change society.[57] This would be accomplished by attaining a rational use of one's physical powers and also through an emphasis on mathematics and physics. Such an intellectual discipline would offer the students a "clear and simple" method independent of the "senses," the enemy of reason.[58] The Socratic method of teaching was used in the school, for the students must train their own will by finding their own rational answers to problems. Typically, Nelson took a dim view of history as a means to "socialist education." Contrary to orthodox Marxist thought, humanity must be freed from historical circumstances and prejudices to work freely on behalf of the ideal.[59]

The adults attending the philosophical-political academy lived in a self-contained community and had to break off all relations with the outside world.[60] At the Walkermühle, Leonard Nelson continued the tradition of Paul Natorp (1854–1924), who much earlier (1899) had called for a socialist education on the basis of Kantian ethical principles. Given the political theories of these figures, education was indeed their best hope to realize their Utopia, however much the tardiness of the process might clash with the urgent need they felt for immediate action.

The Walkermühle was destroyed by the Nazis, but through Nelson's disciple Minna Specht (1879–1961) his ideas were spread after his death to other schools, though for the most part shorn of the socialist desire to change capitalist society.[61] Moreover, through the ISK, Nelson's ideas lived on briefly after the Nazi seizure of power. Despite the "international" in its title, the organization had managed to establish only a tiny branch in England. Throughout the thirties this remained a small, politically isolated group, which, however, was active in publishing a journal (the *Socialist Vanguard*) as well as pamphlets carrying their message. Eventually the group, now calling itself the Militant Socialist International, drew closer to the Labour Party, and by 1940 it publicly dropped Nelson's elitist ideas as well as its own revolutionary stance. Growing ever more revisionist, this group (while broadening its original base) provides some continuity with the present magazine *Socialist Commentary*, and also with the philosophical journal *Ratio*.[62]

The original ISK and the Militant Socialists did have informal ties with like-minded men and women in the rest of Europe. We find, for example, the Italian socialist leader Paolo Treves (1908–1958) speaking at a London meeting.[63] But more important than the personal and institutional links, which were minor in any case, were the common body of ideas and the common outlook shared by German and other European left-wing intellectuals. Nelson's were meaningful but comparatively small, long-range attempts to set this kind of socialism on its way to victory through a properly oriented elite leadership.

Participation in a political party was blocked for the left-wing intellectuals by their own theories. Democracy as popular rule was rejected and with it all ideas of majority rule. It seemed futile to break with the dictatorships of the past in order to fall under the tyranny of the majority.[64] The "parliament game" in which political parties indulged seemed to lead to just such a result. The intellectuals called for a left unified against the menace of the right, and in the same breath castigated political parties as evil, attacking both Social Democrats and communists with impartial bitterness. These intellectuals resented party discipline, which was based on decision and compromise rather than on an absolute governing principle. The SPD were Philistines led by sergeant-majors, and the communists were as totalitarian as the Catholic Church.[65] Stefan Großmann (1875–1935) in his novel *Die Partei* (*The Party*, 1919) summed up this feeling when he wrote of the tainting of a party's ideals by its disciples: there, one mass of humanity unites merely to gain control over the masses. "For us," said the *Tagebuch*, "collaboration with a political party is foreign and unthinkable."[66]

Großmann himself exemplified the consequences of this attitude. Having been active in the Austrian Socialist Party, itself greatly influenced by Kantian idealism, he left it twenty years later, after starting his publishing venture in Berlin. He hesitated so long because he did not want to destroy the "love of my youth," even though for him the Social Democrats had become mere petit bourgeois.[67] Here again the break with a political party led to a stress upon an elite; the first manifesto of the *Tagebuch* had referred to a "secret society of those who really have wisdom."[68]

The road to full participation in the life of the Republic was closed to the left-wing intellectuals, as it was to many of their völkisch adversaries. To be sure, the *Tagebuch* was for a time more positive than the *Weltbühne*, supporting President Friedrich Ebert (1871–1925), for example—but in the end it too succumbed. Both journals did make a further attempt to descend into everyday politics, to suggest a "non-political" figure as President of the Republic, a man who would lead in the direction they desired. The *Tagebuch* early on sent up a trial balloon for Gerhart Hauptmann (1921), only to abandon it in disillusionment a month later.[69] The *Weltbühne* waited until 1932 to put Heinrich Mann's hat into the ring.[70] This effort too collapsed, but both episodes illustrate the journals' ideas of leadership. Neither of these famous authors was meaningfully involved in day-to-day politics; both men were literary figures—in their terms, men of culture.

As the rightist menace became ever more apparent, the intellectuals around the *Weltbühne* made one more effort to take part in organized political activity. They now urged a united front of the left, to stop the disintegration of the Republic and to transform it instead into a state approximating more closely to their socialist ideal. In February 1931, Heinrich Mann presided over a unity conference which encompassed the Communist Party, the SPD, and the ISK. The meeting was attended by 118 delegates. But the new people's front collapsed in mutual recriminations as soon as it was formed. After Hitler's seizure of power, Heinrich Mann attempted to revive it in exile, but this too failed.[71]

In 1931, too, came the possibility of a second chance for common left-wing political action, with the founding of the Sozialistische Arbeiterpartei Deutschlands (SAPD, Socialist Workers Party of Germany). Here was a political organization which, according to Carl von Ossietzky, might save "whatever in the SPD can still be saved in fighting spirit and activism."[72] However, his own friends and colleagues on the *Weltbühne* helped to scuttle this attempt. Some of them had a few years earlier established a "group of revolutionary pacifists" and in the founding of the SAPD they thought themselves (in the words of Kurt Hiller) "shamelessly ignored," though they had worked hard for leftist unity. Instead, the party seemed to prefer alliance with bourgeois pacifists, and so they refused to join the new party, showing clearly how the intellectual attachment to absolutes, the isolation from the mainstream of politics, led to a heightened personal sensibility and pride which had all the hallmarks of sectarianism.[73]

There is no evidence that the left-wing intellectuals joined what may have been, toward the end of the Republic, the most cohesive of the groups that sought to reactivate a revolutionary dynamic lost to communists and Social Democrats alike. The New Beginning (Neu Beginn), as it was known by 1933, was a secret organization which originated in discussion groups formed by disgruntled Social Democrats and communists. The New Beginning was largely composed of young intellectuals, and the concept of acting within each of the two chief left parties as an elite conspiratorial organization should have appealed strongly to the individuals we are discussing. Leonard Nelson's IJB had tried to use much the same tactic inside the SPD. Typically, however, the IJB had worked in the open and not underground. The New Beginning had no scruples about tactics, and though they also stressed revolutionary consciousness as a prerequisite for political action, ideology was closely linked to organization.

This group believed in tight leadership and a disciplined organization, and so for a time it survived as a small resistance group within Nazi Germany.[74] The left-wing intellectuals deplored such discipline, though they might well have sympathized with the hope that through such a group, active within the Communist Party and the SPD alike, the unity of the left would be restored. But the New Beginning's emphasis on organization was combined, not surprisingly, with a positive attitude toward the Marxist dialectic of history, as well as with admiration for Lenin.[75] Perhaps the very fact that the socialism of the left-wing intellectuals, in its idealism, rejected all three of these helps to explain their failure as organizers of political movements, and even of small action groups.

What was left for them to do in politics? After sending up its trial balloon for Heinrich Mann, von Ossietzky advised his readership to give their votes to the communist leader Ernst Thälmann (1886–1944) in the presidential election of 1932, a course of action which the SAPD also advocated. Nothing could better document the dilemma into which their political failures had led these intellectuals than the reasons von Ossietzky gave for supporting the leader of the hated Communist Party. Thälmann was worthy of the vote because he was an "embattled man of the left," and not because he was the communist leader. The old condemnation of the Communist Party was expressly reaffirmed: whoever belonged to it would, in the last resort, place discipline above conviction.[76] Thälmann led that party. How could this communist leader be considered a "man of the left" in the context of the *Weltbühne*'s definition of true leftism? Von Ossietzky does not tell us.

The political failure of the left-wing intellectuals was complete. All their efforts represented a search for means of political action which were bound to be frustrated, whether it was the attempted Council of Intellectual Workers of 1918, Leonard Nelson's organizations, or the attempts at establishing a popular front. None of these seriously influenced the course of events; they remained at best marginal political phenomena. Political isolation become sectarianism was responsible for the intellectuals' failure to join the SAPD, which itself was never an important factor in German political life. But the roots of the political failure of these intellectuals, as of their disappointment in the Republic, lie in their outlook on the world and society. The ethical idealism so central to these intellectuals' thought detached itself ever further from the reality they desired to change. For the earlier neo-Kantians, idealism and reality had been closely linked. Together with the eternal moral imperative, they had tried to maintain something of the Marxist historical dialectic in order to provide a mechanism of revolutionary change. But now idealism not only displaced what remained of the historical dialectic; it dominated the practical programs of socialist change. As we shall see, men like Leonhard Frank (1882–1961) and Ludwig Rubiner (1881–1920), writing during and after the First World War, were already concerned solely with an idealistic road toward a new society. In the *Weltbühne* and the *Tagebuch* also there was to be an increasing emphasis on ethical absolutes at the expense of concrete political involvement.

Typical of this attitude was an open letter which Alfred Döblin wrote in the *Tagebuch* to a young man who had asked whether one should support Marxism against the rising tide of National Socialism; the year was 1930. Döblin could not give an unqualified yes to such a commitment. More important than political ideology was individual human liberty, and the hatred of envy, barbarism, and war. Fear of Marxist dogmatism led Döblin to propose the "spontaneous uniting" of the people. This vagueness was relieved only in the complaint that economic interests rather than the intellectuals were ruling Germany.[77] The primacy of ethical considerations had swamped all other factors.

Döblin included this letter and others "to a young man" in his book *Wissen und Verändern!* (*Know and Change!*, 1931), in which—a year after the Nazis' spectacular electoral successes and only two years before their coming to power—he sums up the heightened idealism of the left-wing intellectuals. In the last resort, socialism was a categorical imperative, a spiritual value derived from a basic moral human instinct. This had been distorted by the materialism of both Social Democrats and communists.[78] To be sure, Marx is praised for his destructive analysis of the bourgeoisie and their capitalism, but the free individual of the future cannot be created through a dictatorship or through force. The means do govern the end.[79]

We have discussed the political efforts and the final failure of these intellectuals, but it is difficult to escape the conclusion that, in the last analysis, politics was irrelevant to the realization of their aim. The ethical idealism which led to failure directed the political awareness of left-wing intellectuals from the very beginning. Self-consciously intellectual, they believed that their task lay outside the normal realm of politics, beyond society and yet relevant to it. For that reason many of their political ventures were somewhat halfhearted.

It was their task to hold aloft the banner of true socialism, to provide a living example for the working classes. Intellectuals had no army and no political power, but this was not important, for their stand was based on absolute human values which exist in each person. Following on the thought of Jakob Friedrich Fries in the nineteenth century and Leonard Nelson in their own time, these intellectuals held that humanity sought ceaselessly to push through to the surface and was only kept from doing so by the "powers of darkness" opposed to the triumph of reason.[80]

These men and women took wing through their optimistic view of human nature based on a shared rationalism which bound all generations together. The novels and plays they wrote about their hopes for humankind may present us with a more meaningful insight into their political aims than their abortive political actions. The young Ludwig Rubiner, in voluntary exile in Switzerland during the First World War, wrote a drama, *Die Gewaltlosen* (*Those Without Power*, 1918), which asserted that men and women who exemplified the pure and unsullied belief in humanity would triumph over the evil of naked force, even if they lost their lives in the process. "Our will weighs heavier than their might."[81] Rubiner was one of the circle grouped around Kurt Hiller.

Leonhard Frank's stories *Der Mensch ist gut* (*Man Is Good*, 1918) appeared immediately after the war, and its very title was meant to symbolize the optimism of this group. It was suggested by Julio Álvarez del Vayo (1891–1975, later foreign minister of the Spanish Republic in its struggle against Franco)—one more indication that this body of ideas was not confined to Germany.[82] In Frank's stories, ideas of love and human brotherhood triumph in a confrontation with naked force. How could this be otherwise, for if the credo "Man is good" could be uttered with sufficient force, it would automatically activate each human being's belief in universal fraternity. No external force could stand against the wellspring of human nature.[83] Frank and Rubiner wanted to stimulate by an appeal to emotion that same force which Leonard Nelson attempted to bring into human consciousness by his socialist education. A basic presupposition about human nature provided the foundation for all these theories: people, Rubiner wrote, perform their deeds on the basis of ideas. These ideas are not bound to one individual but are common to all humanity.[84] Some intellectuals derived them from Kant's categorical imperative and others simply from humanity's love for humanity, but they amounted to the same thing, since these intellectuals held up their banner before the people, leading as they hoped to the spontaneous conversion of the masses.

Humanity was at the center of their hopes, and they believed they were being realistic in emphasizing individual human consciousness as against abstract ideology. Thus Thomas Wendt, the hero of Lion Feuchtwanger's (1884–1958) novel of the same name (1920), learns that in a revolution individuals are more important than abstract, "arid" ideas; and the initial manifesto of the *Weltbühne* demanded that the individual human being be kept always in view. In reality, these intellectuals' view of the individual was itself based on an idealistic abstraction, indeed an "absolute" conception of human nature. But they could not admit this, for their theory combined individualism and idealism leading to action with a consciousness of their lack of power in the modern world. Given the task they set themselves, their view of humanity did indeed provide them with an all-inclusive ideology, a springboard for possible action.

Of course, in direct opposition to Marxism, the super structure was to be brushed aside, together with those concrete economic and social factors which might provide a basic explanation of the present state of society and a guide for the future. Capitalism must go—the intellectuals shared this aim with those socialists who retained a Marxist base to their thought—but it must go because of factors inherent in human nature, not because of exigencies created by an external situation. The socialism of the intellectuals was filled with an idealism about human nature, about humanity's urge to do good in this world.

This idealism was bound to have a negative effect on their relationship to the Weimar Republic, for that state could not live up to their image of the good society, could not even offer hope of approaching such a paradise. It was forced to operate on the basis of realities, and it was precisely the exigencies of real situations which were constantly displaced in the thought of these intellectuals by their idealism. Where, in a parliamentary Republic based on majority rule, was the categorical imperative to be found—that moral impulse so necessary to inspire the right actions?

Carl von Ossietzky called Weimar a "state without an idea, having a permanent case of bad conscience."[85] How close this is to Moeller van den Bruck's analysis of the ills of the times! The conservative also complained that Germany was without "ideas" and linked this in turn to the transcending of political parties. For him and his followers too, as for most adherents of völkisch thought, a self-renewing elite was again the way out of the present dilemma. However different the concepts which went into these ideologies, the Republic as it existed and functioned was criticized in a similar manner by both left-wing and right-wing intellectuals.

The völkisch movement found in Adolf Hitler a man who would devote one half of *Mein Kampf* to ideology and the other half to practical questions of organization. For the left-wing intellectuals there was an indissoluble connection between the means used and the absolute to be realized, whereas Hitler did not decline to enter the arena of practical politics for the sake of a victory which he envisaged as the triumph of his ideology. It is interesting to note that many right-wing intellectuals rejected Hitler precisely because he used realistic tactics and founded a political party; for them also, this could be done only at the expense of principles. Such men often found themselves in the same concentration camp as their erstwhile enemies.

The assessment of National Socialism by the left-wing intellectuals illustrates the growing loss of contact with reality into which their kind of socialism had led them. They realized that the "saint from Braunau" (i.e., Hitler) did attract the discontented *petit bourgeoisie*, but for the *Tagebuch* he was not a real danger, even in 1930. The Nazi Party was intellectually inferior and had a barbaric lack of culture; thus it would inevitably be defeated in any reasonable discussion. For the *Tagebuch* this meant that the parliamentary, legal way to power was closed to the Nazis; the only danger was of a Nazi putsch, which would rely on the element of surprise.[86] Clearly the presupposition here that true politics must be based on an ideal, an absolute standard, led to a gross misreading of the political reality. Thus the faith of these intellectuals in the efficacy of free debate is manifest once more. On the one hand their intellectual standards were absolute, and on the other hand they showed great faith in the political importance of rational dialogue. We have seen this attitude throughout our discussion: in Kurt Hiller's Council of the Wise and in Leonard Nelson's emphasis on the Socratic dialogue as the indispensable mechanism of education for societal change. Nearly ten years earlier, Stefan Großmann had shown more understanding of the importance of National Socialism as an "instinctive" and non-rational movement which by its very nature attracted youth.[87]

The *Weltbühne*'s attitude toward Hitler was very similar. In its pages Heinz Pol (1901–1972) pronounced Hitler and the völkisch movement dead as early as 1925.[88] But here conspiracy theories with a Marxist slant played a role. The villain was monopoly capitalism—Hugenberg was the danger, for this high financier would use Hitler and then discard him when it suited his purpose.[89] Similarly, the *Tagebuch* for many years cast the industrialist Hugo Stinnes (1870–1924) as the villain who manipulated Germany. In the intellectuals' own analysis of National Socialism there is a strange mixture of the Marxist approach, which they otherwise deplored, and the overemphasis of an ethical imperative, which they thought could not be ignored if victory were to be gained in the long run.

Were these then the "free-floating intellectuals" of whom Karl Mannheim (1893–1947) had written?[90] Even earlier than Mannheim, Leonard Nelson had made the same point: these intellectuals were not bound by their class position but had everyone's interest at heart.[91] They cut across all classes, as the *Weltbühne* asserted, in opposition to the class emphasis of orthodox Marxism.[92] One can see in the efforts to actualize their ideas an attempt to link the free-floating intellectual with a position of leadership in the transformation of society toward socialism. But in this process they cut themselves off from meaningful political action within the existing order. They were interested in absolutes, not in possibilities.

III

The fact that German left-wing intellectuals were predominantly of Jewish origin cannot be ignored, whether in analyzing their ideology or accounting for their isolation. Though there were important exceptions, such as Carl von Ossietzky, the widespread correlation between Jew and left-wing intellectual does not lack historical significance. Without doubt this factor contributed to the isolation of these intellectuals within the population. However, the influence of their Jewish origins on their own thought is not easy to determine. The ethical impulse of the Enlightenment, the emphasis on reason which characterized that age, had remained very much alive within the Jewish bourgeoisie throughout the nineteenth century. Jewish emancipation had owed much to the "religion of humanity" of the Enlightenment, and among Jews this tradition never lacked strength. The feeling of being a powerless minority in a Germany where Jewish emancipation had never taken deep roots directed the thoughts of many Jews away from a narrow nationalism and toward the ideal of fellowship and concern with all humanity.

When emancipated Jews, like many Christians, left religious orthodoxy behind them, they were inclined to turn toward such an idealism instead. Many young Jews joined the socialist movement, but from the beginning they were attracted by ethical idealism rather than by the materialist base which Engels had stressed. They contradict the antisemitic picture of the materialist Jew, for these Jews were in most instances the driving force behind the introduction of idealism into the socialist movement.

Hermann Cohen, whose neo-Kantianism was such an important source for left-wing intellectuals, held that it was the mission of the Jews to prepare humankind for the reception of a new social spirit springing from Judaism's belief in monotheism.[93] For Cohen, the monotheistic God was identical with the categorical imperative which demanded a just ethical order for the world. Cohen's thought may well have had relevance to the religious feelings of the intellectuals we have been discussing—and not just in Germany. Quite independently of Cohen, the Italian socialist and antifascist Sabatino Enrico "Nello" Rosselli (1900–1937, brother of Carlo Rosselli) reiterated these ideas in 1924, a few years after Cohen's death. Jewish monotheism meant a social conscience imbued with personal responsibility and a love for one's fellow humanity.[94] The Jewish intellectuals within Italian socialism shared this idealistic outlook with their German contemporaries. Examples from other European countries can be added to show that for many young Jews this commitment to a left-wing idealism provided a new religion.

The specific Jewish religious heritage was transformed into ethical idealism and directed toward bringing about a change in present society. Respect for the individual was the essential attitude the categorical imperative demanded, and this again fitted into the pattern of Jewish development. The Jews were increasingly embattled against the effort to view them as a cohesive, evil group, to transform the individual Jew into a stereotype. The pervasiveness of racial thought before and after the war made this battle of prime concern to every Jew. The individualism in neo-Kantian socialism must have had an especially strong appeal under these circumstances, together with the optimistic belief that idealism could be awakened in every person, Jew and Gentile alike.

For many a Jew the rejection of traditional Judaism led to this new religion. Thus the Jewish heritage gave added impetus to the idealism of these intellectuals. The awareness of minority status, heightened by the increasingly successful antisemitism of the right, also made the self-conscious theories of intellectual leadership attractive. The particular sociology of German intellectuals can serve further to explain the close link between some Jews and this left-wing pattern of thought. German intellectuals were apt to be involved in occupational worlds incidental to their existence as intellectuals. Intellectuals entered the establishment as academics, civil servants, or officially approved authors: the official desk, the name plate on the door, title and pensions became more important than literature. But it was difficult for German Jews to enter into a competition for status, and this gave them a freedom from involvement closely related to their position on the margins of the establishment. To be sure, the Weimar Republic opened up all professions to Jews, but the individuals we are discussing here still came from a Wilhelminian background.

These various considerations may help to explain the high incidence of Jews among the left-wing intellectuals: Cohen, Hiller, Nelson, and Eisner, to take a few examples—though Nelson and Eisner had Christian mothers. Moreover, it is worth noting that once again there was a parallel development outside Germany. Jewish intellectuals in the Austrian socialist movement, such as Max Adler (1873–1937) and Otto Bauer (1881–1938), were also strongly attracted to neo-Kantian idealism. In Italy, Carlo Rosselli identified his Judaism with a religion of liberty and a tradition of social concern, not unlike Hermann Cohen in Germany. Nor is it a mere coincidence that Italian Jewish anti-fascists were especially numerous in Rosselli's Justice and Liberty movement.[95]

The failures of the German left-wing intellectuals can be attributed primarily to their attitudes toward humanity and society and to their lack of a political base and an effective mechanism of social change. But the predominance of Jews within the group served, in Germany at least, to separate them not only from the population at large but also from the working classes they wanted to reach.

Their failures increased their bitterness. It is not without a shudder that one reads in the *Tagebuch*, only two months after Hitler had attained power, that the collapse of the Republic was not "undeserved."[96] But, above all, their isolation and their bitterness led them more and more into becoming critics par excellence, taking up the heritage of such people as the famous Wilhelminian publicist Maximilian Harden (1861–1927). This criticism performed a service, certainly—the *Weltbühne* exposed the Black (i.e., illegal) Reichswehr and fought against militarism and corruption. But, taken on their own terms, these intellectuals wanted to be builders of a new society and not merely critics of the old. Balanced against the aid they gave the Republic by exposing the hostile remains of Imperial Germany must stand their own image of themselves as "activists." It is by adopting their own viewpoint toward themselves that we see the positive, the connection with a constructive reality, receding increasingly into the background. Looking back at the past, Kurt Hiller rightly criticized the editor of the *Weltbühne*, Carl von Ossietzky, for lacking any valid concept of political strategy.[97] But the same might be said for all these intellectuals.

This negativism expressed itself stylistically as well, through an emphasis on paradoxes, on aphorisms, and on cleverness of phrase. In short, these individuals, despite Kurt Hiller's earlier efforts to turn them into prophets, returned to the feuilletonist tradition of the *fin de siècle* and applied this to serious social and political criticism. The end of their efforts was well summarized by Kurt Tucholsky—who, however, cannot be properly classified as a member of any group—even before the triumph of National Socialism: "Sometimes it is very nice to be alone, to belong to no club. Sometimes it is very nice to pass by."[98] These figures not only wanted to be part of a club; they wanted to change society through it. But it proved to be the wrong club. Theirs was not an individualism which could lead to social change. Kantian socialism proved as much a failure in their lives as it had been for Kurt Eisner in the Bavarian Revolution itself.

Heinrich Mann tried to point a way out. He was a thoroughgoing optimist so far as the potentiality of the people themselves went. Did the Weimar Constitution not represent the "better Germany"? Regardless of what happened under the Republic, the love of freedom inherent in all humanity could not be destroyed.[99] Heinrich Mann was to maintain this faith at a time when the left-wing intellectuals were becoming disillusioned and bitter. In 1931 he wrote in the *Tagebuch* that democracy could count on the instinct of self-preservation among the people. The people sensed that the enemies of democracy wanted to suppress them and drive them into war against the foreigner. The Nazis were the creatures of the industrialists, and even if they attained power they would be defeated. The bloodbath which would accompany such a defeat would serve to strengthen democracy for, unlike 1918, this time democracy would be attained through struggle.[100]

His optimism rendered Heinrich Mann ideally suited to preside over the attempt at a popular front to stop National Socialism in the same year (1932) that he reaffirmed his belief in the inevitable survival of democracy. This popular front was supposed to unite all the democratic forces in their struggle against the right. Did not all such parties claim to be the instruments of the people? The attempted popular front failed amid the recriminations of the left-wing groups. Heinrich Mann's political faith proved as ineffectual as the elitist ideas of the left-wing intellectuals that divided their politics from his.

Mann realized that the intellectuals had become the enemies of the Republic, and from his own optimistic worldview he counseled patience. Was it not the essence of the Republic that it was undogmatic and open to all ideas?[101] Significantly, Kurt Hiller criticized Heinrich Mann in the *Weltbühne* "in all admiration" for accepting unquestioningly the democratic ideal.[102] As we have seen, however, the politics of these left-wing intellectuals were not based on such wholesale optimism about the German people in their present stage of development.

Mann was a thoroughgoing rationalist in the Jacobin tradition, which he held up as a model for a "dictatorship of reason." His optimism was based upon faith in the ideals of the French Enlightenment: why should not the beautiful preference of the mature eighteenth century for goodness and the recognition of human equality be recaptured? Mann retained for the rest of his life the belief which he had put forward in his most famous novel, *Der Untertan* (*The Loyal Subject*, 1911), "That power which cannot spread goodness and kindness throughout the world is not destined to last . . ." The abolition of capitalism was desirable in order to create such a power, but more important was a revival of the French tradition of rationalism. For Mann, Kant was the heir of the French Revolution, whereas Nelson, a product of German idealism, had warned against believing in the "all-powerfulness of reason."[103] For Mann again, the ethical imperative would prevail if the maldistribution of riches were redressed and economic considerations no longer predominated over all others.[104] Here he was in line with the other Kantian socialists. Like them, Mann rejected orthodox Marxist historical analysis and method. Economic reform depended in the first place on the *Geist*, which he equated with reason.[105] The primacy of the *Geist* could, at times, lead Mann into an idealism difficult to harmonize with the tradition of the French Enlightenment or indeed with the works of Émile Zola (1840–1902), whom Mann so greatly admired. Once again we are back to the primacy of the "idea."

This primacy led the rationalist, democrat Mann at times into a still closer relationship with the left-wing intellectuals. Thus, in 1928, he reported to the "poetry section" of the Prussian Academy that the *Geist* has an autonomous morality which must not compromise with fleeting reality. Humanity must commit itself to the eternally valid, as Kant had believed; only if all kept their gaze on these heights would he find that existing reality recognized his worth. Here the categorical imperative must at all times uncompromisingly set the goals for reality; hence those who served the *Geist* did become an elite, even for Heinrich Mann.[106]

Who were they? The priest, the philosopher, the poet—above all, the writers, who understand the "power of the word."[107] Just as the other intellectuals had done, Mann grossly overestimated the importance of the written word. And he maintained this viewpoint even after "illiterate" National Socialism had seized power. "Literary talent and the power of a pure will are identical."[108] But the language used to express this power had to be clear and exact. For Heinrich Mann, clarity and precision of language typified the belief in the necessity of a rational approach to all problems, founded on the conviction that humanity was basically rational. It is in this conviction that the differences between Mann and the other intellectuals we have been discussing are most evident.

The elite of writers were, in the image of Mann's beloved Émile Zola, the moralists and educators, who would lead humanity to humanism and justice. They would be successful in a truly democratic environment if belief in rationalism were central in their work, for rationalism is shared by all humankind.[109] Progress would not be achieved by leaving the solid ground of reality for "boundless vistas, the finite or the absolute." Mann condemned the young Expressionists for having such visions. He might at the same time have condemned some of his fellow intellectuals for a similar retreat into unreality. Instead, progress would be achieved by increasing, through example, the allegiance paid to reason within the nation, an increase which would lead not to the immediate dawning of Utopia but to the better ordering of society—approaching ever closer to the categorical imperative.[110] Eventually, reason and humanity would triumph among humanity.

Heinrich Mann attempted to combine belief in a democratic Republic with concepts linking him to the left-wing intellectuals who admired him so greatly. His optimism and rationalism may seem as removed from the reality of the 1920s as their own ideas. And for all his greater "realism," the person whom the *Weltbühne* proposed for the next president could not find a firm footing among the existing political parties. For a time he was close to the liberal Democratic Party, but the same factors which prevented the others from working through the existing political spectrum affected him as well. The communists represented a tyranny seeking to destroy the open-endedness of the Republic which he so admired and the Social Democrats, though sincere, had become wedded to the status quo.[111] It is typical that Mann had the highest praise for Kurt Eisner, whose brief government in Bavaria had meant "more ideas, more joy in rationalism, more activism of the *Geist*" than any other rule.[112]

All in all, Heinrich Mann was a passionate defender of the Weimar Republic, unlike the left-wing intellectuals. But because he shared the basic ideas of their kind of socialism, an ambivalence was introduced into his allegiance, a perspective which prevented him from working in the most effective way for the protection of the Republic through its existing political structure.[113]

It was not Heinrich but his brother Thomas Mann (1875–1955) who had the strength to find a positive relationship to the Republic, as Kurt Sontheimer's (1928–2005) book shows.[114] He was an outsider among the intellectuals we have discussed, and indeed they rarely failed to attack his status and his reputation. The contrast is interesting and significant.

Thomas Mann called for an intellectual balance between extremes on the basis of humanism. During the Weimar Republic he advocated support for the Social Democrats, whom the others despised. Thomas Mann realized that, for all its faults, this was the party which had fought the barbarism that was engulfing the nation. But even Thomas Mann shared some of the attitudes of the other intellectuals. Socialism was not a materialist dialectic for him, but the new humanism. Thomas Mann's objective was always the inner freedom of humanity, and now he realized that this freedom must be linked to society, that there must be a balance between the rational, as exemplified in working through existing political society, and the irrational expression of humanity's metaphysical impulse. Thus he was able to find his way into a concrete political organization rather than regarding such collaboration with reality "foreign and inconceivable."

We have concentrated on one influential type of intellectual during the Republic. The parallels with völkisch intellectuals have already been pointed out: the same concentration on the primacy of an idea, the same rejection of political parties and the tactics of compromise. But whereas the völkisch intellectuals found a leader in Adolf Hitler, who through practical politics transformed ideal into reality, the left-wing intellectuals went into exile and had their books burned. Here is the ultimate consequence of these attitudes, of the contempt for political reality without the attainment of a firm relationship to any actual part of it. It would, however, be wrong to see in this intellectual dilemma merely opposition to the Republic and not the grappling with a real and existing problem. Parliamentary majority rule did help bring Hitler to power; political parties did paralyze the state. The problem of leadership is an important one; Nelson's education for leadership was supposed to be a training in rationalism.

To be sure, even those who did achieve a positive relationship toward the Weimar Republic, who became political pragmatists, failed in the end. Hitler did come to power. It can be argued with some justice that such figures, through their total involvement with existing politics, lacked the strength of principle to provide an effective barrier to the politics of compromise which brought Hitler to office. From this point of view a vindication of the left-wing intellectuals is certainly a possibility.

But the dilemma of the left-wing intellectuals cannot focus merely on what they did at the end of the Republic. It must also take into account their attitudes at its inception and during the Republic's evolution, when this form of government still stood a chance at success. The left-wing intellectuals opposed the Weimar Republic all along the line, without providing what might prove to be a viable alternative method of change. Thus they tended to become critics rather than builders and in that process alienated, almost masochistically, larger parts of the intellectual community from a state which, for all its injustices, provided an almost unprecedented freedom of expression and political action.

Certainly Leonard Nelson attempted to bring about a change within the Social Democratic Party, and others at times also entered the political fray, but politics was submerged under an absolute and uncompromising image of humanity and its possibilities. This contrasted markedly with the irrationalism of popular attitudes on which Hitler was able to build his movement, and yet the intellectuals never made any concessions to such a political reality. The diverse interpretations of National Socialism illustrate this fact. As self-conscious intellectuals, they were never able to link themselves either to a mass movement or to an existing political institution, two possibilities that would have given a basic relevance to their fight against the rightist menace, lost though it was in the end. However, the left-wing intellectuals deserve to be taken seriously on their own terms, though one can criticize their irrelevance to existing reality. They did want to bring about a new society; they called themselves "activists." But they faced the postwar problems in a manner that excluded them from any effectiveness in leading Germany in the desired direction. They were conscious of their failure long before Hitler came to power, but their reaction was not to adjust their basic attitude toward humanity and society: instead, we see an increasing bitterness and a tendency to withdraw into sectarianism.

These German intellectuals were not alone in facing these problems after 1918. We have, from time to time, pointed out the existence of like-minded people and groups outside the faltering Republic. There was reason for Hiller's great and lasting admiration for André Gide and Romain

Rolland (1866–1944). He saw in Gide an activist with a socialism similar to his own, and in Rolland a man who rejected dogmas for a truly spiritual socialist revolution.[115] He was correct. What better summary of the attitudes of these German intellectuals than André Gide's statement about the Communist Party: "It is to the truth that I attach myself; if the party deserts it, at the same moment I desert the party."[116] Hiller might have added to his list the name of Julien Benda, whose intellectual group is so similar to Mannheim's and whose task is not so different from that which Nelson had also given them. Yet there are important differences between the French and German left-wing intellectuals which must not be overlooked. As David Caute (b. 1936) has shown, rationalism for the French was not diffused by the idealist elements which we have seen take an important place among the Germans; nor did French intellectuals, even when they broke with the party, reject Marxist dialectic and historicism with the decisiveness of the intellectuals on the other side of the Rhine.[117] The French tradition was different from the German, and intellectuals were not "free-floating" enough to divorce themselves from the national context.

However, the urge toward Marxist "humanism" and the dilemmas confronted are similar enough to make it possible to maintain that the German story is only one side of a history shared by intellectuals in Western Europe. We have cited French examples. The Italian socialist Carlo Rosselli too shared these ideas of a socialism which was not proletarian but devoted to the realization of eternal ideas of liberty and justice that are innate in every person. The anti-fascist group he founded in the 1920s is strikingly similar in ideology to the group exemplified by the *Weltbühne* and the *Tagebuch*. All these individuals sought social justice on the basis of a common spiritual attitude rooted in an absolute ethic outside history and on such foundations sought a "third way" between the materialism and historicism of orthodox Marxism and the irrational mysticism of the right. Most of them did not find it, though the Italians showed a greater realism than the Germans. Rosselli believed that only if the proletariat became a politically united force would the conquest of power be possible.[118] He did not share the elitism of the Germans. The political party which such intellectuals founded (Partito d'Azione), quite unlike the Council of Intellectual Workers, became, for a time, an effective political force. Contrary to Rosselli and his group in the 1930s, the German left-wing intellectuals removed themselves ever further from the realities of their times. The result was a Marxist impulse translated into the realm of idealism, a "Marxism of the heart" rather than one based on the rational analysis of existing facts.

The German case is especially tragic because there a Republic had to be saved and a growing menace from the right had to be countered. The Party of Humanity in the age of reason had believed in experimentation within society, stemming from the given reality which it represented. The absolute of a categorical imperative distracted some of the best minds of a later generation from the task at hand. In condemning compromise, existing politics, and the exploitation of realistic possibilities, the left-wing intellectuals put forward a vision of society that seemed incapable of realization. Though we have been concerned with only one important group among the many varieties of left-wing intellectuals in the Weimar Republic, their thoughts and dilemmas have a wider application in Germany and Europe.

IV

In our own times, as we witness a revival of interest in the young Marx "filled with human passion," in contrast to a Marxist historical dialectic, the failures and dilemmas of the German left-wing intellectuals are worth recalling.[119] Anyone watching the development of the new radicalism of the early 1960s in the United States must be struck with its inherent similarity to the earlier movement. Once again, a young generation is searching for a way out of a closing political universe, and once more the intellectuals among them are longing for new possibilities of social change. Small wonder, for they believe themselves to be growing up into a world in which the existing communist regimes have betrayed the hopes of earlier generations and in which the establishment at home uses the weapons of war and hypocritical persuasion to make the world over in its own image. It is impossible, we are told, to compromise with such reality: it must be confronted and liquidated.

The ideals which these radicals hold are not merely of American origin, though their devotion to democratic procedure does arise from a specifically American context.[120] Instead, they show striking parallels to the attitudes and dilemmas of the earlier German left-wing intellectuals. The history of the German intellectuals goes on, though many had pronounced it dead with Hitler's seizure of power more than thirty years ago. It is important to discuss this historical continuum, for it widens the relevance of the thought of the Weimar intellectuals even beyond Europe, where their ideas had wide range in their own time.

The American left-wing intellectuals also face a society in which no existing political or institutional force seems committed to basic social, economic, or ideological change. Like the earlier thinkers, they confront the politics of their time imbued with a "noble morality" and, for the most part, a commitment to non-violence.[121] Here also principles must never be compromised, for they are based on the belief (which should be familiar to us) that humanity is an end and must never be made a means.[122] Now, as earlier, it is held that the depersonalization of modern society and modern politics constitutes the barrier to a realization of the human potential. Humanity must not be reduced to the status of "things": the means and the end are intimately related.[123]

With a set of principles at the core of their outlook that parallel those of an earlier generation, such left-wing intellectuals in America reject all compromises and all notions of party discipline. In this search for a new politics, orthodox Marxism is repudiated as inadequate to the task of bringing society under human control, of placing humanity's destiny in its own hands.[124] What, then, is necessary to accomplish this end? The dominant opinion among this so-called New Left comes to conclusions very much like those which men like Leonhard Frank and Ludwig Rubiner reached long before them. The programmatic statement of the Students for a Democratic Society (SDS) calls for activating the capabilities of "reason, freedom, and love" which reside within each human being.[125] Just so, the students at Berkeley called for a community based on a shared humanity and the need people have for each other.[126]

Such idealism, resting on a dominating moral impetus, raises the same dilemmas which we have been discussing. The modern intellectuals cling to an optimistic view of human nature based on the shared potential of humanity, including both reason and creativity. Activating these well-springs of human nature will produce a true community: a "community of friends" in which personal relationships provide the base for an effective politics.[127] This kind of idealism has been castigated by a leader of the New Left as "failure to go beyond our moral position"; indeed, for some the willingness to make a revolution in the present order of things is a personal, not a collective decision.[128]

This New Left, like its predecessors, possesses a sense of the powerlessness of intellectuals to bring about a change in the present order. This sense provides the background for the manner in which these intellectuals propose to transform theory into action. Herein lies a significant difference between the contemporary American radicals and their earlier counterparts. Quite unlike their German predecessors, the Americans work within the university community. A pattern of emigration from the university to organize Blacks and poor whites has become fairly common. But the university base has exacerbated rather than resolved the political dilemma of the new radicals. On the one hand, it emphasizes their distance from the rural or urban poor whom they seek to organize; on the other hand, university reform cannot satisfy the urge to transform society. The fact that America lacks the traditional European concept of the intelligentsia has further intensified the problem. This New Left faces, once again, the problem of the relationship of intellectuals to revolutionary change.

Typically, the program of the SDS holds that the New Left must acquire the intellectual skills which permit action to be informed by reason.[129] Does this entail an elitism such as Leonard Nelson's, whose intellectuals were supposed to lead the masses toward reason and change? Staughton Lynd (1929–2022), one of the intellectual leaders of this New Left, has called for a new Continental Congress which would enable the rest of society to enter into a dialogue with those who advocate the true socialist community.[130] But this is not to be a Council of the Wise. Rather, it would include people from all walks of life.

The self-conscious elitism of the earlier intellectuals has given way to an attempt to link the intellectual to the masses in a more direct sense than the European intellectuals had wished or thought desirable. It is at this point that an American democratic impulse, which was missing among German left-wing intellectuals, becomes predominant; people of the tradition of Frank and Rubiner might have sympathized. "We are the people and we work with the people."[131] Culture-bearing elites cannot be allowed to exist; in consequence the people must be encouraged to work out their own fate.[132] If they are freed from the false ideas which the middle classes have inculcated, then they will make the "right" decisions.[133] This optimistic viewpoint is based on the moral imperative inherent in all humanity.

Thus, unlike the older European generation, this New Left spends itself working within the framework of local communities, trying to get the people to make their own decisions about their future at the grass roots. This "participatory democracy" is built on the hope that the people will make spontaneously correct decisions once they have an opportunity to do so and in that process will further their own education by confronting the oppressive nature of the present social system. Here the intellectuals' function is merely to point out the abstract conclusions which spring from concrete actions taken within the local community.[134]

The American democratic populist tradition helps to overcome the feeling of powerlessness among these young intellectuals. The longing for a meaningful community is all-pervasive and is combined with the goal of giving humanity back control of its own destiny. This is certainly not traditional Marxism, and it is small wonder that at times the moral imperative overshadows the concrete economic and social ideas which the Marxist radicals thought so important. For Staughton Lynd, "the spiritual unity of the group is more important than any external accomplishment."[135] A leader of the Student Non-Violent Coordinating Committee finds that money and power are only the means to the end: it is the end which is important.[136] A general suspicion of power goes hand in hand with a rejection of politics as they are usually defined. The same held true for the older left-wing intellectuals, and for the one as for the other the categorical imperative threatened to swamp specific programs of social and economic change.

The new radicals provide a guide to action that is more negative than positive.[137] This is not the result of a supposed "end to ideology" in America but derives rather from the conflict between ethical idealism and the harsh necessities of politics. The *cul-de-sac* in which these intellectuals find themselves today is directly parallel to the "dead end" from which their German predecessors could find no exit. Where the Germans with their elite ideas became bitter critics rather than builders, however, the new American radicals have been saved from such a fate by their continuing optimism about humanity and their ideal of participatory democracy. Yet, in their groping for a new kind of revolutionary change, the modern left-wing intellectuals find themselves facing the same stone wall as soon as their idealism calls for concrete revolutionary action.

For all their labor among the people, one also hears the complaint that "we don't have working-class contacts."[138] They cannot associate themselves with an existing political party or a mass movement but, since here there is no Hitler to cut off their history, some still believe that participatory democracy might eventually serve to create a popular movement that could make itself felt. The roadblock to the creation of such a movement is not merely the conscious rejection of leadership but the hypothesis that whereas the moral imperative is eternal, the concrete social and economic program which is needed will somehow emerge out of a grassroots movement. By recapturing their moral selves through disinvolvement from and confrontation with the present establishment, people will spontaneously produce the socialist society of love and reason.

In its community work the New Left does try to establish a link with political reality. But the earlier intellectuals in a different way tried to do the same. Moreover, though the democracy of the new differs from the elitism of the old, both work within a common tradition. The ideals of this New Left we have discussed seem to have run dry by the late 1960s.

There are signs of a return to a more traditional Marxism. Concern for economic and social change is no longer so sharply separated from the necessity of leadership and revolutionary tactics. The scene is constantly changing, and any analysis of the movement is likely to be out of date as soon as it is made. However, the parallelism we have pointed out does hold for the mid-sixties, though the attitudes of this New Left as we have seen them continue to provide one constant theme in the often dissonant symphony of protest. It should be clear that we have drawn a parallel with the European experience which does not depend upon direct influence. However, this is not to deny the significance of the common tradition which provided a single framework for their thought, though other factors (both American and deriving from anarchist traditions) also entered into the making of this New Left.

The search for a "third way" between orthodox Marxism and the established order is common to all these groups, and the basis on which this search is conducted relates, however unconsciously, to the neo-Kantian impetus and to the hopes which Frank exemplified in the title of his novel *Man Is Good*. Perhaps Carlo Rosselli best expressed what distinguishes the left-wing intellectuals from the Marxist tradition. Though he wrote for Italian intellectuals in the early thirties, what he had to say holds good for all the intellectuals we have discussed. "Strongly idealist, voluntarist, and pragmatic, the new generation no longer understands the materialist, positivist, scientific vocabulary of the old socialists."[139]

For Rosselli also, voluntarism must inform all revolutionary activity, and this will succeed if one comes to the masses with the "truth," that is, with ideas strongly held. Once more, the scope of this discussion can be broadened beyond Germany and the New Left. It was Rosselli who again best summed up the vision of all left-wing intellectuals when he wrote that the spiritual essence of liberalism can only be preserved in a socialist society. By liberalism he meant freedom of action and thought informed by the categorical imperative. Because of the inherent dignity of humanity, democracy must be preserved at all times in the struggle against existing conditions.[140] Moreover, we confront here still another parallel which deserves mention. Rosselli was a Jew, as were many of the German intelligentsia, and as were a disproportionate number of the new American left as well. Here the factors which we have discussed and which grew out of the persistence of the ideals of the Enlightenment and the problems of assimilation seem still to hold, modified, however, by the peculiarities of the American cultural context.

Clearly, the parallels we have tried to illuminate must await a thoroughgoing history of left-wing intellectuals in all Western civilization before they can be stated with certainty. Yet it is not infringing the boundaries set by historical reality to point to such parallels, in the belief that there exists a dimension to this left-wing tradition which shows sufficient coherence to constitute a meaningful part of our modern intellectual and political life. The important search for a new society continues despite past failures and the hitherto insoluble dilemmas that are intrinsic in this attitude to humanity, the world, and society.

Notes

A Critical Introduction by Sarah Wobick-Segev

1. George L. Mosse, *The Crisis of German Ideology: Intellectual Origins of the Third Reich* (Madison: University of Wisconsin Press, 2021).

2. Shulamit Volkov, "Antisemitism as a Cultural Code: Reflections on the History and Historiography of Antisemitism in Imperial Germany," *Leo Baeck Institute Year Book* 23, no. 1 (January 1978): 25–46, 34, https://doi.org/10.1093/leobaeck/23.1.25

3. Steven E. Aschheim, "German History and German Jewry: Boundaries, Junctions and Interdependence," *Leo Baeck Institute Year Book* 43, no. 1 (January 1998): 315–322.

4. Max Horkheimer and Theodor W. Adorno, *Dialectic of Enlightenment: Philosophical Fragments*, ed. Gunzelin Schmid Noerr, trans. Edmund Jephcott (Stanford: Stanford University Press, 2002).

5. Philipp Stelzel, *History after Hitler: A Transatlantic Enterprise* (Philadelphia: University of Pennsylvania Press, 2019), 3, 6. Stelzel writes that for Ritter, National Socialism "had been a decisive break with all German traditions, and not an integral part—let alone the logical culmination—of modern German history." Additionally, Ritter saw Nazism as "an Austrian-Bavarian import." See also Anna Corsten, "'Unerbetene Erinnerer'? Emigrationshistoriker in den USA als Impulsgeber für die Aufarbeitung von Nationalsozialismus und Holocaust in der Bundesrepublik," in *Forschung zwischen Freiheit und Verantwortung: Die wissenschaftshistorische Perspektive*, ed. Dominik Groß and Julia Nebe (Kassel: Kassel University Press, 2018), 199–231; Gerhard Ritter, *Geschichte als Bildungsmacht: Ein Beitrag zur historisch-politischen Neubesinnung* (Stuttgart: Deutsche Verlags-Anstalt, 1946).

6. Steven E. Aschheim, "The Tensions of Historical *Wissenschaft*: The Émigré Historians and the Making of German Cultural History," in *The Second Generation: Émigrés from Nazi Germany as Historians*, ed. Andreas W. Daum, Hartmut Lehmann, and James J. Sheehan (New York: Berghahn Books, 2016), 177–196, 178.

7. At the time, Rabbi Leo Baeck expressed profound disappointment that Meinecke's book failed to acknowledge the complicity of German academics or churches and made no reference to the deeper roots of German antisemitism. Michael A. Meyer, *Rabbi Leo Baeck: Living a Religious Imperative in Troubled Times* (Philadelphia: University of Pennsylvania Press, 2021), 169. Meyer notes how Rabbi Baeck was disappointed by the fact that "leading German intellectuals failed to condemn [the destruction of the Jews] outright," and how they refrained from placing blame on ideas that had long held sway in Germany.

8. Aschheim, "Tensions of Historical *Wissenschaft*," 182; Stelzel, *History after Hitler*, 79–80.

9. On the attitudes of German historians to the historical approaches and those of émigré historians, see Stelzel, *History after Hitler*, 1, 43, 69. For his part, Aschheim has suggested that "divergent experiential, situational, and identificatory factors played an important role in the genesis, nature, and emphases of their work." Aschheim, "The Tensions of Historical *Wissenschaft*," 180.

10. Stanley Payne notes that Mosse's works have enjoyed their greatest popularity, however, in Italy. Stanley G. Payne, "George L. Mosse and Walter Laqueur on the History of Fascism," *Journal of Contemporary History* 50, no. 4 (2015): 750–767, 758; Philipp Stelzel, "The Second-Generation Émigrés' Impact on German Historiography," in *The Second Generation: Émigrés from Nazi Germany as Historians*, 287–303, 295. Stelzel notes that in the US, Mosse's works were considered "must-reads." On the reception of George L. Mosse's works in Italy, see, for example, Lorenzo Benadusi and Giorgio Caravale, eds., *George L. Mosse's Italy: Interpretation, Reception, and Intellectual Heritage* (London: Palgrave Macmillan, 2014); Emilio Gentile, *Fascination with the Persecutor: George L. Mosse and the Catastrophe of Modern Man* (Madison: University of Wisconsin Press, 2021). The recently published special issue of the *Journal of Contemporary History* on George L. Mosse highlights both Mosse's continued legacy as well as his reception in Italy: "George L. Mosse, Nationalism, and the Crisis of Liberal Democracies," ed. Skye Doney, Laura Ciglioni, and Donatello Aramini, special issue, *Journal of Contemporary History* 56, no. 4 (October 2021).

11. Stelzel, *History after Hitler*, 70

12. Payne, "George L. Mosse and Walter Laqueur," 752–754.

13. Stelzel, "The Second-Generation Émigrés' Impact," 295.

14. Karel Plessini, *The Perils of Normalcy: George L. Mosse and the Remaking of Cultural History* (Madison: University of Wisconsin Press, 2014), 39.

15. This definition has Nietzschean roots, but I find more immediate inspiration in the writings of Judith Shklar on Hannah Arendt. Shklar uses the term to define a type of historical writing that encourages using the study of the past to understand the present and build a better future. Judith N. Shklar, "Rethinking the Past," in *Political Thought and Political Thinkers*, ed. Stanley Hoffman (Chicago: University of Chicago Press, 1998), 353–361.

16. John Hutchinson, "The Continuing Relevance of George L. Mosse to the Study of Nationalism," *Journal of Contemporary History* 56, no. 4 (October 2021): 878–895, 881.

17. Aschheim, "The Tensions of Historical *Wissenschaft*," 186.

18. See Payne, "George L. Mosse and Walter Laqueur," 754; Plessini, *The Perils of Normalcy*, 17; Fritz K. Ringer, "Mosse's Germans and Jews," *Journal of*

Modern History 44, no. 3 (1972): 392–397, 397; Hutchinson, "The Continuing Relevance of George L. Mosse to the Study of Nationalism."

19. Plessini, *The Perils of Normalcy*, 39.
20. Plessini, *The Perils of Normalcy*, 4.
21. Payne, "George L. Mosse and Walter Laqueur," 767.

Introduction

1. Friedrich Nietzsche, "Die fröhliche Wissenschaft," *Nietzsche's Werke*, part I, vol. 5 (Leipzig: C. G. Naumann, 1900), 41.
2. Franz Jung, *Der Weg nach unten* (Neuwied am Rhein: Hermann Luchterhand, 1961), 82.
3. Yvan Goll, "Expressionismus," in Paul Pörtner, *Literatur-Revolution 1910–1925: Dokumente. Manifeste. Programme*, vol. 2, *Zur Begriffs-bestimmung der Ismen* (Neuwied am Rhein: Hermann Luchterhand, 1961), 177.
4. Rudolf Leonhard, "Über Gruppenbildung in der Literatur," in Pörtner, *Literatur-Revolution 1910–1925*, 159–163, 162.
5. George Lichtheim, "The Concept of Ideology," *History and Theory* 4, no. 2 (1965): 165–195, 165, 166.
6. Johann Gottfried Herder and Johann Wolfgang von Goethe et al., *Von deutscher Art und Kunst* (Hamburg: Bode, 1773).
7. Justus Möser, "Deutsche Geschichte," in Herder and von Goethe et al., *Von deutscher Art und Kunst*, 163–182, 166ff.
8. Möser, "Deutsche Geschichte," 166, 172.
9. Herder and von Goethe et al., *Von deutscher Art und Kunst*, 84.
10. Philippe Ariés, *Centuries of Childhood: A Social History of Family Life* (New York: Knopf, 1962), 406.
11. Friedrich Ludwig Jahn, *Deutsches Volkstum* (Leipzig, 1810), 36, 197ff.
12. Thomas Nipperdey, "Nationalidee und Nationaldenkmal in Deutschland im 19. Jahrhundert," *Historische Zeitschrift* 206, no. 3 (June 1968): 529–558, 573–577; for the early history of festivals, see François-Alphonse Aulard, *Christianity and the French Revolution* (New York: Howard Fertig, 1966). Albert Soboul has stressed their religious content, though he does not see their importance as a part of modern mass movements: "Saintes Patriotes et Martyrs de la Liberté," in *Paysans, Sans-culottes et Jacobins* (Paris: Clavreuil, 1966), 183–202.
13. Oswald Spengler, *Der Untergang des Abendlandes: Umrisse einer Morphologie der Weltgeschichte*, book 1, *Gestalt und Wirklichkeit* (Munich: C.H. Beck, 1929), 52.
14. Quoted in Walter Laqueur, *Young Germany: A History of the German Youth Movement* (New York: Basic Books, 1962), 139.
15. Carl Gustav Jung, *Aufsätze zur Zeitgeschichte* (Zürich: Rascher, 1946), 18.
16. George L. Mosse, *The Crisis of German Ideology: Intellectual Origins of the Third Reich* (Madison: University of Wisconsin Press, 2021).
17. José Ortega y Gasset, *The Revolt of the Masses* (London: Unwin, 1969).
18. Friedrich Stampfer, *Erfahrungen und Erkenntnisse* (Cologne: Verlag für Politik und Wirtschaft, 1957), 158.
19. As, for example, in a review of Mosse: Elizabeth M. Wiskemann, "Origins of the Third Reich. Review of: George L. Mosse, The Crisis of German Ideology:

Intellectual Origins of the Third Reich," *Times Literary Supplement* 3355 (16 June 1966): 530.

20. George L. Mosse, "Introduction: The Genesis of Fascism," in "International Fascism 1920–1945," ed. Walter Laqueur and George L. Mosse, special issue, *Journal of Contemporary History* 1, no. 1 (January 1966): 14–27; George L. Mosse, "E. Nolte on 'Three Faces of Fascism,'" *Journal of the History of Ideas* 27, no. 4 (October–December 1966): 621–625.

21. See pages 112–113.

22. Robert Brasillach, *Notre avant-guerre* (Paris: Plon, 1941), contrasted with his *Le Marchand d'oiseaux* (Paris: Plon, 1936).

23. Robert Short, "The Politics of Surrealism, 1920–1936," in *The Left Wing Intellectuals between the Wars*, ed. Walter Laqueur and George L. Mosse (New York: Harper, 1966), 3–27.

24. Robert Brasillach, *Léon Degrelle* (Paris: Plon, 1936), 78.

25. See pages 125–126.

26. Hugh Seton-Watson, "Fascism, Right and Left," in "International Fascism 1920–1945," ed. Walter Laqueur and George L. Mosse, special issue, *Journal of Contemporary History* 1, no. 1 (January 1966): 183–197.

Chapter 1. Culture, Civilization, and German Antisemitism

1. Solomon F. Bloom, "The Peasant Caesar: Hitler's Union of German Imperialism and Eastern Reaction," *Commentary* 23 (May 1957): 406–418, 406.

2. Eleonore O. Sterling, "Anti-Jewish Riots in Germany in 1819: A Displacement of Social Protest," *Historia Judaica* 7 (October 1950): 105–142.

3. It must be understood that we are dealing here with only one trend of German thought and with only one image of the Jew. As background for the Jewish catastrophe in Germany, this image is more important than, for example, the favorable view of the Jew which emerges in Gotthold Ephraim Lessing's (1729–1781) *Nathan der Weise* (*Nathan the Wise*, 1779).

4. Oswald Spengler, *The Decline of the West*, trans. Carles Francis Atkinson, vol. 1 (New York: A. A. Knopf, 1926), 31, 44.

5. Spengler, *The Decline of the West*, 32.

6. György Lukács, *Fortschritt und Reaktion in der deutschen Literatur* (Berlin: Aufbau, 1947), 107.

7. Georg Gottfried Gervinius, *Einleitung in die Geschichte des neunzehnten Jahrhunderts* (Leipzig: Engelmann, 1853), 165–166.

8. Heinrich Spiero, "Wilhelm Raabe und Gustav Freytag," in *Raabestudien: Im Auftrag der Gesellschaft der Freunde Wilhelm Raabes*, ed. Constantin Bauer (Wolfenbüttel: Heckner, 1925), 140.

9. Tüdel Weller, *Rabauken! Peter Mönkemann haut sich durch* (Munich: F. Eher, 1938), 77.

10. *Die Judenfrage vor dem preussischen Landtag: Wortetreuer Abruck der Verhandlungen im Abgeordnetenhauss am 20. und 22. November, 1880* (Berlin: Central Buchhandlung, 1880), 51.

11. Christian Wilhelm Dohm, *Über die bürgerliche Verbesserung der Juden*, part II (Berlin and Stettin: Friedrich Nicolai, 1783), 152, 173, 174, 241. Arthur Hertzberg has recently attempted to demonstrate that for Voltaire all Jews were hopelessly and irretrievably alien. *The French Enlightenment and the Jews: The*

Origins of Modern Anti-Semitism (New York: Columbia University Press, 1968), 286ff. However this might be, it does not destroy the distinction between Jews and Judaism which many thinkers did extract from Enlightenment thought.

12. Joachim Heinrich Campe, *Wörterbuch der deutschen Sprache* (Braunschweig: Schulbuchhandlung, 1808, 1811), vol. 2, 852; vol. 5, 433.

13. Wanda Kampmann, *Deutsche und Juden* (Heidelberg: Schneider, 1963), 110 and 107ff. For an excellent discussion of the educational approach to Jewish emancipation, see J. P. Stern, *Lichtenberg: A Doctrine of Scattered Occasions; Reconstructed from His Aphorisms and Reflections* (Bloomington: Indiana University Press, 1969), 241.

14. Gustav Freytag, "Die Juden in Breslau," *Die Grenzboten*, 8 Jahrgang, II Semester, III Band (1849): 148.

15. Heinrich von Treitschke, *Deutsche Geschichte im neunzehnten Jahrhundert*, vol. 5 (Leipzig: S. Hirzel, 1895), 386–387.

16. *Die Judenfrage vor dem preussischen Landtag*, 68–72.

17. Dietrich Eckart, *Das ist der Jude!* (Munich: Hoheneichen-Verlag, ca. 1916), 55ff.

18. Wilhelm Stoffers, *Juden und Ghetto in der deutschen Literatur bis zum Ausgang des Weltkrieges* (Nymwegen: Wächter Verlag, 1939), 610, 613. Auguste Hauschner (1850–1924) was the daughter of a respected Jewish family from Prague. Max Brod has claimed that Hauschner was a skeptic, without illusions, who believed that small-mindedness dominated all human relationships: *Der Prager Kreis* (Stuttgart: W. Kohlhammer, 1966), 42ff.

19. Stoffers, *Juden und Ghetto in der deutschen Literatur*, 413ff., 473ff.

20. M/1 (3), Doc. 93 (National Jewish Archives, Jerusalem); Alfred Döblin, *Reise in Polen* (Berlin, 1926); Goethe quoted in Adolf Leschnitzer, *The Magic Background of Anti-Semitism: An Analysis of the German-Jewish Relationship* (New York: International Universities Press, 1956), 111.

21. Wilhelm Raabe, "Holunderblüthe," *Gesammelte Erzählungen*, vol. 1 (Berlin: Janke, 1896), 83.

22. Stoffers, *Juden und Ghetto in der deutschen Literatur*, 390; Pierre Sorlin, *"La Croix" et les Juifs (1880–1899): Contribution à l'histoire de l'anti-semitisme contemporain* (Paris: Bernard Grasset, 1967), 176, 208–209. The history of the world Jewish conspiracy has now received scholarly and authoritative analysis in Norman Cohn, *Warrant for Genocide: The Myth of the Jewish World Conspiracy and the Protocols of the Elders of Zion* (London: Eyre and Spottiswoode, 1967).

23. Eduard Rothfuchs, *Der selbstbiographische Gehalt in Gustav Freytags Werken (bis 1855): Ein Beitrag zur Frage der Wechselwirkungen von Erlebnis und Dichtung* (Münster: I.W. Helios Verlag GmbH, 1929), 61–62.

24. Weller, *Rabauken!*, preface; Eberhard Wolfgang Möller, *Das Schloß in Ungarn* (Berlin: Zeitgeschichte-Verlag, 1941), a book which went through seven editions between 1941 and 1943.

25. Horst Seeman, "Das Ostjudenthum-Reservoir des Weltjudenthums," *Die Judenfrage*, 1 July 1943, 214.

26. Pieter Coll (Hans-Walter Gaebert), *Die Menschenfracht der "Ano Wati" Kriminalroman* (Berlin: Osmer, 1939).

27. Hans Hauptmann, *Memoiren des Satans die Menschheitstragödie im 19. u. 20. Jahrhundert; ein satirischer Roman* (Munich: Dt. Volksverlag, 1929).

28. Fritz Halbach, *Genosse Levi, ein Roman für das deutsche Volk* (Leipzig: Weicher, 1921).

29. Nathanael Jünger, *Volk in Gefahr! Deutschvölkischer Roman* (Wismar: Hinstorffsche Verlagsbuchhandlung, 1921).

30. Nathanael Jünger, *Hof Böckels Ende* (1910); *Pastor Ritgerodts Welt, ein Roman aus der Heide* (1910); *J. C. Rathman & Sohn* (1914); *Die lieben Vettern* (1916), the dedication of which Admiral Alfred Peter Friedrich von Tirpitz (1849–1930) accepted.

31. Nathanael Jünger, *Volk in Gefahr!*, 352–353.

32. Fritz Claus, *Der Wucherer, tragikomisches Lustspiel in 5 Aufzügen* (1890), no. 57 in the series *Neues kleines Theater* (Familien und Vereinstheater), Paderborn; Wilhelm von Polenz, *Der Büttnerbauer* (Berlin: Fontane, 1895).

33. Weller, *Rabauken!*, 114.

34. Franz Mehring, *Beiträge zur Literaturgeschichte* (Berlin: Weiss, 1948), 210.

35. Raabe, "Der Hungerpastor," in *Sämtliche Werke*, vol. 1 (Berlin: Klemm, n.d.), 312.

36. Max Nietzki, *Heinrich Heine als Dichter und Mensch* (Berlin: Mitscher & Röstell, 1895), 134.

37. Wolfgang Menzel, *Deutsche Dichtung*, vol. 3 (Stuttgart: Adolph Krabbe, 1859), 465–466.

38. Nietzki, *Heinrich Heine*, 34.

39. Menzel, *Deutsche Dichtung*, 466.

40. Treitschke, *Deutsche Geschichte im neunzehnten Jahrhundert*, vol. 4, 434.

41. Karl Beyer, *Jüdischer Intellekt und deutscher Glaube* (Leipzig: Armanen-Verlag, 1933), 9ff.

42. Beyer, *Jüdischer Intellekt und deutscher Glaube*, 12, 17.

43. Adolf Bartels, *Die Berechtigung des Antisemitismus: Eine Widerlegung d. Schrift v. Oppeln-Bronikowski "Antisemitismus?"* (Leipzig: Weicher, 1920), 50.

44. Kurt Fervers, *Berliner Salons: Die Geschichte einer großen Verschwörung* (Munich: Deutscher Volksverlag, 1940), 19.

45. Heinz Bender, *Der Kampf um die Judenemanzipation in Deutschland im Spiegel der Flugschriften, 1815–1820* (Jena: Biedermann, 1939), 69.

46. Carl Wilhelm Friedrich Grattenauer, *Erster Nachtrag zu seiner Schrift "Wider die Juden"* (Berlin: Joh. Wilh. Schmidt, 1803), 24.

47. Stoffers, *Juden und Ghetto in der deutschen Literatur*, vol. 2, 2; Eduard Fuchs, *Die Juden in der Karikatur* (Munich: Langen Univ. Bibliothek, 1921), 219.

48. Edith Gräfin Salburg, *Erinnerungen einer Respektlosen* (Leipzig: Hammer, 1927), 133, 138.

49. Carl Hauptmann, *Ismael Friedmann* (Leipzig: E. Rowohlt, 1913), 43.

50. Artur Dinter, *Die Sünde gegen das Blut* (Leipzig, 1918).

51. Weller, *Rabauken!*, 91, 114, 196.

52. *Der Stürmer* 38, no. 12 (September 1934).

53. Werner Jansen, *Die Kinder Israel: Rasseroman* (Braunschweig: G. Westermann, 1927).

54. *Der Stürmer* 6, no. 4 (April 1928).

55. See page 53.
56. Jacob Burckhardt, *The Letters of Jacob Burckhardt*, ed. Alexander Dru (London: Routledge & Paul, 1955), 170.
57. Burckhardt, *The Letters of Jacob Burckhardt*, 225.
58. Burckhardt, *The Letters of Jacob Burckhardt*, 117.
59. Burckhardt, *The Letters of Jacob Burckhardt*, 147, 148.
60. Burckhardt, *The Letters of Jacob Burckhardt*, 153, 199.
61. Burckhardt, *The Letters of Jacob Burckhardt*, 169.
62. Burckhardt, *The Letters of Jacob Burckhardt*, 147.
63. Quoted in Karl Löwith, *Jacob Burckhardt* (Stuttgart: W. Kohlhammer, 1966), 196.
64. Joachim Heinrich Campe, *Wörterbuch der deutschen Sprache*, vol. 2, 851.
65. Hans Liebeschütz, *Das Judentum im deutschen Geschichtsbild von Hegel bis Max Weber* (Tübingen: J.C.B. Mohr, 1967), 220–244, esp. 237.

Chapter 2. The Image of the Jew in German Popular Literature

1. Alan Bullock, *Hitler: A Study in Tyranny* (New York: Harper & Brothers, 1962), 434.
2. "Beyond Good and Evil," in *The Philosophy of Nietzsche*, by Friedrich Nietzsche, ed. Geoffrey Clive (New York: Meridian, 1965), 184.
3. Hannah Arendt, *The Origins of Totalitarianism* (New York: Harcourt, 1951), 28.
4. Adolf Hitler, *Mein Kampf* (New York: Reynal & Hitchcock, 1939), 66.
5. William O. Aydelotte, "The England of Marx and Mills as Reflected in Fiction," in *The Making of English History*, ed. Robert L. Schuyler and Herman Ausuble (New York: Dryden Press, 1952): 511–521, 512.
6. Felix Dahn, *Ein Kampf um Rom* (Leipzig: Breitkopf und Härtel, 1904), vol. 1, 276–277; vol. 2, 40ff.
7. Léon Poliakov, *Du Christ aux Juifs de Cour* (Paris: Calmann-Lévy, 1955), 153.
8. Cited in Isaac Eisenstein Barzilay, "The Jew in the Literature of the Enlightenment," *Jewish Social Studies* 18, no. 4 (October 1956): 243–261, 257. An examination of pictorial representations of Jews might serve to underline this point. I think that it could be proven that medieval representations of Jews do not show any of the physical characteristics which were attributed to Jews in modern times, except for caricature.
9. Walter Muschg, "Josef Nadlers Literaturgeschichte," in *Die Zerstörung der deutschen Literatur* (Bern: Francke, 1956), 133–152, 151.
10. Gerhard Loose, "The Peasant in Wilhelm Heinrich Riehl's Sociological and Novelistic Writings," *Germanic Review* 15 (1940): 263–272.
11. Julius Eckardt, *Lebenserinnerungen*, vol. 1 (Leipzig: Hirzel, 1910), 48, 67.
12. Gustav Freytag, *Soll und Haben* (Munich: Droemer, 1953), 16.
13. Bernhard Seuffert, "Beobachtungen über dichterische Komposition," *Germanisch-Romanische Monatsschrift* (1909): 599–617, 604.
14. Friedrich Seiler, *Gustav Freytag: Ein Lebensbild* (Leipzig: Voigtländer, 1898), 113.
15. Friedrich Kreyssig, *Vorlesungen über den deutschen Roman der Gegenwart* (Berlin: Nicolai, 1871), 82, 83. Dahn also praised *Debit and Credit*, which

he reviewed, for its emphasis on a "settled" middle class, and remarked that the novel contained reality and not caricature! Felix Dahn, *Bausteine* (Berlin: Janke, 1882), 13.

16. Walter Bussmann, "Gustav Freytag: Masstäbe seiner Zeitkritik," *Archiv für Kulturgeschichte* 34 (1952): 261–287, 261.

17. Gustav Freytag, "Die Juden in Breslau," *Die Grenzboten*, 8 Jahrg., II Semester, III Band (1849): 148.

18. *Der Streit über das Judentum in der Musik, Aufsätze zur Geschichte, Literatur und Kunst* (Leipzig, 1888), 321ff.

19. Gustav Freytag, *Erinnerungen aus meinem Leben* (Leipzig: Hirzel, 1887), 266.

20. *Mitteilungen des Vereins zur Abwehr des Antisemitismus* 2, no. 52 (25 December 1892): 434; Herbert Oskar Meyer, *Felix Dahn* (Leipzig: Breitkopf & Härtel, 1913), 31.

21. Barzilay, "The Jew in the Literature of the Enlightenment," 245, 246.

22. *Augsburger Allgemeine Zeitung*, 22 October 1871, 1.

23. Eckardt, *Lebenserinnerungen*, 203, 257.

24. See the remark by Felix Goldmann that it is interesting to note how Jews defend a Germanic writer like Freytag in spite of the fact that in *Debit and Credit* he was unkind toward Jews. Felix Goldmann, *Der Jude im deutschen Kulturkreise: Ein Beitrag zum Wesen des Nationalismus* (Berlin: Philo, 1930), 83. Oscar Meyer, a leading liberal during the Weimar Republic, tells us that in the last years of the nineteenth century, literature was produced under the impetus of the Enlightenment and National Liberalism. He not only equates these two very different movements but also lists as "good" writers Heyse, Spielhagen, and Freytag. Freytag is considered "Enlightened" and is classed with writers who could really make a claim to "Enlightenment," and this by a leading democrat. Oscar Meyer, *Von Bismarck zu Hitler* (New York: F. Krause, 1944), 20. Not only liberals like Meyer but even Michael Wolff, one of Marx's most trusted adherents, had Freytag's *Soll und Haben* in his small library. Michael Wolff, *Karl Marx and Friedrich Engels, Briefwechsel*, vol. 3 (Berlin: Dietz, 1950), 247.

25. Freytag, "Die Juden in Breslau," 149.

26. For socialism, see George Lichtheim, "Socialism and the Jews," *Dissent*, July–August 1968, 314–342.

Chapter 3. The Influence of the Völkisch Idea on German Jewry

1. Robert Weltsch, "Deutscher Zionismus in der Rückschau," in *In Zwei Welten; Siegfried Moses zum fünfundsiebzigsten Geburtstag* (Tel Aviv: Bitaon, 1962), 30.

2. Siegfried Bernfeld, "Zionismus und Judenkultur," *Der Neue Weg* 2, no. 2 (February 1915).

3. Frank Fischer, *Wandern und Schauen, Gesammelte Aufsätze* (Hartenstein, I.S.: Greifenverlag, 1921), 54.

4. Siegfried Copalle, "Nach grüner Farb' mein Herz verlangt" (typed manuscript, Archiv der Jugendbewegung, Burg Ludwigstein), 77.

5. Hans Breuer, "Herbstschau 1913," *Wandervögel* 8, no 10 (October 1913): 283.

6. See chapter 5.

7. Jacob Toury, *Die politischen Orientierungen der Juden in Deutschland von Jena bis Weimar* (Tübingen: Mohr, 1966), 281.

8. Verein Jüdischer Hochschüler Bar Kochba, *Vom Judentum* (Leipzig: K. Wolff, 1913), 103, vi.

9. Robert Weltsch, "Über das Wesen des jüdischen Nationalismus," *Jüdische Monatshefte für Turnen und Sport* 14, no. 6 (August–September 1913): 177.

10. Max Brod, *Streitbares Leben* (Munich: Kindler Verlag, 1960), 77.

11. Moses Calvary, "Blau-Weiss" (1916), reprinted in *Das Neue Judentum* (Berlin: Schocken Verlag, 1936), 81.

12. Verein Jüdischer Hochschüler Bar Kochba, *Vom Judentum*, 107.

13. Weltsch, "Deutscher Zionismus in der Rückschau," 30; Weltsch, "Über das Wesen des jüdischen Nationalismus," 176.

14. *Jüdische Turnerzeitung* 11, no. 516 (May–June 1910): 75. For the meaning of the ghetto, see Wilhelm Stoffers, *Juden und Ghetto in der deutschen Literatur zum Ausgang des Weltkrieges* (Nymwegen: Wächter-Verlag, 1939). See also the reactions in *Die Weißen Blätter* 2, no. 2 (November 1915): 1408, 1410.

15. Martin Buber, "Über Jacob Böhme," *Wiener Rundschau* 12 (15 June 1901): 251–253.

16. Martin Buber, *Reden über das Judentum* (Berlin: Schocken, 1932), 139; Martin Buber, "Ein Wort über Nietzsche und die Lebenswerte," *Die Kunst im Leben*, December 1900, 13; for one of the best discussions of Buber's thought, see Gershom Scholem, "Martin Buber's Auffassung des Judentums," *Eranos Jahrbuch* 35 (1966): 9–55.

17. Lulu von Strauss and Torney-Diederichs, eds., *Eugen Diederichs Leben und Werke; ausgewählte Briefe und Aufzeichnungen* (Jena: Eugen Diederichs Verlag, 1936), 52.

18. Buber, *Reden über das Judentum*, 133, 136; see also his letter to Dr. Van Eeden (n.d., 1914?) concerning the "Forte Kreis" (Buber Archives, Jerusalem, Mappe 46, Rubrik 7); Martin Buber, "Tempelweihe" (handwritten manuscript of speech given 19 December 1914, 12; Buber Archives, Jerusalem, Mappe 2, Rubrik 7).

19. Robert Weltsch, "1813," *Jüdische Monatshefte für Turnen und Sport* 14, no. 2 (May 1913): 49.

20. "Der Judenstaat," *Ahasver*, no. 1 (1906): 19 (Siegfried Bernfeld Collection, Hoover Institute and Library).

21. Gustav Landauer, "Martin Buber" (1913), reprinted in *Der werdende Mensch* (Potsdam: Kiepenheuer, 1921), 245, 251; Gustav Landauer, *Skepsis und Mystik* (Berlin: Fontane, 1903), 15, 17, 21, 28, 38; Paul Breines, "The Jew as Revolutionary: The Case of Gustav Landauer," *Leo Baeck Institute Year Book* 12 (1967): 75–85.

22. Gustav Landauer, "Sind das Ketzergedanken," in Verein Jüdischer Hochschüler Bar Kochba, *Vom Judentum*, reprinted in *Der werdende Mensch* (Potsdam: Kiepenheuer, 1921), 123.

23. Robert Weltsch, "Zu jüdischen Festen" (1920), in Hans Kohn and Robert Weltsch, *Zionistische Politik* (Mährisch-Ostrau: Färber, 1927), 134; Martin Buber, "Drei Stationen," in *Kampf um Israel* (Berlin: Schocken, 1933), 223, 224.

24. Robert Weltsch, "Unser Nationalismus," in Kohn and Weltsch, *Zionistische Politik*, 145.

25. Felix Weltsch, *Judenfrage und Zionismus, eine Disputation* (London: World Zionist Organization, 1929), 36, 42, 44.

26. Kurt Blumenfeld, *Erlebte Judenfrage: Ein Vierteljahrhundert deutscher Zionismus* (Stuttgart: Deutsche Vlgs-Anstalt, 1962), 43; Karl Glaser, "Tagebuch für die Jüdische Jugend," *Blau-Weiss Blätter* 4, no. 4 (December 1916): 108–110, 109; Gottfried Fraenkel, "Die Form des Gautages," *Blau-Weiss Blätter*, n.s. 1, no. 4 (July 1924): 145.

27. Gustav Landauer, "Sind das Ketzergedanken," in Verein Jüdischer Hochschüler Bar Kochba, *Vom Judentum*, 201, 209.

28. Weltsch, "Deutscher Zionismus in der Rückschau," 30.

29. See the letters from the front in *Haschachar* (Jugendgruppe Hasmonaea, Bielitz), no. 14 (July–August 1917): 5–8 (Siegfried Bernfeld Collection, Hoover Institute and Library).

30. Willi Warstat, "Der Geist des Pfadfinders und Wandervogels," *Der Säemann*, no. 12 (1914): 431–432.

31. Calvary, "Blau-Weiss," 85; Moses Calvary to Martin Buber (1 December 1916) (Buber Archives, Jerusalem, Mappe 151, Doc. 151a).

32. Jaakow Simon, "Umrisse unseres Menschenbildes," *Binjan*, March 1935, 36, 37.

33. Adelbert Sahs, "Blau-Weiss und seine Gegener," *Jüdische Rundschau* 25, no. 21 (21 May 1914): 220.

34. Hans Goslar, "Jugendtags-Referate: Ein offener Brief an Walter Moses," *Jüdische Rundschau* 23, no. 41 (11 October 1918): 318–320, 320.

35. Landauer, "Sind das Ketzergedanken," 108.

36. Joseph Marcus, ed., *Tagebuch für die jüdische Jugend* (Vienna: R. Löwit, 1916), 184–185. For more detail on the Bund in general and the völkisch movement, see George L. Mosse, *The Crisis of German Ideology: Intellectual Origins of the Third Reich* (Madison: University of Wisconsin Press, 2021), 206–219.

37. Glaser, "Tagebuch für Jüdische Jugend," 109; Heinz Kellermann, "Die Glaubensituation der jüdischen Jugend," in *Gemeinschaftsarbeit der jüdischen Jugend, 1933–1936* (Berlin, 1937), 34.

38. Kameraden Deutsch-Jüdischer Wanderbund, *Bundesblatt*, 1924.

39. Hans Tramer, "Blau-Weiss–Wegbereiter für Zion," in *Die Jugendbewegung*, ed. Elisabeth Korn (Düsseldorf: Diederichs, 1963), 213.

40. Glaser, "Tagebuch für Jüdische Jugend," 109.

41. Moses Calvary, "Geleitwort," *Der jüdische Wille* 1 (April 1918–April 1919): 215.

42. Fabius Schach, "Volk und Führer," *Der Schild* 8, no. 16 (19 April 1929): 129, 130.

43. Leo Löwenstein, "Führung!," *Der Schild* 12, no. 12 (22 June 1933): 87.

44. "Die Kraft" Beilage, *Der Schild* 13, no. 15 (20 April 1934).

45. Anon. conversation with a former Jewish Bund leader, 29 October 1961.

46. Paul Jogi Mayer, "Schwarzes Fähnlein," "Die Kraft" Beilage, *Der Schild* 13, no. 13 (13 April 1934).

47. On Köbel, see Walter Laqueur, *Young Germany* (New York: Basic Books, 1962), chapter 17, "Tusk or the Triumph of Eccentricity."

48. Franz Guttman, in *Der Schild* 8, no. 18 (3 May 1929): 149.

49. Reichsbund jüdischer Frontsoldaten E.V., "Auswanderungs-Vorträge im Sportbund Schild!," *Der Schild* 17, no. 13 (1 April 1938): 1–2, 1.

50. Reichsbund jüdischer Frontsoldaten E.V., "Der Tag der Leichtathletik," *Der Schild* 15, no. 28 (10 July 1936): 5–6; Reichsbund jüdischer Frontsoldaten E.V., "Jüdische Nachkriegskämpfer," *Der Schild* 15, no. 52 (25 December 1936): 1–2, 1. Also for Free Corps, see *Der Schild* 12, no. 15 (15 August 1933): 126, 127.

51. *Der Schild* 12, no. 20 (27 October 1933): 1; *Bulletin* (L'Union Patriotique des Français Israélites) 2, no. 4 (December 1936): 1–7 (Archive de L'Alliance Israélite Universelle, Paris). For German veteran groups in general, see George L. Mosse, *Crisis of German Ideology: Intellectual Origins of the Third Reich* (Madison: University of Wisconsin Press, 2021), chapter 14, "Veterans and Workers."

52. "Die Kraft" Beilage, *Der Schild* 13, no. 1 (12 January 1934).

53. Hugo Hahn, "Der Vortrupp," *Der Morgen* 9, no. 6 (December 1933): 386, 387. Schoeps accepted Hahn's interpretation of the Bund. "Brief an Herbert Löwe" (15 January 1934) (Buber Archives, Jerusalem, Mappe 706, Rubrik 8, Doc. 7a). For Schoeps's own description of the Vortrupp, see "Die Kraft" Beilage, *Der Schild* 18, no. 13 (13 April 1934).

54. Hans-Joachim Schoeps, *Die letzten dreissig Jahre* (Stuttgart: Ernst Klett Verlag, 1956), 48. Nevertheless, their personal relations remained friendly (see Buber Archives, Jerusalem, Mappe 706, Rubrik 8, Docs. 7–16).

55. Schoeps, *Die letzten dreissig Jahre*, 74, 75, 206, 207.

56. Hans-Joachim Schoeps, "Zweimal Martin Buber," *Der Schild* 13, no. 25 (6 July 1934): 4.

57. Hans-Joachim Schoeps, "Die Kraft" Beilage, "Gleiches Los—ungleiche Losung," *Der Schild* 13, no. 13 (13 April 1934): 4–5.

58. *Die Körperliche Renaissance der Juden* (Berlin, 1909), 2.

59. Carl Bösch, "Vom Deutschen-Mannesideal," *Der Vortrupp* 2, no. 1 (1 January 1913): 4. This is not to be confused with Schoeps's Bund.

60. Bernfeld, "Zionismus und Judenkultur," 10–11.

61. Max Naumann, *Vom nationaldeutschen Juden* (Berlin: A. Goldschmidt, 1920), 4, 6–10.

62. Naumann, *Vom nationaldeutschen Juden*, 21.

63. Max Naumann, "Die Miesmacherfrager," *Der Nationaldeutsche Jude*, May 1933, 2.

64. Robert Musil, *Der Mann ohne Eigenschaften* (Hamburg: Rowohlt, 1952), 150.

65. Toury, *Die politischen Orientierungen der Juden in Deutschland*.

Chapter 4. The Corporate State and the Conservative Revolution in Weimar Germany

1. Carl Schmitt, *Die geistesgeschichtliche Lage des heutigen Parlamentarismus* (Munich, 1926), 10ff.

2. Oswald Spengler, *Neubau des Deutschen Reiches* (Munich: C.H. Beck, 1932), 11.

3. Arnim Mohler, *Die konservative Revolution in Deutschland* (Stuttgart: Friedrich Vorwerk, 1950). See also Klemens von Klemperer, *Germany's New Conservatism* (Princeton, NJ: Princeton University Press, 1957).

4. Otto-Ernst Schüddekopf, *Linke Leute von Rechts: Die nationalrevolutionären Minderheiten und der Kommunismus in der Weimarer Republik* (Stuttgart: W. Kohlhammer Verlag, 1960), 85.

5. Arthur Moeller van den Bruck, *Das dritte Reich* (Hamburg: Hanseatische Verlagsanstalt, 1931), 5.

6. Schüddekopf, *Linke Leute von Rechts*, 84.

7. Moeller van den Bruck, *Das dritte Reich*, 237.

8. Joachim H. Knoll, "Der Autoritäre Staat: Konservative Ideologie und Staatstheorie am Ende der Weimarer Republik," in *Lebendier Geist: Hans-Joachim Schoeps zum 50. Geburtstag von Schülern Dargebracht*, ed. Hellmut Diwald (Leiden: E. J. Brill, 1959), 200–224, 216.

9. "Rechtsradikale Welle," *C. V. (CentralVereins-) Zeitung* 9, no. 10 (January 1930): 14.

10. Moeller van den Bruck, *Das dritte Reich*, 5.

11. Moeller van den Bruck, *Das dritte Reich*, 18; Hans-Joachim Schwierskott, *Arthur Moeller van den Bruck* (Göttingen: Musterschmidt-Verlag, 1962), 33.

12. Gerhard Günther quoted in Kurt Sontheimer, "Antidemokratisches Denken in der Weimarer Republik," *Vierteljahrshefte für Zeitgeschichte* 5, no. 5 (1959): 56.

13. Moeller van den Bruck, *Das dritte Reich*, 82.

14. George L. Mosse, "The Mystical Origins of National Socialism," *Journal of the History of Ideas* 22, no. 1 (January–March 1961): 83–96.

15. Friedrich Baerwald, *Das Erlebnis des Staates in der deutschen Jugendbewegung* (Berlin: Deutsche Verlagsgesellschaft für Politik und Geschichte, 1921), 25.

16. Günther Ipsen, "Jugend als Altersklasse und Generation," *Deutsche Freischar*, no. 5 (1929): 2–5, 5.

17. Hermann Siefert, "Politische Vorstellungen und Versuche der Deutschen Freischar," in Diwald, *Lebendiger Geist*, 180.

18. Ipsen, "Jugend als Altersklasse und Generation," 5.

19. Karl Seidelmann, *Bund und Gruppe als Lebensform deutscher Jugend: Versuch einer Erscheinungskunde des deutschen Jugendlebens in der ersten Hälfte des xx. Jahrhunderts* (Munich: Wiking Verlag, 1959), 303.

20. Siegfried Copalle, "Nach grüner Farb' mein Herz verlangt" (typed manuscript, Archiv der Jugendbewegung, Burg Ludwigstein), 73.

21. Seidelmann, *Bund und Gruppe als Lebensform deutscher Jugend*, 304.

22. Felix Raabe, *Die bündische Jugend: Ein Beitrag zur Geschichte der Weimarer Republik* (Stuttgart: Brentanoverlag, 1961), 125.

23. Martin Voelkel, "Heil unserm Bunde," in *Der Naumburger Bund 1920–1925*, Der Weiße Ritter 5 (Potsdam: Der Weiße Ritter-Verlag, 1925), 3–4, 3.

24. Voelkel, "Der Bund," in *Der Naumburger Bund 1920–1925*, Der Weiße Ritter 5 (Potsdam: Der Weiße Ritter-Verlag, 1925), 35–40, 38.

25. Raabe, *Die bündische Jugend*, 122.

26. Ernst Buske, quoted in Raabe, *Die bündische Jugend*, 133. See also Otto Michel, "Die Republik," *Freideutsche Jugend* 7, no. 2 (February 1921): 56.

27. Ipsen, "Jugend als Altersklasse und Generation," 5; Voelkel, "Der Bund," 38.

28. Klaus Hornung, *Der Jungdeutsche Orden* (Düsseldorf: Droste Verlag, 1958), 78–79.

29. Hornung, *Der Jungdeutsche Orden*, 84.

30. Albert Krebs, "Partei und Gewerkschaft," *Nationalsozialistische Briefe* 4, no. 10 (15 November 1928): 149–152, 149.

31. Friedrich Hielscher, *Fünfzig Jahre unter Deutschen* (Hamburg: Rowohlt, 1954), 37.

32. Ernst Michael Jovy, "Deutsche Jugendbewegung und National-sozialismus" (inaugural dissertation, Cologne, 1952), 210.

33. *Bremer Nationalsozialistische Zeitung* 1, no. 3 (17 January 1931): n.p.

34. Hermann Berlak, "Burschenschaftliche Erziehungsarbeit," *K. C. Mitteilungen*, no. 8 (25 July 1928): 69–70. Not surprisingly, the corps and fraternities at the universities were foremost in this thought.

35. Edmond Vermeil, *Doctrinaires de la révolution allemande, 1918–1938* (Paris: Nouvelles éditions latines, 1948), 169–170.

36. Carl Schmitt, *Staat, Bewegung, Volk: Die Dreigliederung der politischen Einheit* (Hamburg: Hanseatische Verlagsanstalt, 1934), passim.

37. Hielscher, *Fünfzig Jahre unter Deutschen*, 52–53; August Winnig, *Der weite Weg* (Hamburg: Wittig, 1932), 228.

38. Winnig, *Der weite Weg*, 392.

39. Quoted in Hielscher, *Fünfzig Jahre unter Deutschen*, 56.

40. Paul Bang, "Sozialpolitik," *Unsere Partei* 10, no. 13 (1 July 1932): 171. This is the official attitude of the Deutschnationale Volkspartei, except that corporate ideals never became predominant in a party that took part in the politics and government of the Weimar Parliamentary Republic.

41. Paul Krannhals, *Das Organische Weltbild*, vol. 1 (Munich: Bruckmann, 1936), 31. First published in 1928, the two-volume work went through two editions between 1934 and 1936 in a cheap *Volksausgabe*.

42. Krannhals, *Das Organische Weltbild*, 238.

43. Krannhals, *Das Organische Weltbild*, 245.

44. Krannhals, *Das Organische Weltbild*, 250.

45. Schüddekopf, *Linke Leute von Rechts*, 324.

46. Schüddekopf, *Linke Leute von Rechts*, 234.

47. Karl O. Paetel, "Otto Strasser und die 'Schwarze Front' des wahren Nationalsozialismus," *Politische Studien* 8, no. 92 (December 1957): 274.

48. "14 Thesen der Deutschen Revolution," in Felix Salomon, *Wilhelm Mommsen and Günther Franz, Die deutschen Parteiprogramme* (Leipzig: B.G. Teubner, 1931), 117–118.

49. Otto Strasser, *Aufbau des deutschen Sozialismus* (Prague: Heinrich Grunov, 1936), 70–73. There were two very different editions of this work. But the corporate ideas were the same.

50. *Osnabrücker Allgemeine Zeitung*, 26 September 1930, n.p.

51. Albert Krebs, "Offener Brief an Ernst Niekisch" (Krebs, Nachlass, Bundesarchiv, Koblenz, "Partei, Privat").

52. Schüddekopf, *Linke Leute von Rechts*, 326.

53. Max Habermann, "Volkstümliche Kunst im DHV," *Deutsche Handelswacht* 37, no. 21 (10 November 1930): 415.

54. Otto Schmidt-Hannover, *Umdenken oder Anarchie* (Göttingen: Göttinger Verlagsanstalt, 1959), 230–231.

55. Otto Strasser, *Exil* (Munich, 1958), 64.

56. Franz von Papen, "Rede des Vizekanzlers von Papen vor der nationalen Studentenschaft am 21. Februar 1933," *Der Ring* 6, no. 9 (3 March 1933): 149–151, 149.

57. Edgar Jung, *Gegen die Herrschaft der Minderwertigen, für deutsche und europäische Neuordnung* (Leipzig, 1930).

58. Max Frauendorfer, *Der ständische Gedanke im Nationalsozialismus*, Nationalsozialistische Bibliothek, no. 40 (Munich: Eher, 1932).

59. Robert Koehl, "Feudal Aspects of National Socialism," *American Political Science Review* 54, no. 4 (December 1960): 921–933.

60. Othmar Spann, *Der wahre Staat* (Jena: G. Fischer, 1931).

61. G. W. F. Hegel, *Philosophy of Right* (London: Clarendon Press, 1942), 152–55.

62. Rupert Emerson, *State and Sovereignty in Modern Germany* (New Haven, CT, 1928), 134–136.

63. Hermann Burte, *Wiltfeber, der ewige Deutsche* (Leipzig, 1921), 106. First published in 1912.

64. Burte, *Wiltfeber, der ewige Deutsche*, 71.

65. "14 Thesen der Deutschen Revolution," 118.

66. *Burschenschaftliche Blätter* (1928), quoted in *K. C. Mitteilungen*, no. 8 (25 July 1928): 68.

67. Erwin Guido Kolbenheyer, *Der Lebensstand des geistig Schaffenden und das neue Deutschland*, vol. 2 (Munich, 1934). A small "Kolbenheyer Society" dedicated to spreading his views exists in the German Federal Republic today.

68. "14 Thesen der Deutschen Revolution." Yet when seeking the support of Oswald Spengler, who was not a racist, Gregor Strasser condemned "primitive antisemitism" on behalf of the "German socialist" revolution. Letter of 8 July 1925, in *Letters: 1913–1936* (New York: Knopf, 1966), 183–186, 184.

69. Walter Frank, *Hofprediger Adolf Stoecker und die christlichsoziale bewegung* (Hamburg: Hanseatische, 1935), 243.

70. Klemperer, *Germany's New Conservatism*, 19.

Chapter 5. Fascism and the Intellectuals

1. Hayden White, "Benedetto Croce and the Renewal of Italian Culture: Croce as a Historian" (manuscript read at the annual meeting of the American Historical Association, 29 December 1966), 9.

2. Aldo Garosci, *La Vita di Carlo Rosselli*, vol. 2 (Rome: Edizione U, 1945), 70.

3. Garosci, *La Vita di Carlo Rosselli*, vol. 1, 143.

4. John R. Harrison, *The Reactionaries* (London: Victor Gollancz 1967), 127; Robert Brasillach, *Léon Degrelle et l'avenir de Rex* (Paris: Plon, 1936), 78.

5. Stanley Payne, *Falange: A History of Spanish Fascism* (Stanford: Stanford University Press, 1961), 49; Joris Van Severen, *La Constitution des Pays-Bas* (St. Nicolas-Waes: Anvers, 1938), 24.

6. Robert Brasillach, "La Poésie du national-socialisme," *Notre Combat*, no. 42 (April 1943): 6, 7.

7. Julie Braun-Vogelstein, *Was Niemals Stirbt* (Stuttgart: Deutsche Verlags-Anstalt, 1966), 282. See also the accusations of Carlo Rosselli against Italian socialism: Garosci, *La Vita di Carlo Rosselli*, vol. 1, 143–144.

8. Christopher Caudwell, *Illusion and Reality: A Study of the Sources of Poetry* (New York: Intnl. Publ., 1955), 288.

9. Henry Silton Harris, *The Social Philosophy of Giovanni Gentile* (Urbana: University of Illinois Press, 1966), 172–173.

10. Louis-Ferdinand Céline, *Journey to the End of the Night* (New York: J. Laughlin, 1960), 10

11. Louis-Ferdinand Céline, *Bagatelles pour un massacre* (Paris: Denoël, 1937), 70.

12. Quoted in Harrison, *The Reactionaries*, 132.

13. Céline, *Bagatelles pour un massacre*, 70; Pound quoted in Harrison, *The Reactionaries*, 137.

14. Céline's manifesto in *Au Pillori* reprinted in *L'Affaire Céline (documents)*, *Les Cahiers de la Résistance*, no. 4 (n.d.): 33; his appointment by Otto Abetz, *Les Cahiers de la Résistance*, no. 4 (n.d.): 32. For Céline's career under the occupation, see Léon Poliakov, "Le cas Louis-Ferdinand Céline et le cas Xavier Vallat," *Le Monde Juif 5*, no. 28 (February 1950): 5–7.

15. André Gide, "Les Juifs, Céline et Maritaine," *Nouvelle Revue Française* 50 (January–June 1938): 631.

16. Gottfried Benn, "Das moderne Ich," in *Der neue Staat und die Intellektuellen* (Stuttgart: Deutsche Verlags-Anstalt, 1933), 129–151; Hans Richter, *DADA, Art and Anti-Art* (New York: Thames & Hudson, 1966), 112. For Benn's nihilism, see Edgar Lohner, quoted in Reinhold Grimm, *Strukturen; Essays zur deutschen Literatur* (Göttingen: Sachse & Pohl, 1963), 309.

17. Benn, "Antwort an die literarischen Emigranten," in *Der neue Staat und die Intellektuellen*, 20, 25.

18. Quoted in Peter de Mendelssohn, *Der Geist in der Despotie, Versuch über die moralischen Möglichkeiten des Intellektuellen in der totalitären* Gesellschaft (Berlin, 1953), 251.

19. Benn, "Antwort an die literarischen Emigranten," in *Der neue Staat und die Intellektuellen*, 31.

20. Ladislao Mittner, "Die Geburt des Tyrannen aus dem Ungeist des Expressionismus," in *Festschrift zum achtzigsten Geburtstag von Georg Lukacs* (Neuwied, 1965), 402–420.

21. Camillo Pellizzi, *Una rivoluzione mancata* (Florence, 1951?), esp. 30–35; Benn, "Antwort an die literarischen Emigranten," 25.

22. Pierre Drieu La Rochelle, *Gilles* (Paris: Gallimard, 1939), 74.

23. Walter Benjamin, "Theorien des deutschen Faschismus," *Das Argument* 6, no. 3 (1964): 136.

24. Drieu La Rochelle, *Gilles*, 393.

25. Harrison, *The Reactionaries*, 32.

26. Gottfried Benn, *Kunst und Macht* (Stuttgart: Anstalt, 1934), 106–107; Harrison, *The Reactionaries*, 137.

27. Drieu La Rochelle, *Gilles*, 385.

28. Lucien Rebatet, *Les Décombres* (Paris: Les Éditions Denoël, 1942), 20.

29. Harrison, *The Reactionaries*, 83.

30. See George L. Mosse, *The Crisis of German Ideology: Intellectual Origins of the Third Reich* (Madison: University of Wisconsin Press, 2021).

31. Alfred Baeumler, "Die verwirklichte Idee," in Léon Poliakov and Josef Wulf, *Das dritte Reich und seine Denker* (Berlin: Arani, 1959), 268.

32. Harris, *The Social Philosophy of Giovanni Gentile*, 172.

33. Quoted in Adrian Lyttelton, "Fascism in Italy: The Second Wave," *Journal of Contemporary History* 1, no. 1 (1966): 75–100, 77.

34. Drieu La Rochelle, *Gilles*, 484.

35. Harris, *The Social Philosophy of Giovanni Gentile*, 92.

36. Julien Benda, *The Betrayal of the Intellectuals* (Boston: Beacon Press, 1955). First published in Paris in 1928.

37. Ernst Jünger, *Der Arbeiter* (Hamburg: Hanseatische Verlagsanstalt, 1932), 66, 129.

38. Quoted in Robert Soucy, "The Nature of Fascism in France," *Journal of Contemporary History* 1, no. 1 (1966): 27–55, 52; Walter Muschg, *Die Zerstörung der deutschen Literatur* (Munich: List, 1961), 143, 145.

39. Robert Brasillach, "Introduction à la pensée d'Alfred Rosenberg," *Je Suis Partout* 12, no. 593 (11 December 1942): 6.

40. Quoted in Franz Schonauer, *Deutsche Literatur im dritten Reich* (Olten and Freiburg: Walter-Verlag, 1961), 44.

41. Gastone Silvano Spinetti, *Vent'anni dopo Ricominciare da Zero* (Rome: Edizioni di Solidarismo, 1964), 109. I owe this reference, as well as others on Italian Fascism, to Michael Ledeen and his PhD thesis, "Fascimo Universale: The Theory and Practice of the Fascist International, 1928–1936" (University of Wisconsin, 1969).

42. Arnolt Bronnen, *Arnolt Bronnen gibt zu Protokoll; Beiträge zur Geschichte des modernen Schriftstellers* (Hamburg: Rowohlt, 1954), 302.

43. *L'Universale* (1931–1941) and *La Sapienza* (1933ff.).

44. As reported in *L'Oeuvre*, 24 August 1937.

45. Marc Augier, *Götterdämmerung: Wende und Ende einer grossen Zeit* (Buenos Aires: Editorial Prometheus, 1950), 116.

46. Hans Naumann and Eugen Lüthgen, *Kampf wider den undeutschen Geist* (Bonn: Scheur, 1933).

47. Cesare Rossi, *Mussolini com'era* (Rome: Ruffolo, 1947), 227.

48. Quoted in Lionel Trilling, *Matthew Arnold* (New York: Meridian Books, 1955), 211.

49. George L. Mosse, *Nazi Culture: Intellectual, Cultural and Social Life in the Third Reich* (Madison: University of Wisconsin Press, 1966), 162.

50. Dante L. Germino, *The Italian Fascist Party in Power* (Minneapolis: University of Minnesota Press, 1959).

51. Drieu La Rochelle, *Gilles*, 419.

Chapter 6. Left-Wing Intellectuals in the Weimar Republic

1. Quoted in Kurt Richard Grossmann, *Ossietzky, ein deutscher Patriot* (Munich: Kindler, 1963), 155.

2. *Sperlings Zeitschriften und Zeitungs Adressbuch 1931* (Leipzig, 1931). Istvan Deak, *Weimar Germany's Left-Wing Intellectuals: A Political History of the Weltbühne and Its Circle* (Berkeley: University of California Press, 1968), came out as this book was about to go to press. It is a good straightforward account of the *Weltbühne* and its circle.

3. Kurt Hiller, "Linke Leute von Rechts," *Die Weltbühne* 28, no. 31 (1 August 1932): 157; "Tagebuch der Zeit," *Die Weltbühne* 4, no. 24 (16 June 1923): 837; Stefan Großmann, "Die Hitlerei," *Das Tagebuch* 4, no. 16 (21 April 1923): 550–554, 550. In spite of the postwar feud between Siegfried Jacobsohn (1881–1926) of *Die Weltbühne* and Stefan Großmann of *Das Tagebuch*, at times contributors to one journal also wrote for the other. Kurt Hiller is a good example of this in the 1920s.

4. Joseph Schumpeter, "The Sociology of the Intellectuals," in *The Intellectuals: A Controversial Portrait*, ed. George Bernard de Huszar (Glencoe: Free Press, 1960), 68–79, 79.

5. Kurt Hiller, *Der Aufbruch zum Paradies* (Munich: Desch, 1952), 203, 221–222. This passage seems to date from 1922.

6. Friedrich Engels, *Herrn Eugen Dührings Umwälzung der Wissenschaft* (1876–1878), reprinted as *Anti-Dühring: Herr Eugen Dührings Revolution in Science* (Moscow: Foreign Languages Publ. House, 1954).

7. Franz Mehring, "Kant, Dietzgen, Mach und der historische Materialismus," in *Zur Geschichte der Philosophie* (Berlin: Soziologische Verl.-Anst., 1931), 225–226.

8. Walter Kinkel, *Hermann Cohen: Eine Einführung in sein Werk* (Stuttgart: Strecker und Schröder, 1924), 63ff., 344, 345.

9. Kinkel, *Hermann Cohen*, 63.

10. Kinkel, *Hermann Cohen*, 207.

11. Kinkel, *Hermann Cohen*, 169; Hermann Cohen, "Immanuel Kant," *Allgemeine Zeitung des Judentums* 68, no. 7 (12 February 1904): 76–77.

12. Kinkel, *Hermann Cohen*, 180–181, 197ff., 213; Hermann Cohen, *Briefe* (Berlin: Schocken, 1939), 32–33.

13. Cohen, *Briefe*, 242.

14. Steven S. Schwarzschild, "The Democratic Socialism of Hermann Cohen," *Hebrew Union College Annual* 27 (1956): 417–438, 425, 427.

15. Wolfgang Heise, *Aufbruch in die Illusion* (Berlin: Deutscher Verlag, 1964), 106; V. I. Lenin, *Materialism and Empirio-Criticism* (Moscow, n.d.), 320.

16. Hugo Marx, *Werdegang eines jüdischen Staatsanwalts und Richters in Baden 1892–1933* (Villingen: Neckar Verlag, 1965), 193–197.

17. Karl Vorländer, *Kant und Marx: Ein Beitrag zur Philosophie des Sozialismus* (Tübingen: Mohr, 1926), 210–211.

18. Kurt Eisner, "Hermann Cohen," *Münchner Post*, no. 154 (6 July 1912): 2.

19. Kurt Eisner, "Hermann Cohen," *Münchner Post*, no. 153 (5 July 1912): 2.

20. See the summary of Cohen's thought in Friedrich Albert Lange, *Geschichte des Materialismus*, book 2, 9th ed. (Leipzig: Brandstetter, 1915), 48–51, 422. Hermann Cohen's influence was acknowledged especially in the later editions.

21. See Alf Enseling, *Die Weltbühne: Organ der intellektuellen Linken* (Münster: J. Fahle, 1962), 93–94.

22. Kurt Hiller, "Linke Leute von Rechts," in *Die Weltbühne*, 157.

23. Willi Eichler and Martin Hart, eds., *Leonard Nelson* (Paris: Editions Nouvelles Internationales, 1938), 162, 239–240.

24. Leonard Nelson, *Die bessere Sicherheit, Ketzereien eines revolutionären Revisionisten* (Stuttgart: "Öffentliches Leben," 1927), 17, 18, 19.

25. G. W. F. Hegel, *Philosophy of Right* (London: Clarendon Press, 1942), 6.

26. Minna Specht, *Jakob Friedrich Fries der Begründer unserer politischen Weltansicht* (Stuttgart: "Öffentliches Leben," 1927), 14–15.

27. Kurt Hiller, "Schiefer Revisionismus," *Die Weltbühne* 28, no. 28 (28 July 1932): 50, 51.

28. Kurt Hiller, "Über die Ursachen des Nationalsozialistischen Erfolges I," *Die Weltbühne* 28, no. 34 (17 August 1932): 270–274, 274.

29. Eichler and Hart, *Leonard Nelson*, 181; Kurt Hiller, "Nach Thomas Mann: Franz Werfel," *Das Ziel*, quoted in Pörtner, *Literatur-Revolution*, 418–429, 427.

30. George L. Mosse, *The Crisis of German Ideology: Intellectual Origins of the Third Reich* (Madison: University of Wisconsin Press, 2021), 94–95. The similarity between the "soul dynamic" of the left-wing intellectuals and the völkisch intellectuals has been noted in Kurt Sontheimer, *Antidemokratisches Denken in der Weimarer Republik: Die politischen Ideen des deutschen Nationalismus zwischen 1918 und 1933* (Munich: Nymphenburger Verlagshandlung, 1962), 393.

31. Hiller, "Zur Offensive gegen den Materialismus," *Die Weltbühne* 28, no. 43 (25 October 1932): 608–612.

32. Aldo Garosci, *La Vita di Carlo Rosselli*, vol. 1 (Rome: Edizione U, 1945), 144 and passim.

33. Leo Valiani, *Questioni di storia del Socialismo* (Turin: Einaudi, 1958), 439.

34. *Das Tagebuch* 4, no. 4 (20 October 1932): 1465; Enseling, *Die Weltbühne*, 125.

35. *Das Tagebuch* 4, no. 4 (20 October 1932), 1465.

36. Kurt Tucholsky, *Ausgewählte Briefe* (Hamburg: Rowohlt, 1962), 115. He made this statement in 1920.

37. Admiration for the Saxon communist terrorist Max Hoelz (1889–1933): Stefan Großmann, "Oberbefehlshaber Hölz," *Das Tagebuch* 2, no. 26 (2 July 1921): 802.

38. Thomas Wehrlin, "Unterhaltung mit Kommunisten," *Das Tagebuch* 2, no. 13 (2 April 1921): 386.

39. Enseling, *Die Weltbühne*, 94.

40. Nelson, *Die bessere Sicherheit*, 332.

41. Kurt Hiller, *Geist werde Herr: Kundgebungen e. Aktivisten vor, in u. nach d. Kriege* (Berlin: Reiß, 1920), 56.

42. Hiller, quoted in Pörtner, *Literatur-Revolution*, 423, 457.

43. Hiller, *Geist werde Herr*, 34–38, 56, 57.

44. Kurt Hiller, ed., *After Nazism—Democracy? A Symposium* (London: Drummond, 1945), 14.

45. Otto Wilhelm von Tegelen, *Leonard Nelsons Rechts und Staatslehre* (Bonn: Bouvier, 1958), 71; "Tagebuch der Zeit," *Das Tagebuch* 3, no. 4 (28 January 1922). See also Enseling, *Die Weltbühne*, 122n.

46. Nelson, *Die bessere Sicherheit*, 289.

47. Kurt Hiller, "Logokratie," in *Ziel. Viertes der Ziel-Jahrbücher* (Munich: Kurt Wolff, 1920), 220.

48. Enseling, *Die Weltbühne*, 74; Stefan Großmann, "Zwei Nein," *Das Tagebuch* 1, no. 4 (31 January 1920): 114; *Das Tagebuch* 2, no. 46 (19 November 1921): 1399; Hiller, *Geist werde Herr*, 101.

49. Hiller, *Geist werde Herr*, 84. For an account of these councils, see Franz Schoenbrenner, *Bekenntnisse eines europäischen Intellektuellen* (Munich: Kreisselmeier Verlag, 1964), 127–130.

50. Kurt Hiller, "Kongressbericht," in *Ziel. Viertes der Ziel-Jahrbücher*, 213, 215.

51. Typically, Hiller hoped that the anti-putsch communists would join with USDP. Hiller, *Geist werde Herr*.

52. Alfred Döblin, "Offene Antwort an einen jungen Menschen," *Das Tagebuch* 2, no. 2 (5 July 1930): 1061–1070, 1070.

53. Werner Link, *Die Geschichte des Internationalen Jugend-Bundes (IJB) und des Internationalen Kampf-Bundes (ISK): Ein Beitrag zur Geschichte der Arbeiterbewegung in der Weimarer Republik und im Dritten Reich* (Meisenheim am Glan: Anton Hain, 1964), 62–63.

54. Link, *Die Geschichte des Internationalen Jugend-Bundes*, 122.

55. Link, *Die Geschichte des Internationalen Jugend-Bundes*, 14.

56. Link, *Die Geschichte des Internationalen Jugend-Bundes*, 53.

57. Leonard Nelson, *Politics and Education* (London, 1928), 77.

58. Nelson, *Politics and Education*, 87, 92.

59. Nelson, *Politics and Education*, 90–91.

60. See Hannah Bertholet, "Gedanken über die Walkermühle," in *Erziehung und Politik, Minna Specht zu ihrem 80. Geburtstag*, ed. Hellmutt Becker (Frankfurt am Main: Verlag Öffentliches Leben, 1960), 269–278.

61. Minna Specht, "Minna Specht über sich selbst," in Becker, *Erziehung und Politik*, 371–372.

62. Werner Link is concerned with Germany only. This information was obtained in an interview with Allan Flanders (1934–1974), for a time the leader of the English group (21 October 1965).

63. Louis Lévy (1895–1952) from France was also present at that meeting, as was Jef Reus from Belgium, Willi Eichler (1896–1971) from Germany, and George Green (1908–1989), the only trade-union official who belonged to ISK in England. *Calling All Europe* (London: International Publishing, 1942), n.p.

64. Hiller, *After Nazism—Democracy?*, 19.

65. Großmann, "Wir Marionetten," *Das Tagebuch* 10, no. 24 (15 June 1929): 976; Kurt Tucholsky, *Lerne lachen ohne zu weinen* (Berlin: Ernst Rowohlt, 1931), 243.

66. Thaddäus Beerenbremser, "Glossen," *Das Tagebuch* 8, no. 4 (22 January 1927): 158–159, 158.

67. Stefan Großmann, *Ich war begeistert* (Berlin: S. Fischer, 1930), 198.

68. Großmann, *Ich war begeistert*, 292.

69. "An Fritz Ebert," *Das Tagebuch* 2, no. 1 (8 January 1921): 1–3; "Aus dem Tagebuch," *Das Tagebuch* 2, no. 5 (5 February 1921): 155–156.

70. Enseling, *Die Weltbühne*, 85.

71. Link, *Die Geschichte des Internationalen Jugend-Bundes*, 170. For Mann's politics, see Ulrich Weisstein, *Heinrich Mann: Eine historisch-kritische Einführung in sein dichterisches Werk* (Tübingen: Niemeyer, 1962).

72. Hanno Drechsler, *Die Sozialistische Arbeiterpartei Deutschlands (SAPD) e. Beitr. zur Geschichte d. dt. Arbeiterbewegung am Ende d. Weimarer Republik* (Meisenheim am Glan: Hain, 1965), 158.

73. Drechsler, *Die Sozialistische Arbeiterpartei Deutschlands*, 137, 138.
74. Hans J. Reichardt, "Neu Beginn," in *Jahrbuch für die Geschichte Mittel- und Ostdeutschlands*, ed. Wilhelm Berges and Hans Herzfeld, vol. 12 (Berlin: De Gruyter, 1963), 151ff.
75. Reichardt, "Neu Beginn," 151. And see their indoctrination courses: Reichardt, "Neu Beginn," 156n.
76. *Die Weltbühne* 28, no. 9 (1932); Drechsler, *Die Sozialistische Arbeiterpartei Deutschlands*, 184.
77. Alfred Döblin, "Offene Antwort an einen jungen Menschen," *Das Tagebuch* 2, no. 27 (5 July 1930): 1069–1070.
78. Alfred Döblin, *Wissen und Verändern! Offene Briefe an einen jungen Menschen* (Berlin: Fischer, 1931), 141.
79. Döblin, *Wissen und Verändern!*, 100.
80. Specht, *Jakob Friedrich Fries der Begründer unserer politischen Weltansicht*, 15, 18.
81. Ludwig Rubiner, *Die Gewaltlosen* (Potsdam, 1919), 10.
82. Leonhard Frank, "Links ist wo das Herz ist," *Gesammelte Werke*, vol. 5 (Berlin: Aufbau, 1959), 494.
83. Leonhard Frank, *Der Mensch ist gut* (Potsdam, n.d.), 41.
84. Ludwig Rubiner, "Die Erneuerung," in *Die Gemeinschaft, Dokumente der geistigen Weltwende* (Potsdam: Kiepenheuer, 1919), 75.
85. Quoted in Grossmann, *Ossietzky*, 107.
86. *Der Nationalsozialismus* (3 articles of the *Tagebuch*) (n.p., 1930), 5, 15.
87. Stefan Großmann, "Die Hitlerei," *Das Tagebuch* 4, no. 16 (21 April 1923): 552.
88. Heinz Pol, "Das Ende der völkischen Bewegung," *Die Weltbühne* 21, no. 11 (17 March 1925): 387.
89. Enseling, *Die Weltbühne*, 82–83.
90. Karl Mannheim, "The Sociological Problem of the 'Intelligentsia,'" in Bernard de Huszar, *The Intellectuals*, 62–68, esp. 67.
91. Eichler and Hart, *Leonard Nelson*, 331–332. From Vienna, the socialist Max Adler held as early as 1917 that the class interests of the intellectuals were neither proletarian nor bourgeois but cultural: *Der Sozialismus und die Intellektuellen* (Vienna: Wiener Volksbuchhandlung I, 1923), 5.
92. Kurt Hiller, "Über die Ursachen des Nationalsozialistischen Erfolges II," *Die Weltbühne* 28, no. 35 (30 August 1932): 309–314, 310.
93. Kinkel, *Hermann Cohen*, 264–265.
94. Ludwig Stein, *Die Juden in der neueren Philosophie* (Berlin: M. Poppelauer, 1919), 9. See also Hermann Cohen, "Der Sabbat in seiner Kulturgeschichtlichen Bedeutung" (written 1869), in *Jüdische Schriften*, vol. 2 (Berlin, 1924), 58; Nello Roselli, "The Jew and Italy: I Am Not a Zionist," in *Neither Liberty nor Bread*, ed. Frances Keene (New York: Harper & Bros., 1940), 285–289, 287.
95. Renzo De Felice, *Storia degli ebrei italiani sotto il fascismo* (Milan: G. Einaudi, 1961), 104, 492.
96. Leopold Schwarzschild, "Tagebuch der Zeit," *Das Tagebuch* 14, no. 10 (11 March 1933): 365–369, 365.
97. Kurt Hiller, *Köpfe und Tröpfe: Profile aus einem Vierteljahrhundert* (Hamburg: Rowohlt, 1950), 342.

98. Tucholsky, *Lerne lachen ohne zu weinen*, 13.

99. Heinrich Mann, *Essays* (Hamburg: Claassen, 1960), 492, 545.

100. Heinrich Mann, "Die deutsche Entscheidung," *Das Tagebuch* 12, no. 39 (26 September 1931): 1966–1967.

101. Mann, *Essays*, 545, 443.

102. Kurt Hiller, "Meisteressays," *Die Weltbühne* 28, no. 44 (1 November 1932): 667–678.

103. Heinrich Mann, quoted in Alfred Kantorowicz, *Heinrich und Thomas Mann; Die persönlichen, literarischen und weltanschaulichen Beziehungen der Brüder* (Berlin: Aufbau, 1956), 24; Heinrich Mann, *Der Untertan* (Leipzig: Kurt Wolff, 1918), 489; Nelson, quoted by Hiller, "Zur offensive gegen den materialismus," *Die Weltbühne* 28, no. 43 (25 October 1932): 612.

104. Mann, *Essays*, 446.

105. Mann, *Essays*, 443.

106. Heinrich Mann, "Dichtkunst und Politik," in *Sieben Jahre* (Berlin, 1928), 501.

107. Mann, "Dichtkunst und Politik," 500; Heinrich Mann, *Es kommt der Tag* (Zürich: Europa Verlag, 1936), 225.

108. Mann, *Es kommt der Tag*, 225.

109. Heinrich Mann, "Zola Vortrag in Prag" (1916), in *Essays*, 154ff.

110. Heinrich Mann, "Deutsche Literatur um 1920," in *Sieben Jahre*, 26–28.

111. Mann, *Es kommt der Tag*, 16.

112. Herbert Jhering, *Heinrich Mann* (Berlin: Aufbau, 1951), 84. From the memorial oration of Heinrich Mann for Eisner, 16 March 1919.

113. For Heinrich Mann in exile after 1933, see George L. Mosse "The Heritage of Socialist Humanism," in "The Legacy of German Refugee Intellectuals," *Salmagundi* 10, no. 11 (Fall 1969–Winter 1970): 123–139.

114. Kurt Sontheimer, *Thomas Mann und die Deutschen* (Munich: Nymphenburger, 1961). Our analysis of Thomas Mann follows this book.

115. Chapters on Romain Rolland ("Zwischen den Dogmen," 238–246) and André Gide ("André Gide," 181–220) in Hiller, *Köpfe und Tröpfe*.

116. André Gide, quoted in David Caute, *Communism and the French Intellectuals* (London: A. Deutsch, 1964), 238.

117. Caute, *Communism and the French Intellectuals*. However, an idealistic neo-Kantian tradition also existed in France. See A. Fouilée, "Le Néo-Kantisme en France," *Révue Philosophique* 2 (1881): 1–45.

118. Carlo Rosselli, *Socialismo Liberale* (n.d.), cited in John Hirsch, "Radical Anti-Fascism: Origins and Politics of the Italian Action Party" (PhD dissertation, University of Wisconsin, 1965), 67; Emilio Lussu, *Sul Partito d'Azione e gli altri* (Milan: Murisia, 1968), 40.

119. Erich Fromm, *Marx's Concept of Man* (New York: Ungar, 1961), 30.

120. Contrary to Paul Jacobs and Saul Landau, *The New Radicals* (New York: Vintage Books, 1966), 3.

121. Thomas Hayden in *The New Student Left*, ed. Mitchell Cohen and Dennis Hale (Boston: Beacon Press, 1966), 7.

122. Mario Savio in Cohen and Hale, *The New Student Left*, 257.

123. Port Huron Statement of Students for a Democratic Society, in Jacobs and Landau, *The New Radicals*, 154.

124. Todd Gitlin in Cohen and Hale, *The New Student Left*, 125.

125. Port Huron Statement of SDS in Jacobs and Landau, *The New Radicals*, 155.

126. Gerald Rosenfield, "Generational Revolt and the Free-Speech Movement," in Jacobs and Landau, *The New Radicals*, 214.

127. Port Huron Statement of SDS in Jacobs and Landau, *The New Radicals*, 155.

128. Jacobs and Landau, *The New Radicals*, 315; Robert A. Haber in Cohen and Hale, *The New Student Left*, 47.

129. Port Huron Statement of SDS in Jacobs and Landau, *The New Radicals*, 222.

130. Randy Battle in Jacobs and Landau, *The New Radicals*, 131.

131. Carl Wittman and Thomas Hayden, "An Interracial Movement of the Poor?," in Cohen and Hale, *The New Student Left*, 218.

132. Thomas Hayden in Cohen and Hale, *The New Student Left*, 282.

133. Bruce Payne, "SNCC: An Overview Two Years Later," in Cohen and Hale, *The New Student Left*, 98.

134. Earl Wittman in Cohen and Hale, *The New Student Left*, 178.

135. Staughton Lynd, "The New Radicals and 'Participatory Democracy'" (mimeographed, Chicago, IL, 1965), 10.

136. Barbara Brandt in Jacobs and Landau, *The New Radicals*, 127.

137. Jacobs and Landau, *The New Radicals*, 75.

138. Interview with SDS staffers in Jacobs and Landau, *The New Radicals*, 176.

139. Garosci, *La vita di Carlo Rosselli*, vol. 1, 153.

140. Garosci, *La vita di Carlo Rosselli*, vol. 2, 70; Roselli quoted in Lussu, *Sul Partito d'Azione e gli altri*, 40.

Index

About the Improvement of Jewish Citizenship (Dohm), 27
Adler, Max, 141
Adorno, Theodor, xiv
aesthetics, 41. *See also* artistic movements; beauty; "ideal type"
Against the Jews (Grattenauer), 37
America. *See* United States
antisemitism, xii–xiii, xvii, 15, 24–28, 33, 40–56, 113–117, 140, 156n7
Arendt, Hannah, 43
Aristotle, 128
artistic movements, 4–5, 21, 41, 144. *See also* aesthetics; Expressionism; Surrealism
Aryanism, 25, 92
Aschheim, Steven E., xiii, xv, 156n9
Auerbach, Berthold, 30
Austria, 18, 28, 132, 141

Baeck, Rabbi Leo, 156n7
Bang, Paul, 89
Bar Kochba, 57–59, 64–66
Bartels, Adolf, 31, 36
Bauer, Otto, 141
Bavaria, 142, 145
Bavarian Revolution, 142
beauty, 41. *See also* aesthetics; "ideal type"
Benda, Julien, 147
Benjamin, Walter, 108, 169n23
Benn, Gottfried, 102, 106–114, 169n16
Bergmann, Hugo, 58
Berlin, Germany, 35–36, 51
Bernfeld, Siegfried, 55, 76

Beyer, Karl August Friedrich Albrecht, 36
Beyond Good and Evil (Nietzsche), 43
Biarritz (Goedsche), 32
Black Flag (youth group), 69, 72–73. *See also* Youth Movement
Blau-Weiss (youth group), 66–70. *See also* Youth Movement
Bloom, Solomon F., 24
Blüher, Hans, 128
Blumenfeld, Kurt, 66
Böhme, Jacob, 59–60
Bolshevik Revolution, 81
Bolshevism, 74, 81
Bonus, Arthur, 61
Bourgeois Society (Riehl), 46
Brasillach, Robert, 20
Bronnen, Arnolt, 112–113, 170n42
Buber, Martin, xiii, 17, 59–65, 68, 75–77, 83, 163n16
Bullock, Alan, 43
Bund, 56–58, 68–69, 73–76, 82, 85–87, 114–116
Bund Deutscher Studenten, 17
Bünde (Jewish), 73, 86–87
Bündische Jugend, 72, 84–85
Burckhardt, Jacob, 26, 40–41
Burte, Hermann, 116

Calvary, Moses, 58, 66–70
Campe, Joachim Heinrich, 28
capitalism, 4–6, 12–14, 19, 86–92, 113–117, 122–126, 136–139, 143
categorical imperative, 5, 121–126, 137, 140, 144, 148, 151–152. *See also* Kant, Immanuel

Catholicism, 114–118, 128, 132. *See also* religion
Caute, David, 147
Céline, Louis-Ferdinand, 104–107, 169n10
Chamberlain, Houston Stewart, 125
The Children of Israel (Jansen), 39
Choice of a Bride (Hoffmann), 38
Christianity, 28, 37, 117, 139. *See also* religion
Christian Social Party, 117
civilization (concept of), 25, 35–42
class: bourgeoisie, 3–4, 46, 54–57, 80, 85, 116–117, 122–123, 128, 135, 139; Jews and, 47, 139–141; peasants, 9, 46; proletariat, 47, 73, 126, 147; and *Volk*, 46–47, 85, 116; working, 88–89, 151
Claus, Fritz, 35
Cohen, Hermann, 67, 121–125, 130–131, 140–141
Cohn, Norman, 106, 159n22
Coll, Pieter, 33
communism, 21, 33–35, 122, 126–128, 132–135, 144, 147
Communist Party, 35, 126, 147
community (concept of), 62–64
Comrade Levi (Halbach), 34
The Comrades (youth group), 69, 72. *See also* Youth Movement
conservatism, 12, 81–90, 112–113, 116–118
Copalle, Siegfried, 56
Corneille, Pierre, 7
corporatism, 12, 82–92, 113–118
Council of Intellectual Workers, 129, 135, 147
Council of the Wise, 127, 130, 138
The Crisis of German Ideology (Mosse), xi, xvi–xvii
Croce, Benedetto, 119–120
culture (concept of), 36–42, 64
C.V. Zeitung (organization), 71, 74, 78

Dahn, Felix, xii, 44–53
Das Ziel (*The Goal*), 128. *See also* Hiller, Kurt

Debit and Credit (Freytag), 26, 36, 39–40, 44–49, 162n24
The Decline of the West (Spengler), 11, 25
Degrelle, Léon, 21
democracy, xv, 80, 83–84, 92, 113, 116–118, 132, 142, 151–152
Der Büttnerbauer (Polenz), 44
Der Stürmer, 39
determinism, 124–126
Deutsche Jungendschaft, 72, 77–78
dialectic of history, 134–135, 143, 147–148. *See also* Marx, Karl
Dickens, Charles, 50
Dictionary of the German Language (Campe), 28, 41
Diederichs, Eugen, 61
Die Familie Lowositz (Hauschner), 31
Ding an sich (thing-in-itself), 125. *See also* Kant, Immanuel
Dinter, Artur, 38–39
Disraeli, Benjamin, 39
Döblin, Alfred, 32, 135
Dohm, Christian Wilhelm von, 27–30, 35, 49
Drieu La Rochelle, Pierre Eugène, 107–111, 116

Ebert, Friedrich, 133
Eckardt, Julius Wilhelm Albert von, 51
Eckart, Dietrich, 31
Eckhart, Meister, 59, 61, 63
Ecstatic Confessions (Buber), 61
Edith, Countess of Salburg, 38
education, 131, 138, 145
Eigenschaften, 79
Eisner, Kurt, 123, 128, 141–144
The Elderberry Blossom (Raabe), 32
Engels, Friedrich, 126, 140
Enlightenment, 27–32, 49–50, 57–58, 139, 143, 152, 159n11, 162n24
Expressionism, 5, 144. *See also* artistic movements

family, 8–9, 12
fascism, xv–xvii, xix, 16, 19–22, 88, 115, 119–120, 131

Fascism (Italian), 88, 115
Feuchtwanger, Lion, 137
feudalism, 114
feuilletonism, 127, 142
Fichte, Johann Gottlieb, 77
Fight for Rome (Dahn), 44, 50
fin de siècle, 55, 59, 64, 76, 142
Fischer, Frank, 55
Fourteen Theses of the German Revolution (Strasser), 91, 116
France, 6, 10, 16, 33, 74, 143, 147
Frank, Leonhard, 135–136, 149–152
Franklin, Benjamin, 33
Franzos, Karl Emil, 31–32
freedom, 124–125
French Revolution, 6, 10, 16, 143
Freytag, Gustav, xii, 14, 18, 24–26, 30–40, 44–53, 162n24
Fries, Jakob Friedrich, 124, 131, 136
Führerprinzip (leadership principle), 88
Futurism, 106, 113

Geist, 125–129, 143–145
Gentile, Giovanni, 119
George, Stefan, 85
The German Catastrophe (Meinecke), xv
German History (Möser), 7
German National Party, 12–17
German Volk (Jahn), 8
Gervinus, Georg Gottfried, 26
ghetto, 32–35, 51, 59
Gide, André, 146–147
Gierke, Otto Friedrich von, 115
Goedsche, Hermann, 32–33
Goethe, Johann Wolfgang von, 32
Goldstein, Moritz, 66
Goslar, Hans, 68
Grattenauer, Carl Wilhelm Friedrich, 37
Großmann, Stefan, 132, 138, 171n3
Günther, Hans Friedrich Karl, 77

Habermann, Max, 113
Hackländer, Friedrich Wilhelm, 46
Halbach, Fritz, 34
"half Asia," 32–33

Hamsun, Knut, 68
Harden, Maximilian, 141
Hasidim, 59–61
Hauptmann, Carl, 38
Hauptmann, Gerhart, 38, 133
Hauptmann, Hans, 33
Hauschner, Auguste, 31, 159n18
Hebrew (language), 68
Hegel, Georg Wilhelm Friedrich, 6, 115, 122–124
Heine, Heinrich, 36–40
Herder, Johann Gottfried, 6–10, 14, 18–19
Herzberg-Fränkel, Leo, 31
Hielscher, Friedrich, 86
Hiller, Kurt, 124–130, 133, 136–138, 141–143, 147. See also *Das Ziel* (*The Goal*)
Hindenburg, Paul von, xv
History of Materialism (Lange), 123
Hitler, Adolf, xiv–xv, 15, 32, 43–49, 54, 82, 112–118, 127, 133, 138–151
Hoffmann, Ernst Theodor Amadeus, 38
Hölderlin, Friedrich, 67
Hugenberg, Alfred, xv, 89, 139
The Human Cargo of the Ano-Wati (Gaebert), 33
humanism, 31, 57, 145–147
Hutchinson, John, xix

idealism, 21–22, 121–126, 134–137, 140, 143, 147–149, 151
"ideal type," 41. See also aesthetics; beauty
identity, 4–5. See also *point d'appui*
ideology, xi, 6, 21
Il Duce. See Mussolini, Benito
Independent Socialists. See Unabhängige Sozialistische Deutsche Partei (USDP)
individualism, 84, 137, 140
industrialization, 4, 8, 16, 56–57
Industrial Revolution, 16
intellectuals: American, 148–149, 152; and class, 117, 129; definition of, 120, 141; European, xvii, 3,

intellectuals (*continued*)
147; and idealism, 21, 123, 126;
Jewish, 139–140, 156n7; left-wing,
4–6, 16, 21–22, 122–127, 132–148,
151–152, 172n30; modern, 149,
151; and politics, 20, 119, 130,
138, 147; and *Volk*, 145, 172n30;
young, 134, 148, 151
International League of Militant
Socialists (ISK), 130–132
International Youth League (IJB),
130–131, 134
*Introduction to the History of the
Nineteenth Century* (Gervinus), 26
Ismael Friedmann (Hauptmann), 38
Italy, 19, 88, 92, 115–116, 126, 140–
141, 147
Itzig, Veitel, 39

Jacobsohn, Siegfried, 171n3
Jahn, Johann Friedrich Ludwig
Christoph, 8–10, 18
Jansen, Werner, 39
Jewish Intellect and German Faith
(Beyer), 36
*Jewish Monthly of Sports and Gym-
nastics*, 76
The Jewish Question (Rosenberg), 33
Jews: and antisemitism, xiii, 15, 24,
43, 50, 117, 140; and assimilation,
28–30, 42, 52, 76–77; and class,
47, 139–141; and conspiracy,
34–35, 159n22; Eastern European,
31–33, 51–54, 57, 65, 77; emancipation of, 26–30, 45, 51, 54,
159n13; and Germanism, 36,
162n24; and intellectuals, 139–141,
152, 156n7; and Judaism, 28–35,
159n11; and politics, 37, 49, 58,
63, 76; and race, 37–39, 77–78, 92;
and reeducation, 28–29; stereotypes
of, 14, 25–27, 38–59, 75–77, 90,
158n3, 158n11, 161n8, 162n24;
and *Volk*, xiv, 13–15, 30–32, 54,
61–67, 71, 75–78; and youth,
55–59, 67–79, 139–140. *See also*
"world conspiracy"
Joseph II of Austria, 28

Judaism, 27–37, 57–60, 69, 75, 140,
159n11
Jung, Carl, 13
Jung, Edgar, 114
Jünger, Ernst, 111–112, 115
Jünger, Nathanael, 34–35, 38

Kafka, Franz, 57
Kant, Immanuel, 5–6, 57, 120–125,
128, 137, 142–143, 152. *See also*
categorical imperative; *Ding an sich*
(thing-in-itself)
Kaufmann, Jacob, 30, 49
Kellermann, Heinz, 69
Kerr, Alfred, 128
Kierkegaard, Søren, 75
Klosters, Jacob, 38
Köbel, Eberhard, 72
Kolbenheyer, Erwin Guido, 116–117
Krannhals, Paul, 90
Krebs, Albert, 86–87, 92, 113

Lagarde, Paul de, 58–59, 84
Landauer, Gustav, 63–64
Langbehn, Julius, 58, 84
Lebensgestaltung (forming of life), 76
Le Bon, Gustave, 127
Leers, Johann von, 32
Lenin, Vladimir, 122, 129–130, 134
Letter to M. D'Alembert on Spectacles
(Rousseau), 10
liberalism, 32, 49–50, 57, 62, 71–74,
84, 121–124, 152, 162n24
Lichtenberg, Georg Christoph, 29
literature, 44–48
The Loyal Subject (Mann), 143
Luther, Martin, 75
Lynd, Staughton, 150–151

Machiavelli, Niccolò, 15
Malraux, André, 120
Man Is Good (Frank), 136, 152
Mann, Heinrich, 128–129, 133–134,
142–145
Mann, Thomas, 145
Mannheim, Karl, 139, 147
Marx, Karl, 47, 121–126, 148. *See
also* dialectic of history

Marxism, 4–6, 19, 84, 113–117, 122–129, 134–139, 143, 147–149, 151–152
materialism, 5–9, 14, 21–25, 35, 40, 57, 79, 112, 120–126, 140
Mazzini, Giuseppe, 19
Mehring, Franz, 35
Meinecke, Friedrich, xv, 156n7
Mein Kampf (Hitler), 127, 138
The Memoirs of Satan (Hauptmann), 33
Middle Ages, 7, 113–115
middle class, 21, 46–48, 150
Mill, John Stuart, 128
Mittner, Ladislao, 107, 169n20
modernity, xi, 8, 55, 60, 149
Moeller van den Bruck, Arthur, 61, 82–84, 137
Möller, Eberhard Wolfgang, 33
Möser, Justus, 7
Musil, Robert, 79
Mussolini, Benito, 19, 114, 120
mysticism, 61–63, 125–126, 147
myth, 13–16, 25
The Myth of the Twentieth Century (Rosenberg), 25
Mythos (German), 10, 60–61, 82–83

Napoleonic Wars, 36
nationalism, xx, 3–6, 11, 15, 18–21, 28, 58, 63–65, 71–72, 139
Nationalism and Sexuality (Mosse), xix
nationalist mystique, 8, 16, 19
Nationalist Union of Commercial Apprentices, 113
National Socialism, xi–xx, 14–25, 33–42, 49–53, 112–114, 125, 135–146, 155n5
National Socialist Party, 86, 91, 113
Natorp, Paul, 131
nature, 55–56, 66–68, 76, 89
Naumann, Hans, 114, 170n46
Naumann, Max, 77–78
Nazism, xiv–xvii, 16, 71, 74, 78, 114, 131, 138, 142, 155n5
Nelson, Leonard, 123–138, 141–147, 150. *See also* Walkermühle

New Left, 23, 149–152
New Scouts, 86. *See also* Voelkel, Martin
Nietzsche, Friedrich, 4, 19, 43, 61, 67
Nipperdey, Thomas, 10
nostalgia, 20
Nüchternheit (absence of feeling), 27

Oliver Twist (Dickens), 50
Ortega y Gasset, José, 16
Ossietzky, Carl von, 133–134, 137–139, 142
Our Visitors (Sessa), 37

Palestine, 66–67, 70, 76
Papen, Franz von, 113–114
parliamentary government, 80–81, 84–86, 90, 116, 145
The Party (Großmann), 132
Party of Humanity, 148
patriotism, 49, 58
The Peasant from Büttner (Polenz), 35
Pelizzi, Camillo, 110
Peter Mönkemann Fights His Way (Weller), 27
petit bourgeois, 35, 138
Philistinism, 35–36, 42
philosophes, 26–29
Philosophy of Right (Hegel), 124
Plato, 127
Plessini, Karel, xx
point d'appui, 5. *See also* identity
Pol, Heinz, 138
Poland, 31, 51–52
Polenz, Wilhelm von, 35, 44–46, 49
Poliakov, Léon, 45
Polish Jews (Herzberg-Fränkel), 31
Poor Pastor (Raabe), 36
Pound, Ezra, 119
pragmatism, xii, 146
Prague, Czech Republic, 32, 57
public festivals, 9–10

Raabe, Wilhelm, 24–26, 31–33, 36–37, 40
Rabauken! (Weller), 33–35, 39
race, 25, 37–39, 77, 116–117
Racine, Jean, 7

Index

racism, 14, 27, 37–40, 45, 55, 77–78, 92, 116
radicalism, 148–151
Ranke, Leopold von, 15, 40
Räte (workers' councils), 82
rationalism, 57–59, 90, 125–126, 143–147
Reichsbund Jüdischer Frontsoldaten, 72–76
religion, 25, 28, 139. *See also* Catholicism; Christianity; Judaism
Riehl, Wilhelm Heinrich, 46–48, 73
Robespierre, Maximilien, 16
Röhm, Ernst, 72
Rolland, Romaine, 146–147
Romanticism, 29, 56, 61, 78
rootedness, 11–13, 19, 30
rootlessness, 41–51
Rosenberg, Alfred, 25, 33
Rosselli, Carlo, 120, 126, 141, 147, 152
Rosselli, Sabatino Enrico "Nello," 140
Rothfels, Hans, xv
Rousseau, Jean-Jacques, 10
Rubiner, Ludwig, 135–137, 149–150
Russia, 21, 129

Schleicher, Kurt von, 113
Schmitt, Carl, 80, 88
Schoeps, Hans-Joachim, 73–75
Scholem, Gershom, xiii, 66
Scott, Walter, Sir, 45
Sessa, Karl Barromäus Alexander, 37–38
Sin Against the Blood (Dinter), 38
Social Democratic Party (SPD). *See* Social Democrats
Social Democrats, 21, 121–122, 130–135, 144–146
socialism, 57, 82–92, 116–147
Socialist Workers Party, 133
Sombart, Werner, 90
Sontheimer, Kurt, 145
Soviet Union. *See* Russia
Spann, Othmar, 114
Specht, Minna, 131
Speeches on Judaism (Buber), 63

Spengler, Oswald, 11, 25, 40, 80–82
Spielhagen, Friedrich, 38
Stampfer, Friedrich, 17
Stelzel, Philipp, xvii, 155n5
Stern, Fritz, xvi
Stifter, Adalbert, 12
Stinnes, Hugo, 139
Stoecker, Adolf, 30, 117
Strasser, Gregor, 72, 86, 89–91, 112–113, 116–117
Strasser, Otto, 91–92
Streicher, Julius, 39
Students for a Democratic Society (SDS), 149–150
Sudetenland, 18
Surrealism, 21. *See also* artistic movements
symbols, 13–16

Tagebuch (journal), 126–135, 138–142, 147, 171n3
Thälmann, Ernst, 134
Third Force, xii–xiv, 4–6, 17–20, 23, 74, 81, 84, 118, 152
The Third Reich (Moeller van den Bruck), 82
Those Without Power (Rubiner), 136
Toynbee, Arnold J., 27
Trade and Change (Hackländer), 46
Treitschke, Heinrich von, 30, 36
Treves, Paolo, 132
Tucholsky, Kurt, 126, 142

Unabhängige Sozialistische Deutsche Partei (USDP), 128
United States, 22, 148–152
urbanization, 4, 8
Usurer (Claus), 35

Vayo, Julio Álvarez del, 136
Voelkel, Martin, 86. *See also* New Scouts
Volk: and class, 46–47, 85, 116; as ideology, xiii–xvii, 6–11, 16–22, 34–41, 54, 60–61, 68–79, 89, 138; and intellectuals, 59, 145, 172n30; and Jews, 13–15, 30–32, 54, 61–67, 71, 75–78; and morality, 5,

19; and nationalism, xx, 8; and
politics, 12, 19, 81–84, 87, 90–91,
114–116; and racism, 25, 113; and
the soul, 7–10, 13; and youth,
55–56, 70, 88
Volk in Danger (Jünger), 34, 38
völkisch ideas. See *Volk*
völkisch movement. See *Volk*
Volkov, Shulamit, xiii
Voltaire, 27, 30
Vom Judentum (Bar Kochba of
Prague), 57

Wagner, Richard, 49
Walkermühle, 131. *See also* Nelson,
Leonard
Wandervogel, 55–56, 67–68. *See also*
Youth Movement
Weimar Republic, xi, xiv, 12–16, 69,
117–118, 128–130, 133, 137–138,
141–148
Weller, Tüdel, 27, 33–35, 39–40
Weltanschauung, xix, 83

Weltbühne (journal), 124–128, 133–
144, 147, 170n2, 171n3
Weltsch, Robert, xiii, 54, 58, 62–67,
76–77
Wendt, Thomas, 137
Werfel, Franz, 128
Wiltfeber, the Eternal German (Burte),
116
Winnig, August, 88–89, 112
Witiko (Stifter), 12–13
Wohlfahrt, Anton, 36
"world conspiracy," 32–35. *See also*
Jews

Youth Movement, 11, 14–16, 55–59,
64–79, 84, 87–88, 112, 117. *See
also* Black Flag (youth group); Blau-
Weiss (youth group); The Comrades
(youth group); Wandervogel

Zehrer, Hans, 87
Zionism, 57–59, 64–66, 70–76
Zola, Émile, 143–144

The Collected Works of
George L. Mosse

*Nationalism and Sexuality: Middle-Class Morality and
Sexual Norms in Modern Europe*
With a critical introduction by Mary Louise Roberts

Toward the Final Solution: A History of European Racism
With a critical introduction by Christopher R. Browning

*The Crisis of German Ideology:
Intellectual Origins of the Third Reich*
With a critical introduction by Steven E. Aschheim

The Fascist Revolution: Toward a General Theory of Fascism
With a critical introduction by Roger Griffin

*The Culture of Western Europe:
The Nineteenth and Twentieth Centuries*
With a critical introduction by Anthony J. Steinhoff

*The Nationalization of the Masses:
Political Symbolism and Mass Movements in Germany from
the Napoleonic Wars through the Third Reich*
With a critical introduction by Victoria de Grazia

*Germans and Jews: The Right, the Left, and the
Search for a "Third Force" in Pre-Nazi Germany*
With a critical introduction by Sarah Wobick-Segev